Preparing for Blended e-Learning

Allison Littlejohn and Chris Pegler

Routledge
Taylor & Francis Group

LONDON AND NEW YORK

First published 2007
by Routledge
2 Park Square, Milton Park, Abingdon, Oxon, OX14 4RN

Simultaneously published in the USA and Canada
by Routledge
270 Madison Ave, New York, NY 10016

Routledge is an imprint of the Taylor & Francis Group, an informa business

© 2007 Allison Littlejohn and Chris Pegler

Transferred to Digital Printing 2008

Typeset in Baskerville by
Keystroke, 28 High Street, Tettenhall, Wolverhampton
Printed and bound in Great Britain by
Cpod, Trowbridge, Wiltshire

British Library Cataloguing in Publication Data
A catalogue record for this book is available from the British Library

Library of Congress Cataloging in Publication Data
Littlejohn, Allison, 1962–
Preparing for blended e-learning / Allison Littlejohn and Chris Pegler.
p. cm. – (Connecting with e-learning)
Includes bibliographical references and index.
ISBN 0–415–40361–8 (pbk.) – ISBN 0–415–40360–X (hardback)
1. Education—Data processing—Planning. 2. Computer-assisted
instruction—Design. 3. Computer-assisted instruction—Planning.
I. Pegler, Chris, 1956– II. Title.
LB1028.43.L563 2007
371.33′44678–dc22   2006036689

ISBN10: 0–415–40360–X (hbk)
ISBN10: 0–415–40361–8 (pbk)
ISBN10: 0–203–96132–3 (ebk)

ISBN13: 978–0–415–40360–3 (hbk)
ISBN13: 978–0–415–40361–0 (pbk)
ISBN13: 978–0–203–96132–2 (ebk)

Preparing for Blended e-Learning

Are you an education professional seeking to design innovative courses that 'blend' different sorts of media learning activities across time and space? Do you find it challenging to decide what might be the best blend of activities and media for effective learning? In an age where innovations in social computing and the mainstreaming of e-tools are unlocking new opportunities for blending online with face-to-face interactions, this book will help you to design and implement effective blended e-learning.

With practical, accessible advice for teachers and support staff, *Preparing for Blended e-Learning* reviews practice and research in planning blends of e-learning and scopes the core skills and knowledge required by teachers. Drawing on the experiences of expert practitioners worldwide and citing examples across a range of institutions and countries, it offers a readable, non-technical and comprehensive introduction informed by practice and research. Issues discussed include:

- designing quality, appropriate, effective online learning;
- efficient and sustainable e-learning activity;
- providing appropriate feedback to learners;
- devising student activities and sourcing learning resources;
- managing online and offline interactions.

Preparing for Blended e-Learning offers a careful analysis of strengths and opportunities of blended e-learning, but is realistic about the possible pitfalls. With guidance for both newcomers to teaching and experienced teachers who are developing their practice online, it will appeal to teachers, academics, librarians, managers and educational support staff who are involved in e-learning. It is also a useful text for accredited courses for teachers in further and higher education internationally.

Allison Littlejohn is the Chair in Learning Technology and Director of the Caledonian Academy at Glasgow Caledonian University, UK. She has led international research, development and implementation of innovative learning methods, including blended e-learning, in both further and higher education in the United Kingdom and United States.

Chris Pegler is a lecturer and researcher into educational technology at The Open University, UK. She has led a wide range of educational initiatives in both further and higher education and has studied and taught online since 1995. In 2004 she was awarded a National Teaching Fellowship as a 'Rising Star'.

Connecting with e-Learning series
Edited by Allison Littlejohn and Chris Pegler

e-Learning is rapidly becoming a key component of campus-based education as well as a cornerstone of distance learning. However, although e-learning is an increasingly essential skill for effective teaching, it remains challenging for most teachers in higher and further education. There are four major reasons for this:

- Learners increasingly expect effective application of technologies; this can be intimidating to teachers/lecturers who are novices at using these technologies themselves.
- Already under pressure for time, teachers need to understand how to design an appropriate blend of online and offline, otherwise their learners may end up working unproductively and unhappily.
- Courses need to be created sustainably, so that learning materials can be easily generated, stored, retrieved and repurposed.
- Teachers/lecturers are understandably uncertain about how to invest their time and effort in a fast-moving field.

This exciting new series provides relevant guides for both newcomers to teaching in higher and further education and experienced teachers/lecturers who are developing their practice online. Featuring practical, accessible advice that draws on recent research and the experiences of expert practitioners, each book is structured, accessible and relevant to teachers and lecturers worldwide.

Books in the series include:

Preparing for Blended e-Learning
Allison Littlejohn and Chris Pegler

The Educational Potential of e-Portfolios: Supporting personal development and reflective learning
Lorraine Stefani, Robin Mason and Chris Pegler

The web site for this series is **connecting-with-elearning.com**

Contents

Figures

Tables

Examples

Series editors' foreword
Preparing for blended e-learning

The integration of our physical world with the digital domain is becoming ubiquitous. Every day thousands of new digital communities are created across the world and online social spaces are gaining rapid popularity. MySpace (w) has over 110 million registered accounts and is growing at a rate of 250, 000 new accounts each day. Many individuals are choosing the digital domain as a primary source of information with 77 per cent of Americans choosing the internet as their primary source of news. These phenomena are bound to impact on formal education, yet the educational world does not appear to have corresponding, startling claims.

Many educational institutions across the world have implemented electronic learning environments. Learners and teachers increasingly are integrating physical and electronic resources, tools and environments within mainstream educational settings. Yet, these new environments are not yet having a major impact on learning. This is partly because the 'blending' of 'real' and 'virtual' domains – or 'blended learning' – is challenging for most teachers, yet it is becoming an essential skill for effective teaching. On the one hand this new way of teaching and learning opens up a range of opportunities. At the same time it adds a degree of complexity to educational development and curriculum design. The key to success is to move away from thinking of how to integrate different sorts of content resources and towards developing educational processes that 'blend' online with face-to-face interactions.

Preparing for Blended e-Learning offers a careful analysis of what educators and managers in further and higher education could expect from 'blended e-learning'. It looks at the research, but also draws on the experiences of practitioners to address teachers, academics, librarians, managers and educational support staff who are involved in e-learning. It will help both novices and those who are looking to extend their e-learning practice further, offering guidance on how to change existing practice, with insights into key issues and what may appear to be intractable problems. Everyone is talking about blending and e-learning; this book goes further to explore a variety of contexts, a number of different views of blending, and to examine what works, and why.

The authors, Allison Littlejohn and Chris Pegler, have drawn on years of experience working with a range of staff in tertiary education who are implementing blended e-learning. Ideas are illustrated by case studies drawn from a range of institutions and across many different countries.

The book offers a readable, non-technical and comprehensive introduction to the field. It is the first in a new series, 'Connecting with e-learning'. This series is aimed at teachers, academics, librarians, managers and educational support staff who are involved in ensuring e-learning becomes an important facet of mainstream teaching and learning practice. We hope this book will help you develop ideas for your own practice.

January 2007

Acknowledgements

Writing a book is a landmark. This book is no exception and has marked a series of milestones for us. Firstly, it integrates years of our work in supporting colleagues in planning, developing and implementing blended e-learning with the practice of colleagues from around the world. Secondly, it marks the beginning of a new book series, which we have been planning for a couple of years. Thirdly, the process of writing and editing a book series has illustrated the patience and understanding of those closest to us! Consequently there are lots of people around the world to thank for their contributions to this text.

Allison would like to thank the case study authors who freely shared their experiences of blended e-learning: Professor Lorraine Stefani (University of Auckland, New Zealand), Jane Tobias (Bell College of Further and Higher Education, UK) and Matthew Riddle (University of Melbourne, Australia, though currently at Cambridge, UK). She is grateful to Professor Loretta Jones, her American 'mom' from the University of Northern Colorado, USA, for introducing her to blended e-learning many years ago. Thanks also to long term collaborator and friend Dr David Nicol (University of Strathclyde) who helped devise the principles for LDLite and to ASCILITE (the Learning Technology Association in Australasia) for the award of a Fellowship in 2006 that allowed development of these ideas.

There are many close colleagues, friends and family Allison would especially like to mention. In particular Harriet Buckley for years of valued advice and practical support while developing ideas. Thanks to Catherine McKernan for treasured comradeship and long hours of helpful discussions. Dr Isobel Falconer, a superb colleague and friend, offered invaluable comments and ideas on representations of practice. Special thanks go to Dr Anoush Margaryan who helped maintain momentum through her sparkling friendship, cheerful encouragement and distinctive contributions to the text. And to her father, George Littlejohn, for his unshakeable patience and extraordinary wisdom. Thanks also go to Karen Berry for her support in preparing the final manuscript. Finally, Allison would like to say thank you to Chris for creativity, patience and humour. All three were essential ingredients for the book, the series and our sanity.

Chris has a few personal thanks in addition to the above. She would like to thank everyone who has contributed to her knowledge about e-learning, but there are too many to mention, so she will content herself with thanking colleagues at the Institute of Educational Technology and The Open University, particularly Robin Mason, Martin Weller and Patrick McAndrew, who have all had to be patient while she worked on this project rather than another one. On the home front Steve lent his knowledge of Further Education at key stages, while Rhys and Mum tried to take her mind off the book when it all got too obsessive. Allison deserves special thanks for starting the whole thing rolling and for being (as always) such a great colleague.

Finally, we both thank the many people who helped us with the practical problems of making the series, and this book, a reality.

Introduction

This book offers practitioners in further and higher education a broad view of what is happening in 'blended e-learning'. It reviews practice and research in planning blends of e-learning and explores the range of issues that you will need to consider to be effective in preparing to use blended e-learning with your students. We draw on examples across a range of institutions and across many different countries to offer a readable, non-technical and comprehensive introduction informed by their own practice and research.

The art of blending

Blending is an art that has been practised by inspirational teachers for centuries. It centres on the integration of different types of resources and activities within a range of learning environments where learners can interact and build ideas. Over the past few decades, blended learning has extended learning methodologies, opening up opportunities for open and distance learning as well as challenging more traditional methods. Most recently the term 'blend' has been attached to e-learning, and this blending of e-learning with traditional methods is attracting the interest of many teachers in further and higher education. This contrasts with the relatively poor take-up of predominantly or exclusively e-learning methods, particularly where e-learning has been expected to offer an unproblematic cost-saving replication of traditional teaching methods.

The term 'blended e-learning' recognizes that the opportunities for using e-learning on its own are far fewer than where e-learning is integrated into (blended with) other approaches as a form of blended learning. Education has not been the driver in the use of new technologies in learning. These developments have often been driven by new trends that originated outside formal education. Electronic tools, such as DVDs, iPods, digital cameras, mobile phones and computers, are becoming ubiquitous and are very familiar to our students. The most recent innovations in social software are changing the ways we meet people and interact. They challenge the social norms, opening up opportunities as to how we broadcast personal information and collaboratively explore topics of mutual interest. Students' expectations are being moulded by changes in the use of technologies in their social lives, and the update of these technologies in education has been rapid. All this must have an impact on the potential and future directions of blended learning and e-learning. It also signals a new confidence in using technologies and blended them with existing teaching.

Tutors are making lectures available via podcasts (downloadable videos or audio files of lectures), and at the same time many of their students will be using personal broadcasting technologies to disseminate videos, still images and audio clips captured on their mobile phones. Many of the technologies are easy to 'connect' to and also connect or blend easily with each other. The blends in blended e-learning have become richer, more complex and variable – more rewarding, but also more difficult to predict.

Interest in where these new ideas are taking this area and an appreciation of what has brought us here have both shaped this book. Developments in blended e-learning are not isolated from the changing needs of institutions, and changing practice in education. Staff trying to implement blended e-learning need practical advice that will help them rapidly develop and implement ideas. This book offers that advice, but also acknowledges and examines the impact of the broader environment and the wider expectations of students and teachers in further and higher education today.

The potential of blending

Blended e-learning offers the possibility of changing our attitudes not only as to *where* and *when* learning takes place, but in terms of *what* resources and tools can support learning and the *ways* in which these might be used. Blended e-learning adds extra dimensions to blending. It fosters integration of different *spaces*, allowing students to learn from college, university, the work environments, from home or on the move. It can offer flexibility in the *time* when learners can participate in courses, reducing or removing restrictions arising from that balancing of work or home commitments with study. It opens up the range of *media* resources that can be used for learning. The blend of space, time and media offers new possibilities as to the sorts of *activities* students can carry out and the ways they can collaborate using available electronic tools. Blended e-learning adds extra dimensions to learning. The integration of physical and online spaces means that communities can form and interact in ways that were previously unimagined. It introduces the possibility of interacting in real time (synchronously) in conjunction with opportunities to collaborate over a period of time (asynchronously). This in turn allows exploration of different forms of dialogue and new types of learning. New media resources and tools open up possibilities for students to create their own resource banks, integrating self-generated assets with more 'formal' materials sourced from libraries around the world. This brings into question some of the traditional values of education, such as who owns, creates and controls resources and knowledge. New types of learning activities challenge our thinking as to how learning might be facilitated, creating new etiquettes of learning and teaching, and shifting the locus of control from the teacher to the learner.

Although blended learning and e-learning have the potential to provide the kinds of flexibility required by learners, there are some major obstacles clustered around four key themes. First, the drivers for change should be identified and capitalized on. Second, new possibilities in delivery are available at a cost, so we must find sustainable approaches to these learning methods. Third, new methodologies add a layer of complexity for all those preparing for blended and e-learning. Fourth, new ways of interacting and the free exchange of information require careful consideration of ethical issues.

These considerations impact upon a range of stakeholders within institutions. Senior management and policy makers have to think of new opportunities and reasons why they might adopt blended e-learning. e-learning managers have to consider the levels of support required as well as the cost implications. Support staff have to offer advice to tutors and students in universities, colleges or in work-based environments – or to individuals working across these domains. Tutors have to think about new contexts of learning in addition to the different factors involved in blending and how these items interrelate. Students must be prepared to assume new roles and responsibilities within these new forms of learning. And everyone has to consider the ethical implications of new forms of interaction and freedom of information.

The problems with blending

This book aims to provide all those involved in the development and implementation of e-learning with a general guide to blending e-learning. We have worked over a number of years with a range of different stakeholders planning, designing and implementing blended and e-learning within a number of universities and colleges. We have tested their ideas with students and practitioners worldwide. Ideas within this book are grounded in real-life opportunities, issues and problems raised by their own practice and that of their colleagues. The text contains many illustrative examples and case studies.

We have based our review of blended e-learning around eight key questions associated with the design, development and implementation of blended e-learning. These issues cluster around the four key themes: drivers for change, costs and benefits, educational design and development, and ethical considerations.

I What is blended e-learning and why do we need it?

Implementation of new learning methods cannot be effective without identifying and considering a range of compelling drivers for change. Therefore, the book begins by exploring the meaning of 'e-learning' and 'blended e-learning', identifying factors that have so far driven the implementation of e-learning. Chapter 1 tracks the origins of modern e-learning functions from the adoption of personal computers. It notes the development in the technology and the progress in arguments put by proponents and protesters against e-learning. What this chapter reveals is how the wider political environment of higher and further education today affect what we may expect and what we may achieve in blended e-learning. While showing us how far we have progressed in the past two decades, it also notes the lack of progress, and persistent concerns in several areas.

2 What do we mean when we talk about blending?

The idea of blending different sorts of media and learning tasks is not a new concept. But blended e-learning has an added degree of complexity because blending extends beyond media and activities. e-Learning allows us to blend different spaces. For example, we can use electronic learning environments within physical teaching spaces; we can work across time zones in real time or asynchronously. For effective blending, we need to have a clear idea of why we want to blend (might blending save teachers' time, yet enhance learning?) and what we might blend.

Chapter 2 takes you through a range of blending decisions, considering the impact of factors such as the location and experience of students. It looks at blending from the point of view of informal and formal, work-based and on campus, personal and institutional, new formats and traditional, and personalized or individualized blending. The choice of blend is challenging in a way that it never has been before. Blending offers students and educators choices, but choosing is not an easy process for either group.

3 What sorts of blended activities are useful to the students?

Teachers across a range of institutions have told us that one of the biggest challenges for them is to design learning activities that motivate students and capture their imagination. To understand how to design engaging tasks within blended e-learning, we have to have some knowledge of why we might design specific learning activities in particular ways. Why is one sort of activity appropriate for one learning situation, but not so effective in another? What sort of student activity are we expecting to see online and how might this differ from what we are accustomed to?

Chapter 3 focuses on the potential of online and blended e-learning activity and interactivity. It offers examples of how to approach the blending of asynchronous and synchronous activities, looking at a range of student online activities and in particular how to make sure that you, and your students, communicate effectively. Some of the assessment approaches to online interactivity are compared and we start to look forward to the impact of social computing. That has the potential to change radically the type of student interactivity within courses. It is less formal not only in the use of the tools by students, because of their familiarity with these in other contexts, but in terms of the ownership of the tools. Chapter 3 concludes by considering the impact of bended e-learning on making learning more accessible for disabled students.

4 How can we plan the blend?

Once teachers have decided what sort of learning activities they require, they face a further problem. This is the question of how to plan so that there is integration of these activities with appropriate resources, e-tools and environments, using a range of teaching methodologies. Thinking through all the possible combinations and solutions is complex and demanding. Our conversations with teachers internationally confirmed that this is a problem that needs to be addressed. This led us to develop a framework that would help teachers think through all the possibilities of course design and in considering 'how to blend'. We have called this framework LD_lite, since it is broadly based on a notional system for Learning Design.

We present this framework in Chapter 4, outlining the thinking behind its development. We begin by reflecting upon the different components we might blend – from learning strategies to learning environments, resource activities, space and time. We look at teachers' strategies for planning course design and consider the sorts of problems teachers have told us they face when designing blended and e-learning. We then illustrate ways in which LD_lite might help tutors integrate activities, resources and e-tools for their own blended learning courses.

5 Which e-tool can best support a learning activity?

Another complicating factor for tutors lies in choosing an e-tool for a particular learning task. There are now a wide variety of e-tools to support the range of learning activities that tutors design, so choosing the right one can be complex. In Chapter 5 we map tools with tasks; we explore the relationships between different types of learning activities set for students and the e-tools that can support them.

Within Chapter 5 we go on to explore a range of case examples constructed by tutors from a variety of disciplines and countries. These case studies outline the ways in which colleagues have used the LD_lite framework to plan different sorts of learning activities in real-life teaching and learning situations. It illustrates how LD_lite helped them to map appropriate e-tools and resources with each activity – including materials generated by the students themselves. These case studies look at simple learning activities that can be viewed as small 'chunks' of learning. The chapter does not address issues associated with more complex designs; these are considered in Chapter 6.

6 How can resources and activities be integrated within learning environments?

Students are motivated by solving authentic problems based on real-world activities that may be carried out non-sequentially and iteratively. Such problems contrast with the sequential orchestration of tasks frequently planned in 'formal' education. Planning non-sequential activities is more complex and may involve integrating a variety of media and e-tools across 'real' and 'virtual' spaces. In Chapter 6 we examine different sorts of electronic and physical learning environments available for learning. Through two case studies we explore the relationships between physical and virtual environments and illustrate potential interplay across these domains.

7 How can blended e-learning be designed to be sustainable?

Implementing blended learning requires considerable investment in sourcing and creating learning materials. In Chapter 7 we investigate a range of strategies for cost-effective blended learning. These strategies focus around the reuse or adaptation of existing learning resources. Associated with this, we examine ways in which we can design courses in small, reusable chunks and examine how we might make repurposable resources and learning designs available for reuse.

8 How does blended e-learning affect the support structures and how we use them?

Successful implementation of blended learning and e-learning requires efficient support structures that meet the needs of staff and students. Yet the fast pace of change in this area, coupled with the fact that students (and staff) may be working at a distance, makes it challenging for e-learning managers and support staff to offer effective support.

Chapter 8 examines the experience/location nexus and considers what the options for learner support are within blended e-learning. The internet already offers the potential to offer pre-emptive support, anticipating a range of academic and non-academic student requirements. Just as with other aspects of blended e-learning, there is a wide variety of e-tools to choose from. We consider some options and also look at the role of librarians as we move towards emphasis on 'information literacy' rather than 'information technology' as a prerequisite for effective online study.

9 What are the wider strategic and ethical issues associated with blended e-learning?

Blended e-learning brings with it a new order. With effective design, the locus of control should, in theory, shift from the teacher to the learner. This shift, combined with the free flow of information, requires the development of new sorts of relationships and trust. Ethical issues are of primary importance, and institutions may need to develop or revise strategies to reflect this fact.

Some of the ethical issues that this chapter explores are ones which are familiar, but made more urgent by e-learning, for example issues about intellectual property rights (IPR) and student codes of conduct. As regards, the former, the internet and self-publication online by students and staff create a new set of dangers and concerns in terms of intellectual property rights. The physical separation of teacher and student(s), as well as the magnification of risk mentioned above, create issues around student etiquette (or 'netiquette'). The potential of the internet to allow anonymous communication is one issue that we need to explore, especially as many younger students now enter education with prior experience of online behaviour that may not translate well to a more formal online learning community.

The issues associated with blended e-learning are exciting, complex and ever-changing. From reviewing the literature we know there is little practical advice for staff in institutions moving into this rapidly developing area. Through a thorough exploration of the issues central to this book we present useful and usable guidance for those at the 'digital chalkface'.

This book introduces readers to a new form of educational practice. We have drawn on our own research and experiences in blended and e-learning and then tested our understanding and assumptions with many other practitioners at a variety of institutions. This is a rapidly changing field and we have needed to be selective in choosing the topics that readers might most need support in as they prepare for blended and e-learning. We hope this book will help align the creativity and brilliance of teaching staff within institutions with the exciting opportunities and new directions taking place in students' everyday lives.

Chapter 1

What is blended e-learning?

Blended e-learning is:

- access to a wide choice of alternative resources on your personal computer drawn from international, as well as institutional, digital repositories, accessed via a single log-in that personalizes the 'blend' of learning you are offered;
- studying online with tutors as facilitators and emphasis on co-creation within a course that is rich in online collaboration;
- downloading content to mobile devices, using podcasts and e-books as resources, tablet PCs with wireless connections to take and share notes in class, and using text messaging to receive course updates while on the move;
- immersion in online multi-player gaming or multimedia role-playing using extended, authentic simulations to explore real-life problem solving;
- personalized content delivered through a customized interface with RSS alerts to flag new content relevant to individual interests;
- using a virtual learning environment (VLE) to access course materials and ask questions whether on- or off-campus;
- uploading notes to your own blog (weblog) while the lecture is in progress and using hand-held voting devices to offer instant feedback to the presenter;
- learning on a just-in-time basis using computer-based tutorials;
- staying in contact with study buddies away from the class through use of instant messaging and other informal 'social computing' mechanisms;
- assembling and publishing an e-portfolio of your work from courses studied across several institutions;
- seamless integration of physical and virtual learning spaces that integrate and accommodate technology, but focus on student learning;

- successful and rewarding student–teacher relationships initiated and maintained through online communication without ever meeting face to face.

You are probably already familiar with the term 'e-learning' and recognize that this approach to learning almost never exists in isolation. Even where a CD-ROM is attached to a textbook, there is an element of blending of print and computer-based instruction. The more complex learning activities in higher and further education will generally be examples of blended e-learning. The word 'blended' may refer to a blend within the 'e-learning mix' of media, or a blend of the e-learning with other approaches. As we move towards educational exploration of 'social computing' with emphasis on sharing and working informally, we also see a blend of technologies and skills that students use in their wider lives overlapping with and integrating into their studies.

You may already be using blended learning or e-learning as terms to describe at least some of your own activity. If so, you will have already wrestled with some of the questions posed by use of these terms. Is e-learning really about learning (the student experience), or does it primarily describe 'e-teaching'? To what extent is existing effective practice in teaching and learning transferable to blended e-learning? Is *any* use of computers within education, for example e-administration, an aspect of e-learning? Is a good teacher a good teacher whatever the medium? Is the investment in blended e-learning really paying off?

Each of these questions invites a positive response, but the strength of that response will differ, depending on context and experience. Just as with any other aspect of teaching and learning, differences in expectations and experiences of blended e-learning exist within the same department, institution and discipline. What distinguishes e-learning and 'blends' of e-learning is a further layer of complexity associated with its reliance upon technology, and the uncertainty about technological developments.

Within education in general there is growing awareness of the potential and implications of blended e-learning, not just among the techno-enthusiasts (early adopters who embrace the novel and new), but also across the majority of teaching and support staff. This rise in interest in and enthusiasm for e-learning, although extremely timely, is not merely a matter of chance or coincidence. Neither is the popularity of e-learning purely a matter of politics, technological obsession or aggressive marketing – although all three have played a part.

The interest in the role of computers in education is not a new one, although use of the term 'e-learning' is relatively recent. What we currently understand to be e-learning is the latest stage in a gradual evolution spanning over a quarter of a century. The main difference now is that awareness and interest are becoming more extensive, more 'mainstream'.

Where did e-learning come from?

Many of the constituent parts of e-learning, in particular the move towards students using computers for self-directed study, have been evident in education (particularly in higher and further education) since the early 1980s. This period was significant because personal computers (PCs) then became sufficiently affordable for some colleges and universities to buy them in quantity for student use. Tertiary institutions moved quite rapidly to equip computer suites with the new PCs and allow students access to networked packages and applications. Computers prior to this point were usually not trusted in the hands of many students (or even most staff). Earlier computers in universities were protected and cosseted in special environments, with access controlled by specialist staff who acted as interpreters and gatekeepers.

Even when personal computing in education started, the PCs were not 'personal' in the sense that we now understand. Students today often own at least one computing device for their exclusive use. Some may be carrying a computer in their backpack and another in their pocket, and perhaps even have one in their car. A modest mobile phone offers more functionality and computing power than the earliest PCs. For example, the Acorn/BBC 'B' microcomputer was introduced in 1982 as a popular and affordable computer geared to educational use. It remained in use for the next ten years, yet in its basic form it offered only 64 kilobytes (kb) of memory. In 2002/3, colleges of further education in the United Kingdom reported that they would not consider purchasing machines for student use with less than 2 gigabytes (Gb) of memory, a 300,000-fold increase (Becta, 2003).

Back in the early 1980s the reasonable assumption was that neither students nor tutors would be familiar with how a computer worked, yet most PCs did not offer a user-friendly interface. They were also slow (compared to today's machines) and relatively scarce. Nonetheless, they represented a massive leap forward when compared to the previous use of computers on campuses. For the first time, students were now able to use computers without first learning how to program them, or relying on someone else to do the programming.

The arrival of user-friendly, relatively inexpensive, compact computers led to a dramatic transition. Computers changed from being a relatively

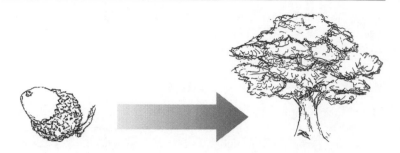

1982: The Acorn BBC 'B' Microcomputer was launched as the first popular and affordable computer for education. It featured 64kb of memory as standard.

2002: UK further education colleges considered 2Gb of memory the minimum for new machines for students – a 300,000 fold increase. (Becta, 2003)

Figure 1.1 Increase in computing power, 1982–2002

limited and very expensive educational resource tied to the classroom, to being powerful, relatively inexpensive, portable and usable tools. While the technology has improved dramatically, so too has the design of learning to take advantage of those improvements.

This journey continues today, but set in the context of developments in teaching and learning approaches, the progress in adapting to use of computers in education has been very fast. We need to remember that education is in many ways a very conservative arena, where the face-to-face lecture remained relatively unchanged for centuries.

As we would expect, the use of computers in education has changed as the functionality has developed. Many of the systems used to develop and deliver this early form of e-learning (called computer-based or computer-assisted learning/training) are now no longer in use, but some of the early approaches to using e-learning have been remarkably robust. Several notable innovations at the start of personal computing in education are still recognizable in today's blended e-learning. For example:

- *Personalization*: The early PCs were able to 'recognize' and use the student's name, personalizing responses to student activity, e.g. 'Well done, Chris, now try this new question'. Now, more refined personalization of the environment is possible, using a student home page or portal that recognizes each student when they log in, and can offer them tailored content based on preferences, performance and permissions.

- *Saving individual work-in-progress:* While students at one time would save work on to floppy disks (carried along to every session), they are now more likely to save progress to a central server that they can access from many locations. Or they may save files to a USB device so that they can work on these using their own off-campus machines. Being able to save work-in-progress allowed students to complete more complex tasks across several, separate sessions and led to widespread word-processing of notes and assignments.

- *Self-paced learning:* A significant virtue of computers is that they never grow weary of explaining the same point repeatedly. Computers do not generally impose a time limit on the student's activity. If the student is working one-to-one with the computer, there need be no suggestion that they are slowing down the rest of the class, or moving ahead too fast. Computer-based courseware can permit a student to revisit content as often as necessary, when they wish. It works at an individual student-centred pace, rather than at a speed set by others.

- *Multiple choice and automated feedback:* The multiple-choice quiz (MCQ) was often a substantial element within early computer-based learning packages. MCQs were easy to generate, and if students provided the wrong answer, the computer could address this through constructive feedback, providing information on why that answer was incorrect. Unfortunately, this element was sometimes overdone in early computer-based tests. Students could become so bored with repetitive question answering that they would randomly select options in order to be allowed to continue. MCQs in computer-based learning became discredited, but they remain a feature of e-learning, now presented with a much greater degree of sophistication. Online programs such as Hot Potatoes (www.hotpot.uvic.ca/) are readily available to teachers under educational licences that allow use free of charge if there is dissemination of the tests created. Modern MCQs offer variety, are easy to use and can be highly effective in some contexts.

- *Tracking student progress.* Using a computer not only makes testing easier to do, but makes it easier to collect data on individual student performance in a form that allows analysis of the class or student, or even comparison across classes. Refinements in data mining and student tracking now mean that it is possible to see how individual students, or groups of students, tackle a particular activity (time spent on each screen, use of help screens, number of attempts, etc.), as well as noting scores. This level of information can act as an early warning of which parts of the course students find difficult. It can also alert teachers to parts that are habitually skimmed or omitted.

- *Using third-party content*: It was not feasible for most tutors to create their own computer-based learning packages. Even today, with availability of powerful and intuitive 'what-you-see-is-what-you-get' (WYSIWYG) word processors and web editors, there remains a tradition of using third-party computer-based resources. With the growth in the internet, there are many more externally produced resources to use, and it is easier to locate and tailor suitable material for e-learning. High-profile international educational initiatives such as the MIT Open Courseware initiative (www.ocw.mit.edu), and the emergence of national repositories such as Jorum (www.jorum.ac.uk) in the United Kingdom and MERLOT (www.merlot.org) in Canada, increase the ease with which suitable educational resources can be found. So, although it is now easier to make your own online or computer-based material, this remains an unusual approach in the face of the greater quantity and higher quality of third-party resources available for reuse or repurposing.

Those are only some of the elements of computer-based learning which persist in e-learning today. It is perhaps inevitable that while key teaching features have been retained and refined over time, so have several of the concerns that educators have expressed about use of computers for teaching or learning.

We can broadly classify the most persistent and significant concerns into three types:

- *Concerns about quality*: These can arise as technical, pedagogical and/or operational questions. Will the learning experience be comparable with that which the student would obtain through more conventional teaching? If the content is devised by someone else, will it be relevant to the context in which *your* students are being taught? Is this content as good (e.g. as accurate and topical) as that which you could generate yourself? Will the application prove robust in use? Will the service on which it relies continue to be available when, and as long as, you and your students need it? Will the service remain affordable?
- *Concerns about control*: The question of how to maintain control of a class is one that all teachers wonder about, and not just in respect of e-learning. In that sphere the questions may include 'How can I make sure that your students are not wandering off and aimlessly exploring the package (or the computer or internet more generally)?';

'Will they access applications, or information, which they should not be allowed to see, or which should be released in a staged way?'; 'How can you be sure that they are understanding and learning, rather than unreflectively pressing the "Next" button until they reach the end?'; 'If student performance is assessed using a computer, without the tutor being present, how can you be sure that the work is their own?'

- *Concerns about change*: These are perhaps the most significant set of concerns. How is it possible to keep up with the demands of the technology as well as with the demands of teaching a syllabus that includes student activity and course content which you have not yourself devised? Will this ultimately lead to a reduction in the status of tutors while increasing the numbers of students that they are expected to teach? Where is all this change leading?

Concerns about quality, control and change were voiced when personal computers first started to be used in education. Although we now know far more about the design of effective e-learning environments, similar concerns are still expressed today. One of the advantages in embracing e-learning may be that it requires us to address these questions. These concerns are relevant to other forms of teaching and learning, but rarely applied. For example, plagiarism is not new. Is e-learning simply making more visible something that was previously easier to ignore? Is plagiarism detection software the solution to preventing plagiarism, or should we be looking at ways of assessing courses which make plagiarism less tempting and less rewarding? Should we find a solution that is effective across all forms of teaching, not just e-learning?

It is important not simply to focus on the anxieties that e-learning raises. We need also to recognize that e-learning offers exciting opportunities. Students can now communicate about their learning using mobile devices, hold discussions with other students from around the globe, access course resources and conduct academic research on a 24/7 basis all year round using online databases and repositories.

Examples of how far we have travelled in our thinking and acceptance of educational technologies can be seen in recent designs for 'wired' buildings. These spaces offer flexible spaces that can be transformed by use of portable technologies, whether the personal technology of the learner or the presentational technology of the tutor. The centrally timetabled computer suites that supported computer-based learning in the 1980s are now giving way to more exciting and inviting spaces such as the Saltire Centre at Glasgow Caledonian University (JISC, 2006) – versatile, social spaces that integrate and accommodate technology, but principally focus on student learning.

Definition of e-learning

Although initially used in the corporate sector to describe computer-based or online training, the term 'e-learning' has increasingly been taken up within education. This has been a gradual transition, and a variety of other terms continue to be used to cover much the same sort of activity. Terms such as 'telematics' and 'telelearning' were at one stage popular, and are still sometimes used. They reflected the impact of telecommunications at a time when the use of information technologies (IT) in education was starting to expand into information *and communication* technologies (ICT), noting the contribution of computer-based interactivity and communication. The term 'e-learning' was not in general use in education until 2002; other terms were used as being synonymous with e-learning. A search in the literature throws up 'networked learning', 'online learning', computer-assisted learning', 'web-based instruction' and 'computer-mediated learning', but e-learning is increasingly an umbrella term used to describe them all. As Chapter 2 points out, e-learning is often only part of the approach, being blended with other – perhaps traditional – approaches as blended learning.

One of the reasons that it is difficult to be precise about what e-learning means and what it covers is that the technologies that make it possible continue to change and develop. What we each mean when we talk about e-learning in the context of teaching and learning may differ, but e-learning is commonly taken to mean the use of computers *and the internet* for learning. This can be taken to mean only using e-learning at a distance, for remote students. However, there are a growing number of applications of e-learning with campus-taught students in either blended or fully online mode.

Other terms may emerge to reflect further changes in the way we use technologies in education. Currently there is considerable interest in mobile learning, or m-learning as it is sometimes called. Is this simply a part of e-learning, or does it suggest a new and fundamental shift?

There is also a tendency, particularly when trying to measure the impact, or influence, of e-learning, to adopt an even broader definition of what it may cover. For example, does this term include the provision of online registration systems for students, or the availability of computer-based overviews for student support? Is providing online timetables an aspect of e-learning? Does it include the use of Microsoft PowerPoint for presenting lectures? These are relatively easy things to measure, allowing comparisons of 'e-learning activity' between institutions. But such measures do not give any clear picture of the level and richness of integration of e-learning into teaching and learning. Publishing slides and handouts from lectures within the electronic learning environment (ELE) may indicate a low level of compliance with organizational directives rather than any real progress towards changes in teaching and learning. There may be little expectation that students or staff will *use* e-learning apart from as means of publishing or retrieving certain limited resources (a form of e-content). It may be simply a means of making contact about administrative matters through email or through the intranet (a form of e-administration). e-Learning in the sense used in this book requires a broader range of e-activity. It is about the process of learning and teaching using computers and other associated technologies, particularly through use of the internet. Some aspects of e-administration and e-content publishing may be part of that e-learning process, but they are not our focus here and, some would argue, are not what e-learning is all about.

Educational and not so educational e-drivers

Should you accept this picture of sustained and expanding interest in use of computers in learning and teaching at face value? As a very general overview it may suffice, but this view disguises the fact that progress was made through a succession of high-risk ventures, a complex network of individual – often unrelated – initiatives worldwide. The progress towards effective e-learning is littered with many abandoned projects, such as the development of laser disk resources including a specially compiled copy of the Domesday Book (the first English census). This update of the 1086 original was published in 1986 and used extensively in UK schools until laser disk technology disappeared from general use. Even among the most promising e-learning projects there have been developments like this, which ultimately proved unsustainable, because of shifts in technology or lapses in funding. In the light of such expensive and short-lived experiments, what is the appeal in e-learning – an often risky and expensive enterprise?

Drivers to adopt e-learning

Although one of the more obvious advantages of using computers in education is that it presents exciting pedagogical opportunities, these are not usually the most talked-about reasons for adopting e-learning. Other motives are often pushing the political and funding agendas in education. We have identified here four major drivers: cost, quality, widening participation and student expectations. These are likely to have played a part in your own institution's decision making about e-learning. You will notice that only one of these relates directly to improvements in learning and teaching.

Can e-learning cut costs?

There is a certain irony in cost reduction being so often proposed as a reason for embarking on e-learning. Not only is this likely to excite academic resistance to change if it is the main reason proposed (see, for example, Noble, 2003), but it is extremely difficult to accurately estimate the costs of e-learning, let alone any cost savings. Notwithstanding estimates of significant cost savings based on work in the corporate world, for example EPIC's estimates of a 700 per cent return on investment from a project for the Royal Bank of Scotland (Clark, 2001), and impressive efficiencies suggested by studies in the United States (Twigg, 2003), it is very difficult to prove that e-learning has led to any savings within colleges or universities. Research into costing e-learning by Bacsich, Asch, Boniwell and Kaplan in the United Kingdom identified many of the 'hidden' costs of networked learning (Bacsich *et al.*, 1999, 2001). Their extensive study of UK universities found that accurate cost data for e-learning activity are rarely collected. Where they are, many of the significant hidden costs of changing to and supporting e-learning are ignored. A report with a similarly informative title, *Costing e-Learning: Is It Worth Trying or Should We Ignore the Figures?*, was prepared by the Observatory of Borderless Higher Education and concluded that e-learning activity was likely to be more expensive than traditional forms of instruction, but that it is so complex that collecting full information about costs was unlikely to be an efficient use of time. This report suggested that using informed estimates would be equally useful, and a more realistic goal in most cases: 'there is little point in costing small scale use of e-learning when it is being developed and used within departments' (Fielden, 2002).

One of the reasons for the existence of conflicting views of cost savings from e-learning arises from trying to draw conclusions from data about corporate e-learning. In Clark's Royal Bank of Scotland example a substantial saving followed from not having to pay travel expenses for staff and overnight stays for residential courses, but the largest cost saving of all was in reducing the amount of staff time lost through attending training courses away from the branch. These dramatic cost reductions do not figure in the costing of e-learning in non-corporate settings. The saving of time and expense for students may well be an important issue and recognized as an advantage, but it does not translate into cost savings for their college or university.

One possible cost saving in education could be through scaling up courses so that the costs of presenting a course are shared with many more students. If students are taught wholly online without the requirement to attend classes, then it becomes possible to offer courses nationally or even globally from a single location. That could massively increase the audience (student revenue) for the same course without disproportionately increasing the costs of the product. Several high-profile initiatives have sought to capitalize on this. One example was the UKeUniversities project, which sought to provide premium-priced online courses worldwide but in 2004 was forced to wind down operations because it failed to secure sufficient students (Bacsich, 2005). There have been other failures of government or consortium-led initiatives for similar reasons, and the experience of supporting mass online courses such as the UK Open University's 'You, Your Computer and the Net' (which attracted 12,000 students in a single year) suggests that the costs of mounting a very popular e-learning course may be significant (Weller, 2004) because of the high costs of support. e-Learning may, after all, offer relatively few cost advantages for smaller-scale presentations – at least in current forms.

It is worth remembering that it is the multitude of small-scale initiatives that are taking blended e-learning forward, even though they do not attract the attention of the press when they succeed, or fail.

Can e-learning improve quality?

As the examples at the start of this chapter indicate, e-learning makes possible many things that would be unfeasible without the use of technology. In particular, it lends itself to personalization, tailoring content and delivery to better suit the needs of individual students. For example, students with a disability can access certain types of resources using assistive technologies, and e-learning can thus expand their range of study options. However, other students could find that they are unable to use these technological aids because the resources have not been designed to be accessible. The potential is there, but the realization of that potential may be flawed. This is a similar effect to using a gifted researcher in a relevant area to teach without preparation. The researcher may find that they have failed to communicate effectively with some students even though the content is academically excellent.

Although improving the quality of learning and teaching design may be a stated motive for blended and e-learning, there is also a sense in which transition to ICT is, more obviously, a means to improve quality in the process of delivery and recording of learning. Here the emphasis is not on pedagogical innovation but on the development of systems that support accountability, recording and transparency. The ease with which student records of achievement can be exchanged, or shared, between and within institutions is one potential advantage of a shift to e-learning. There is a further possible advantage if learning materials and learners' conversations are captured in digital form. It allows them to be disseminated and developed more systematically, and can make them visible for quality control and staff development in ways that other teaching material rarely are. In today's climate of regular quality audits, both internal and external, having convenient access to data on individual students and being able to make comparisons across a class, or between courses, offers a significant advantage.

Improvements in the quality of student administration are easier to quantify than the impact on learning and teaching quality. This is particularly the case with e-learning, where the approach to teaching and understanding of learning may be substantially different from what has gone before. How is it possible to judge the impact of e-learning on teaching and learning quality? Russell, in his massive 1999 'No Significant Difference' review of 355 research reports (Russell, 2004), found that there was no significant overall difference between the teaching quality of courses that used new technology and those that did not. However, we might bear in mind that when Walker and Schaffarzick (1974) tried to answer the question 'Are new (school) curricula better than the old curricula?' they found that new curricula were better at teaching the things that new curricula emphasize, and old curricula produced a better understanding of the things that they emphasize. So, perhaps Russell should have been looking for significant *new* differences and we should expect to see these, depending on what we are trying to do and how. More recent research suggests that in specific contexts there are significant quantifiable improvements through use of e-learning (Pepicello and Pepicello, 2003).

Can e-learning widen participation?

There are many prospective students who cannot attend courses that are taught exclusively full time and on-campus. This has always been the case, although recent growth in the availability of places in further education and higher education means that, in most developed countries other than the

United Kingdom, the majority of school leavers now engage in some form of higher or further education (OECD, 2006). There is at the same time a growth in accredited professional development and the demand for lifelong learning opportunities, which both bring substantial numbers of mature students into higher education. Overall, more students now choose to engage in post-compulsory education than ever before. These 'new' students offer a much more diverse profile than that of the 18- to 24-year-old entering higher education following a record of successful academic study and formal schooling. With the extension of disability discrimination legislation into education, such as the UK's Special Educational Needs and Disability Act (SENDA) (JISC, 2001), there are now also greater numbers of students entering higher education with some form of pre-existing disability that must be accommodated.

Harold Wilson, then prime minister of the United Kingdom, in establishing The Open University (OU), described it as 'the University of the Second Chance'. When it started in 1971, it intentionally set out to attract students for whom the standard route to higher education was unavailable. Having no prior record of formal educational achievement was not a barrier to obtaining an OU degree. Many of the OU's early students had left school before taking exams, and nearly 9,000 of its 200,000 current students have some form of disability that could impact on their learning. The OU has always been 'open' in the sense of widening access to undergraduate studies. At the same time, it has been open to new teaching approaches, particularly the use of technologies, notably use of radio and television, in which it was a pioneer. It has acted as a model for other large open universities and mega-universities such as the Indira Gandhi University in India (Daniel, 1996). Many other institutions are now widening participation in further and higher education, and have adopted new teaching approaches, including blended learning and e-learning, to meet the needs of students from diverse academic, social and cultural backgrounds.

Recognizing the challenges that their students face, the emphasis at the OU is on 'supported open learning', with considerable emphasis on the 'support' and the significant resource devoted to this. That support has always included face-to-face and telephone support options, but increasingly offers online and computer-based alternatives and extensions.

Other educational institutions are also using e-learning as a form of support for students both on- and off-campus. They may use it as a form of distance or distributed learning, to offer access to education to those who cannot attend campus-based activities. They may also use it to offer additional or alternative support to students on more conventionally delivered courses.

If we broaden our horizon and think globally, the challenge of meeting demand for higher education becomes even startling. Asia is already home to nearly half of all higher education students, but a substantial increase is expected over the next fifteen years (from 17 million in 1995 to 87 million by 2020). The demand in China alone is overwhelming – 20 million places by 2020. 'Asia is seeing a massive and insuperable demand for higher education,' said Alan Olsen, director of the Hong Kong-based think tank Strategy Policy and Research in Education. 'It is beyond the ability of the world's universities to satisfy that need by physical campuses' (DFID, 2003). He suggests that e-learning is the way ahead, and many universities are now engaged in 'e-China' projects to take that approach forward.

Within more developed countries there also is a struggle to meet demand through full-time courses. For many potential students this delivery format is inaccessible, and in the United Kingdom the number of part-time students now accounts for 40 per cent of all registrations. However, potential part-time options that require regular attendance for face-to-face teaching may still be out of the reach of many. In this context, e-learning off-campus, or blends of e-learning with campus-based teaching, could provide the answer.

Do students expect (and want) e-learning?

The growth in use of personal computing has not been restricted to education. In the home and workplace, personal computing has grown at an even more startling pace. Some would argue that it is now necessary for colleges and universities to recognize this by making technology use inside the classroom comparable with use of technology outside it. As many students now carry mobile phones (even into examination halls as revision aids! (*Guardian*, 2006)), there is a sense in which the learner cannot be separated from technology and will use it with or without explicit instruction from the tutor. For example, deaf students have been reported as using text messages to 'whisper' to each other in class – a more discreet alternative to sign language, and one that is less visible to the presenter.

Marc Prensky has talked about students as having a familiarity with the use of computers (and wider technologies) that makes them interact with learning technologies as confident 'digital natives'. He argues that younger students grew up using this type of technology for leisure and for schoolwork, and are very familiar with it. In his words, 'Today's average college grads have spent less than 5,000 hours of their lives reading, but over 10,000 hours playing video games. . . . Computer games, email, the

Internet, cell phones and instant messaging are integral parts of their lives' (Prensky, 2001a). This is in contrast to older students, and most university staff, who are more in the nature of what he calls 'digital immigrants'. They are unfamiliar with the technologies, used to different ways of getting the job done, need reminding how to use different applications and are generally less fluent in using computers and the internet. They are relatively inexperienced users of technology in comparison to their students, which may erode their confidence in teaching using ICT.

Prensky (2001b) and others have suggested that educational design should learn from games design in order to engage and retain younger students. The computer games player learns through mistakes, reflects and moves forward through many attempts. This contrasts with traditional approaches to assessment, which offer only limited opportunities to improve performance following an initial failure.

Exciting as these ideas may be, there is also a sense in which it is simply not possible to hold back the use of computers in education, as students are now used to using these tools in everyday life. Recently, commentators such as Stephen Downes (Downes, 2006) have suggested that students, if unhappy with the e-learning tools offered by the institution, will forge their own, substituting personal online tools for those that the institution has provided. School-age students use instant messaging, outside the control of their schools, to keep in contact with homework buddies. It will seem natural to them to continue this practice when they leave school and start studying elsewhere. Many children are confident users of technology from an early age, using online encyclopedias such as Wikipedia to complete homework assignments, learning how to use technology as part of their K-12 curriculum and augmenting that use through experience of online and computer-based games outside school.

Where researchers have tried to assess how much e-learning students entering higher education expect as part of their university courses, they have found that the expectation is lower than the 'digital native' argument might anticipate. The technologies do not play the same role in formal learning contexts and there are mismatches in the learning processes involved in classroom settings and social situations (Kukulska-Hulme and Traxler (2005). An extensive survey of students at the University of Strathclyde (Wojtas, 2001) showed that although, over a four-year period, students changed their use of ICT for informal learning, social and play activities, they did not display a corresponding shift in how they expected e-tools to be used in formal learning at university.

Whether or not students see the e-learning activity as being something that the university or college itself provides as 'e-teaching', what is clear from recent studies (e.g. Golden *et al.*, 2006) is that e-learning in a broad sense is having an impact on learning and teaching in post-16 education. This happens even when e-learning tools are not specified by the tutor (for example, students may be using Google for homework without being directed to do so). There is therefore a certain powerful logic to the driver that courses should be devised that make use of these tools, even though there is scant evidence, as yet, that students actively choose courses on the basis on the e-learning technology employed.

e-Learning in online, conventional and blended courses

e-Learning, and particularly the potential offered by online learning (using the internet to deliver or support learning activity), has been long recognized as offering important advantages to distance teaching institutions. It represents a fundamental shift in distance education – effectively a move into the 'third generation' of distance education (Nipper, 1989). Now communication and interaction at a distance can be as rich at a distance as it would be in face-to-face campus-based settings. Where distance-taught students had previously met other students and their tutors infrequently by travelling to a central or regional location, online learning now offers an alternative. Its flexibility and relatively low cost – compared to setting up face-to-face workshops and the time and travel costs to attend – provides many more opportunities for dialogue than would otherwise be possible within print- or broadcast-based distance learning courses. Such dialogue opens up the opportunity for more effective learning on courses that rely upon developing argument through discussion with others (philosophy was one of the first UK Open University courses to use online forums for discussion). It was also now possible for distance-taught courses to offer a more engaging social experience to their students, with the kind of serendipitous conversation and peer interaction normally associated with attendance at a campus-based university (Rennie and Mason, 2004).

There has not been the same enthusiastic take-up of online teaching in conventional (non-DL) teaching. One of the biggest pedagogical barriers to adopting fully online teaching approaches in campus-based institutions is often presented as being that students may feel isolated, or that tutors would lack the feedback that they require to teach effectively (e.g. body language). Of course, the reason why DL institutions are keen to adopt online learning is that *for them* these two aspects are improved by online interaction. Campus-based students and tutors have a number of face-to-face alternatives for meeting and conversing with other students and their tutors, hence the popularity of blended learning. But for distance-taught students, online discussion, particularly where there is also use of audio or video, offers a much better level of interaction with others than was previously possible. Unlike telephone conferencing or regional seminars, these means of establishing and maintaining dialogue are also scalable and can be experienced asynchronously (that is, without the need for all participants to be online together at the same time). This particularly benefits those students who are studying at a distance precisely because they cannot easily predict their availability for study.

Online courses are a popular and logical alternative for distance learning students, and all the OU's 200,000 students now have access to computer conferencing and online access to their library and other support mechanisms. These students already expect *not* to see or meet with other students and tutors on a regular basis. The systems that are needed to support students studying away from the campus (e.g. distributed tutors and regional support) are already in place.

Within more conventional institutions there is a greater cultural gap. Here the norm for tutors and students is to see each other at regular intervals at scheduled events and on an *ad hoc* basis. Offering fully online interaction in place of face-to-face can be perceived as a second-best alternative. Where it is offered, it may be as an extension to distance learning provision, which is already targeted at students who are not able to attend the campus – for example, overseas students studying for an MBA by distance learning. Sometimes, online courses from other institutions may be 'bought in'. These are offered to students to allow study of courses that would not normally be offered within that institution, or as alternatives to support a more flexible timetable. For example, 80 per cent of the undergraduate students registered at Athabasca University (described as 'Canada's Open University') are registered for their degrees with other institutions and take online courses at Athabasca as an addition to taking conventional classes elsewhere (Ally, 2006).

Even within distance education, fully online courses remain fairly uncommon. One of the reasons given for the £62 million collapse of the UKeUniversity (Bacsich, 2005) was that there was no significant global market for wholly online courses. Some mass online courses (e.g. 'You, Your Computer and the Net', launched by the OU in 2000 with 12,000 students) have been successful, but remain as yet isolated examples of how popular such courses *could* be.

Most courses that offer opportunities for online or e-learning, particularly those offered in conventional colleges and universities, are 'blended': they blend the online experience with more conventional approaches, or may use some elements of e-learning, usually as optional or additional resources that the student can opt to use, or not. The most common example of the use of additional resources is the use of electronic learning environments (ELEs) and intranets as a place to publish the course resources and handouts (Becta, 2005). This, and the use of software such as Microsoft PowerPoint to prepare lectures, are the most frequently observed uses of computers in education (Golden *et al.*, 2006).

The term 'blended learning' is increasingly being used to describe a hybrid model of e-learning that allows coexistence of conventional face-to-face teaching methods and newer e-learning activities and resources in a single course. Described more fully in Chapter 2, the blend can refer to several aspects of the course design, including the activity and media blends. Ideally, what determines the mix of different elements will be the relative strengths and weaknesses of each. The designer of the course will have chosen the best approach to each activity, or the best medium reflecting the most effective instructional practice. However, as with other ideals in course design, the determination of what part of the course is online can be led by considerations such as the cost of developing new resources, availability of and commitment to existing resources, or simply the access that students or tutors may have to certain technologies at particular stages in the course.

When used effectively, blended approaches can address some of the problems that have yet to be resolved within e-learning. For example, it has been noted (Weller, 2003) that some large online courses have relatively high drop-out rates. One way to counter the tendency to drop out may be by building in opportunities for groups to meet face to face, to help students to feel more committed to the group that they are studying with. Where the students are already in a single geographical location on a regular basis, such opportunities are usually easier to arrange.

Another approach to blending is to use this to overcome specific difficulties in campus-based teaching. For example, the online or e-learning elements of a course can be used to 'wrap around' the face-to-face (or printed distance learning) elements, adding additional activity, assessment or support. New online elements are created which can extend the interactivity of the classroom, giving students a greater range of opportunities to explore, discuss and work together using online or offline resources. This approach is especially useful with courses where the students have diverse educational backgrounds and different motivations for study. For example, each student studying a work-based course will have different requirements from the course, depending on their work context. They may have very different access to work-based resources depending on the size and type of organization and their position within it. Using e-learning to prepare students in advance of the face-to-face teaching can make the task of in-class learning easier for everyone. Timetabled sessions can then be focused on activity such as lab work and group discussion rather than used to 'level the playing field' for some students, or as a means of information transmission to fill in gaps in knowledge.

Blended learning could be seen as a stage in the adoption of e-learning which is less threatening and less risky than a move to fully online or fully computer-mediated courses. It does not rely upon the complete revision of existing courses – a huge enterprise and one that most established institutions would not be sufficiently resourced or motivated to undertake. For some institutions it may simply be a 'comfort zone', popular because it allows academic staff to continue to teach as they have previously done, with some online and peripheral resources. This level of blending is unlikely to produce convincing evidence that e-learning has anything significant to add to the educational experience. For example, a video lecture that is simply a recording of a talking head offers little advantage to students apart from the possibility of saving travel time. An interactive video conference over three sites, requiring students at each location to research and then role-play parties to oil pricing negotiations, is an entirely different type of e-learning experience. It allows students to experience the excitement of the negotiation process, pitting their skills against others in real-time discussion. Alexander (2002), when reporting on this use of multi-site two-way videoconferencing, pointed to the impact that the exercise had on students. Some were so 'into' their roles that they dressed in costume.

The challenges of designing blended e-learning

This chapter has given you an overview of what is new and not so new in e-learning. We can recognize several persistent concerns about the use of computers in education. We also see a growing trend for optimism, backed by confidence based on positive experiences.

If we return to the concerns about quality, control and change mentioned at the start of this chapter, we see that one of the reasons why these have persisted is because sharing of knowledge of what works in e-learning has been very patchy in the past. Even where we recognize that good practice exists, it is not usually easy to transfer what we learn there into our own teaching and support of learners; it is not clear *why* this is good practice. e-Learning is no longer primarily about pioneering experiments, something that the time-pressured educator has little time for, although it can sometimes appear that e-learning is still on the nursery slopes in terms of its maturity and reliability. In reality, we already know a lot about how to make e-learning work, and many institutions have been putting what they know into practice, increasingly effectively, for at least a decade.

This book focuses on the factors that you should take into account when approaching the design of e-learning. In particular, it focuses on the design of *blended* e-learning. It offers you a framework (the LD_lite approach to learning design) that will ensure that appropriate designs are easier to recognize and share. Before then, Chapter 2 will take you into the world of choice that underpins blended learning.

Chapter 2

Different approaches to blended e-learning

As the use of computers in education has grown, e-learning has become increasingly prevalent in colleges and universities. Its use may be central to the courses offered, or it may be entirely incidental, available as an optional 'extra', or offering an alternative route. The combination of conventional teaching approaches and e-learning elements within a single course or programme is commonly referred to as 'blended learning', but we can also think of it as *blended e-learning*. The blend refers to the proportion of e-learning content within the course. It can be a strong blend (almost exclusively e-learning) or a weak blend (virtually none).

It is also possible to think of blends in terms of the *media blend* or the *activity blend*. For example, a course could be a media blend of audio and video (webcast or otherwise), and print resources or readings with face-to-face lectures. These could work together in a very integrated way, each referring to and building on each other, or they could work as stand-alone resources with the tutor providing an overarching narrative. They could even be offered as a menu that students are encouraged to navigate for themselves, making their own personal blend based on preferences for specific topics, or particular formats.

An e-learning *activity blend* focuses on what we do and where. Is the discussion going to happen online or offline? If it is happening in both ways at different times, how can these support each other? How can the activities be sequenced and supported so that they work well? This activity blend is often what people mean when they talk about 'blended learning', but that term can often refer to the proportion of e-learning (blended learning), the mix of media (media blend), or the way in which activities are used together (activity blend). We are usually thinking about blends of media resource and blends of activities and tools whenever we consider blended learning.

Blending in chunks

While the word 'blended' implies a seamless integration or intermingling of e-learning and conventional teaching approaches and environments, this is not usually what is offered in colleges and universities. To achieve that level of seamless integration would require the remaking of courses from scratch, creating a precise balance and blend of media use across the course from the earliest design stage. In practice, 'blended learning' more often means the introduction of e-learning alongside, or as a substitute for, specific elements within an otherwise conventionally taught course. The e-learning works alongside 'legacy' materials that were designed for the course in its earlier form and that are proven and familiar. The experience, for learners and educators, is therefore often not finely blended, but somewhat 'lumpy', with the joins between the newer e-learning and older-established material being apparent to students. Where there is lack of confidence in e-learning, those sections of the course may be presented and identified to learners as optional extras or experiments (e.g. an additional online conference in which participation is invited, but not required or recognized). A more elegant 'solution' is to wrap one approach around another, for example using conventional teaching to wrap around e-learning resources, or extending traditional approaches by wrapping these around e-learning activity. As with any approach to blending, a 'wraparound' will work best when attention has been given to how the resources relate to, and complement, each other (see Figure 2.1).

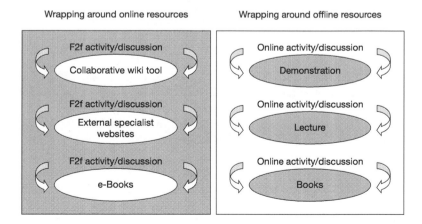

Figure 2.1 Two approaches to 'wraparound' activity blending

The proportion of online to offline, and the type of offline activity favoured, will be informed by both the pedagogical and the operational preferences of the institution and course developers. On the side of pedagogy will be decisions about which activities in the course are best accomplished through e-learning with particular groups of students, what level of assessment these parts should carry, where in the course e-learning will occur, how it will be introduced, what sorts of e-learning students can access and where they will be studying. On the operational side, concerns will centre on how to resource and support new approaches as these blend with established teaching – what the cost considerations may be, staff development implications and issues of technical support for staff and students. Chapters 4 and 5, which introduce the design of e-learning using the LD_lite framework, examine the pedagogical considerations in more detail. This chapter looks at the broad issues affecting the why, which, what, where, when and how of blended learning – why is it often proposed as the most effective approach to e-learning within further and higher education (Garrison and Kanuka, 2004; Golden *et al.*, 2006)?

Why blend at all?

We hope that by now you are convinced that there *are* virtues in using e-learning. Incorporating e-learning into a course can introduce variety into the way that teaching is approached; it can accommodate elements of personalization that would be problematic where there are a large number of students being taught by a single tutor; it can extend the range of resources and allow the course to be offered more flexibly.

The question with blended learning is, why offer a blend at all? If e-learning is so good, then perhaps the course should be offered entirely through e-learning, perhaps as a wholly online course? Different media offer different opportunities for e-learning, just as they do for conventional teaching and learning. Factors that the tutor will consider in making choices will include the impact on space (e.g. the physical location of the students), the impact of time (synchronous or asynchronous) and the level of interaction. All three concerns are addressed over the following three chapters.

e-Learning and only e-learning?

Courses that rely entirely upon e-learning, whether campus based or distance-taught, remain unusual (Sener, 2002; Becta, 2005) and are generally offered only where there are special requirements that preclude any face-to-face teaching. This can lead to the perception that e-learning only works when it is at a distance. There are, however, a number of motives for adopting a wholly e-learning approach. These can include any or all of the following:

1   Most of the learners are located at some distance from the institution, perhaps even spread internationally. The population density may be low, and travel distances between institutions and students very great. It is no coincidence that some countries have well-established distance learning institutions, and students who are used to learning without face-to-face teaching (e.g. Australia with its Deakin and Monash Universities, and Canada with Athabasca University). Such courses may have previously been offered through more conventional (print-based) distance learning.

2   The course covers such a specialist area that insufficient students could be found to make a viable cohort for face-to-face teaching. Postgraduate-level courses are particularly likely to be offered as e-learning variants. Here the student numbers are likely to be low, and the students may already have a successful record of achievement in more conventional study. They could meet on-campus (with some travel), but e-learning is a desirable and convenient alternative.

3   The courses may be offered to students who already have experience of learning at a distance, in using computers for communication, and perhaps also in e-learning. Students and employees who are already successful e-learners may seek further courses delivered in this way (Murray, 2001). Such courses and students are so far concentrated in a few discipline areas, notably computing and business. In these areas, students may actively choose e-learning.

4   The availability of places at colleges and universities may be restricted, and insufficient to meet demand. For example, the Syrian Virtual University (www.svuonline.org/sy/eng/about/mission.asp) was established to meet the need for an Arabic-based higher education opportunity, in recognition that only half of Egypt's 600,000 potential university students could secure places to study at a physical campus and that taking up places at universities overseas may be culturally inappropriate (Syrian Virtual University, 2003). Local e-learning is in this case preferable to residential face-to-face teaching elsewhere.

5   The times at which individual students are studying may vary widely and there is no common pattern of availability for face-to-face

sessions. This will be particularly the case for courses that are work based, or that offer some sort of just-in-time dimension to the learning. Collis *et al.* (2005) at the University of Twente in the Netherlands have commented on the use of online only, just-in-time activity as a supplement or adjunct to on-the-job informal learning at Shell Exploration.

6   Wholly online sessions or segments within a course may be offered as a means of extending the reach of teaching in order to share teaching resource across more than one site. In this model the tutor typically teaches face to face at one location only (his or her 'home' location), with simultaneous recording and broadcasting of that session to students in other locations (their homes or other institutions). An example of this would be the use of videoconferencing by Duke University on its Global Executive MBA programme to teach internationally, or by the University of Ulster to share teaching across a multi-site campus. Another, slightly different example is the UHI Millennium Institute, which connects geographically dispersed, independent colleges across the Highlands and Islands of Scotland (www.uhi.ac.uk). Unlike Duke and Ulster (where there is one multi-site institution), UHI has been formed from many separate institutions. Collaboration has helped to secure viable numbers across their degree programmes. Learners use a variety of means of electronic communication, from their homes, outreach centres and college campuses.

7   Students at some locations may be asked to accept e-learning as a means of accessing an otherwise scarce resource.

8   The learning is based upon a stand-alone, wholly e-learning package designed to be studied independently. Local institutions may offer additional campus-based teaching on an optional, additional cost basis, but the courses were originally developed to be studied online. An example of this would be the African Virtual University, which offers online distance learning material from the OU alongside its own courses. The e-learning is bought in as a stand-alone.

While the opportunities for increasing the amount of e-learning in conventional teaching are expanding, most courses do not fall into the categories identified above and so have not – yet – migrated to a wholly online delivery. As more courses are offered online, more students and tutors will become used to this delivery format, and some may seek this out in preference to other forms – in the same way that face-to-face teaching, being familiar, is often highly valued by current students. At present, a positive preference for e-learning is only likely to be a decision-making factor for 'early adopters' (either students or staff), with perhaps more students being interested in these approaches than staff. The most likely reasons for adopting wholly online delivery will be that some operational factor precludes learners from accessing the same course through more traditional approaches.

Before choosing an e-learning blend

Any advice on how to choose an optimal blend of e-learning must be conditional upon the provision and support of e-learning being in place, or attainable. Where the students have never used a computer before, they will require some introduction and an opportunity to acquire and practise basic skills. If the institution cannot provide sufficient access to computers, then this must also be addressed. If teaching and support staff have no experience in delivering courses using e-learning, then this needs to be remedied. As with other ideals in course design, the determination of which part of the course uses e-learning will be influenced by operational considerations. These will include the anticipated cost of developing resources in a new format, availability and allegiance to existing resources and approaches, and the availability of certain technologies at particular stages in the course.

It is tempting to think that by adding on e-learning as an extra you are managing risk, creating an effective blend and at the same time allowing students to fall back on conventional face-to-face sessions if this does not work. However, perhaps unsurprisingly, research shows that where use of new media is optional or incidental, students will typically not value material presented in that way as much as material that is clearly core or assessed (Kirkwood and Price, 2005). This creates a vicious circle whereby lack of experience and confidence in using e-learning feeds into approaches to blending that are undervalued by students and unused by many, contributing to the overall lack of positive experience and confidence. This lack of experience covers not only lack of practical skill in using e-tools, but also an absence of what we might think of as 'e-learning literacy skills', for example skills in searching and browsing, without which finding and discriminating between internet sources can appear overwhelming.

Ideally, what will determine the use of conventional or e-learning delivery for the different elements within a blended course should be the strengths and weaknesses of each medium rather than the prejudices and fears of the course designer. Where e-learning elements are selected, they fulfil a necessary function. For example, Laurillard's conversational framework (Laurillard, 2001) emphasizes the need for educational activity designs using different media to support interactivity and to be communicative (enabling reflection on learning in progress), as well as the requirement to be adaptive (subject to necessary modification while teaching is in progress) and narrative (articulating the conception of teachers to students, and vice versa). Media strengths differ, and it is important to obtain a suitable blend so that learning can be enabled and enriched. Some media have been traditionally inclined towards broadcast communication rather than dialogue and negotiation, so their use would need to be balanced with opportunities to review, reflect on and practise what has been learned. It is interesting to observe how changes in format (e.g. from web site to wikis) can alter the interactivity of an e-learning approach.

Increasingly, the format in which the media are made available will also affect decisions about which media to blend and how these should be introduced to students. As Table 2.1 shows, evolution in the formats in which we use even familiar media has made these more portable and more adaptive than previously. As well as improving the potential access, greater prevalence of portable media playback and recording devices in everyday life builds expertise and acceptance of these among learners. We are seeing a movement in use of these technologies from 'geeks to grannies', with some countries showing extensive use among atypical users of technology such as senior citizens (Oksman, 2005). Where everyday use of such devices is extensive, for example in Norway and Japan, they provide a natural extension to the media traditionally used to communicate with students.

One way in which the potential of media can be understood is in terms of the affordances that they offer. This term is derived from the work of Gibson (1979) and Norman (1999), and can be taken to mean the perceived as well as the obvious, almost visible, features of the medium. Just as a ball lends itself to kicking, throwing, catching, rolling, etc., audio lends itself to listening to voice or sounds, recording, storing and perhaps editing (changing) and sharing them. The first row of Table 2.1 shows how different formats of audio present different affordances in terms of the different learning and teaching behaviour that they can support. For example, an MP3 recording will lend itself to being carried about on a just-in-case basis rather more than an audio tape would, and this makes it more possible that learners will be able to access a recording precisely when they need it as well as increasing the likelihood that they will share it with others. (This table covers only a selection of the most commonly used media, and some of the more popular uses; Conole and Fill's DialogPLUS taxonomy in Chapter 5 shows the extent of the learning

Table 2.1 Comparing the affordances of traditional and e-learning formats across commonly used media

Medium	Affordances of traditional formats	Affordances of e-learning formats
Audio	As audiotape or recordable CDs, this medium has been used in language teaching to offer students recordings of native speakers, or to provide opportunities to polish and review students' own spoken language skills. This takes advantage of the capability to record and re-record speech. Across a range of disciplines it is used to provide variety in terms of interviews with experts, or verbatim accounts presented as case history. In music teaching it can provide access to performances. As with language teaching, audio is central to learning in this discipline. Audio can be listened to in a group or on an individual basis. However, the tapes or CDs can be damaged and the players (even the Walkman-type players) are relatively bulky.	With MP3 recording devices and the capability to download and upload recordings from the internet, the access to recordings has increased exponentially and the portability of the devices has also dramatically improved. These devices can carry such quantity of audio that it is common for them to allow organization as playlists, simple browsable sets of recordings that can be shared online with others. In music, the digital form allows musicians to compose and perform material virtually, without meeting face to face. Students can create their own individual audio artefacts, or create ensemble pieces, and upload these as podcasts and to share with peers and tutors. Many radio programmes are now available as podcasts and some colleges and universities are making audio resources available in this form as part of their courses.
Video	Video has often been used with large groups, as trigger material or to bring to the class real-life examples. It can be an engaging experience, but lighting conditions may make taking notes difficult and it can present viewing and accessibility problems. For individual viewing, videotape requires access to relatively bulky, non-portable devices and a television. Although most homes possess a video recorder, access to this device may be restricted because of competition with other household members. There are many different video recording	Use of DVDs has largely overtaken use of videotape, as this format offers additional functionality in terms of navigation, storage capacity and smaller physical size. Many DVDs can be viewed on computers as well as dedicated players (although there may be format incompatibilities). Digital-format video allows students to edit using a home computer or laptop and compact video recording devices.
Streaming video allows students to view remote events as they are happening, while video downloads allow them to access relevant video over a fast internet connection. Video diaries and portfolios are easier to create and update.

	formats and students will need access to specialist editing suites to create viewable video output. Cruder, unedited, video recordings are often used to help refine performance skills. As with audio tape, this format is relatively fragile, with a finite lifespan.	Several mobile computing devices (e.g. 3G phones) now also incorporate video recording/messaging capability.
Static images	Images displayed in print, 35mm, on acetates or as posters have been used extensively in the teaching of highly visual subjects such as art and medicine. Projecting a static image so that it can be viewed by the whole class presents some logistical problems, and access to individual copies can be limited, as full-colour images are relatively expensive to reproduce. Locating static images to use as in-class resources can offer challenges, as the size and format are likely to vary between sources, and the potential to resize these is limited, and can be time-consuming. There is little opportunity to reuse images produced in a non-digital form. Copying from copies will degrade quality.	Digital images can be shared and displayed more easily. In particular, they can be used and reused in presentation software such as PowerPoint much more easily than the 35mm or acetate equivalents. The resolution of digital images can be such that it is possible to drill down through a succession of images to reveal more and more detail, as for example on the GoogleEarth project (earth.google.com/.) Students and staff can manipulate images, resizing, changing colours, morphing, cutting and pasting, to create integrated and original documents. Students of photography can create a variety of effects using their computer without access to a darkroom. This freedom to change the appearance of images can be a problem where accuracy of colour and tone are required, as each student's computer may show a slightly different image. There may also be concerns about the infringement of digital rights.
Animation	Traditional animation, because of high cost, was relatively little used in conventional teaching before the advent of digital techniques.	Digital animation is cheaper, easier and far quicker to produce and has the advantage of being easier to reuse and update. It is also easier to share, both as work-in-progress and as a finished product. This has opened up the potential for a wider range of visual arts students to develop skills in animation as well as opening up the potential for educational technologists to employ this medium. There is now significant interest in games-based education, and several projects offer extensive simulations based on computer-based imaging (CGI) (e.g. Ha and Dobson, 2005).

continued

Table 2.1 continued

Medium	Affordances of traditional formats	Affordances of e-learning formats
Artefacts	Access to artefacts may be important so that students can appreciate intangible aspects of the object in a way that they could not by viewing static or moving images of it, or because the student needs to handle and use the object. Unfortunately many artefacts that students are asked to access, e.g. original artworks, are rare items which are protected and confined to specific locations. Access may not be permitted to all those students who could benefit, and for some items (e.g. historical documents) facsimiles may be used instead. Where students use the object or equipment themselves there may still be problems of rarity and access, although on a smaller scale. While it is feasible to provide every student with a rat for dissection practice, it is not feasible to provide medical students with enough human bodies for their practical studies. While students may be able to have hands-on experience of an electron microscope, this will probably be a very limited experience because of the numbers sharing the equipment.	While it is not possible to replicate the experience of viewing an important artefact *in situ*, it is possible to supplement that experience with additional and unusual (e.g. aerial or panoramic) views of the object, or allow close examination of the content of artefacts that students could not hope to otherwise examine in detail. Examples of the latter include Leonardo da Vinci's diaries and Mozart's handwritten scores via the British Museum at www.bl.uk/onlinegallery/ttp/ttpbooks.html. Students are able to rehearse practical experiments using virtual equipment such as microscopes. That particular application is now so popular that it has given rise to the term 'web microscopy' to describe how slides are digitized for sharing over computer networks. Some set-ups allow the student to control settings, position and magnification while others primarily offer a database for comparison. While access to simulation facilities is not new, the possibility of accessing these remotely and via a personal computer offers more flexibility to learners. Web sites reviewing the step-by-step process that students will need to undertake in handling artefacts are also popular. For example, the virtual frog dissection site www.curry.edschool. virginia.edu/go/frog/ created at the University of Virginia in 1994 was revised in 2002 and has spawned many other virtual dissection sites. These resources cannot substitute for the experience of 'being there', or having 'hands-on' experience, but they can provide valuable preparation, particularly for off-campus students, or – in the case of vocational students – on-campus students.

| Text | Print is a familiar and largely portable format which is relatively inexpensive to produce and reproduce. Digital forms of print are now extensively used in education to create resources. Although many texts will have been created digitally, they may only be available to students in physical (book) form. | With the onset of word processing it has been easier for tutors to create, reuse and share their handouts with students and colleagues. With the introduction of hyperlinks and web formatting into even standard word processing, web publishing became feasible for many students and staff and gave rise to writing as a form of 'connected document' allowing weaving of links to online resources (in a variety of media) into the text-based online document. The arrival of blogging and wikis now makes publishing online and creating documents collaboratively a possibility for most students.

Although most colleges and universities still rely upon libraries with print-based stock, there has been a growth in access to online journals and ebooks. Authentification systems can allow students to access online resources held at other academic libraries internationally, and work is ongoing to digitize legacy materials as well as inputting fresh content. One project, EThos (based at Warwick University), is attempting to do this for all the UK PhD theses held by the British Library.

In terms of accessibility, text in digital form opens up the potential to use assistive technologies, from simple reformatting and resizing to use of magnification and read-out packages. When one is inputting text, voice recognition is now a feasible option, allowing some disabled students to take notes and prepare written work without the need for human scribes.

For able-bodied users there are some trade-offs as text on-screen has been rated in some early studies to be over 25 per cent less efficient reading material than the equivalent print (Muter and Maurutto, 1991), so some students may spend extra time printing off copies for reading off-screen. |

activities that *might* be designed into a course.) In that chapter we also consider cases that involve the use and blending of different media and activities.

Media and mobile manifestations

One of the most exciting recent developments in e-learning is the use of web-based applications that allow streaming of audio and video within web pages, enabling the integration of several types of media within a single space. This is a significant move towards a more seamlessly blended experience of multiple media within a single course, or even inside a single learning activity.

Learners can now access audio, video, print, online games/simulations that might previously have been supplied as separate print (handouts and reading lists), audio and video items. They can access and move easily between the different media without swapping between devices. This solves several of the operational difficulties that formerly restricted use of multimedia (for example, ensuring that each student has the correct version of the item and access to a device suitable to review the content). It also removes some of the problems of how to use the various media within a single activity. Prior to this, an activity that required a student to make notes on an offprint, then view a video and then contribute opinions in a discussion would require changes in location and involved an amount of wasted time in setting up and transferring between each medium (unless the institution had the capability to create interactive DVD or CD-ROMs incorporating web links). This inconvenience is now reduced, although the effect of switching from library search to note taking, then on to viewing video and into discussion, will still not be entirely seamless, as each requires different skills.

Another significant development in the blending of online media is the increase in access to portable and mobile wireless computing devices. These offer even greater opportunities to learners by allowing access to multimedia resources in a variety of locations where such access would otherwise be impossible. Greater mobility of the playback and recording devices also opens up the pedagogical potential – although use of these devices in education is still quite new. Example 2.1, which involved using mobile devices on an experimental basis with schoolchildren, offers an insight into what is possible.

In this example the mobile devices were loaned to students for the day. They first needed to be trained in using the handheld personal digital assistants (PDAs), and they had no opportunity to continue to use these in

Example 2.1:

Mudlarking in Deptford

This project headed by Futurelab (a spin-off from NESTA, the National Endowment for Science, Technology and the Arts) equipped groups of schoolchildren with hand-held mobile devices which they could use to write in, record audio, take pictures, access reference resources online and, with satellite navigation, pinpoint their exact location. The students made a multimedia map of their walks around Deptford, carrying out experiments and recording findings – capturing all that they found significant about the environment. These records could then be accessed by later groups and extended or edited into an evolving and increasingly rich and diverse resource.

(*Source*: www.futurelab.org.uk/showcase/mudlarking/mudlarking.htm)

other settings. Many adult students now carry devices such as mobile phones and PDAs that have much of the capability of those used at Deptford. They may prefer the use of familiar applications and devices, which could in some cases be superior to the college-provided equivalent (this has led to the suggestion that in the future there should be personal learning environments owned by students rather than virtual learning environments owned and controlled by institutions (Downes, 2006). Some colleges and universities are already starting to make use of the technology in their students' pockets – for example by texting urgent messages and reminders to students' phones (Soon and Sugden, 2003) or distributing handouts in electronic form for uploading to students' PDAs, flash memory drives and notebooks. This form of e-administration is often seen as non-contentious, although there are ethical barriers to taking its use further, for example by tracking absent students using satellite navigation. Encouraging students to submit multimedia records using mobile devices is still unusual and most often ignores the technology owned by the student in favour of technology loaned by the institution (Attwell, 2006). In Chapter 9 we return to some of the ethical issues this presents for blended e-learning.

One of the big concerns about expecting students to use their own mobile technologies is that there are still a significant number of students who do not have access to such devices. There remains a 'digital divide' between computer haves and have-nots in terms of access to mobile devices and the capability to use them (training, confidence and infrastructure). The following example shows the progress that is being made in bridging the divide. Although targeted at the very poorest countries and school-children, the development of affordable and robust mobile computing devices is likely to have a much broader impact.

Example 2.2:

One child, one laptop

Announced in January 2005, this initiative is set to address the need for affordable mobile computing in classrooms beyond those of the developed world. The aim is to create a robust laptop for $100 that will be supplied to students via government initiatives. It is proposed that the laptops will use a free-of-charge open source operating system (Linux), have wireless broadband and, among other things, allow each laptop to communicate with its nearest neighbours, creating an *ad hoc* local area network. Pictures of prototypes such as that shown here feature a hand crank to provide an innovative power source. It is suggested that these laptops will be able to do almost everything that a conventional laptop can except store huge amounts of data.

(*Source:* www.laptop.media.mit.edu/ and www.laptop.org/)

The significance of student location

Another way of looking at blending is as a combination of on-campus and off-campus activity, where traditional teaching approaches are used more extensively with students who are physically present, and e-learning is used at other times to bridge the distance between student, tutor and other students. Developments in e-learning, particularly the sort of format changes in new media outlined in Table 2.1, have transformed the potential of distance education, in which a wide range of media formats were already extensively used. But e-learning also allows on-campus courses to take a more flexible view of the type of student activity that may be going on outside the formal classes, in particular the potential for the learning conversations that Laurillard (2001) values. Use of e-learning, and particularly online learning, significantly extends the options for part-time courses to facilitate communication between classes, while mobile learning can accommodate the needs of part-time students, who can study at home, in their workplace, on trains and buses, at airports, in hotel rooms, on park benches and anywhere else where the opportunity arises.

While students are studying full time on campus they have a range of opportunities to engage in discussions with their fellow students and tutors. Even where e-learning options are available they may prefer to attend a lecture face to face so that they can discuss the content there and then, with peers if not with the tutor. Forming social relationships online can appear daunting to many students. However, distance-taught students have a much more limited opportunity for *any* interactivity, so e-learning (the synchronous webcast or asynchronous recorded lecture, or online discussion) is perhaps their only or best option for social interaction. It would be naïve not to recognize that e-learning often requires more initiative on the part of the student than they may be expected to exert in a face-to-face teaching environment. However, it is realistic to recognize that the opportunities for off-campus students to engage with the course community are often necessarily limited, so their motivation to use technology is likely to be stronger.

The level of student experience with e-learning as well as their location relative to campus can be important factors in determining how, where and when to blend e-learning with conventional teaching. Put simply, if the student is located at a distance from campus, then they are likely to value e-learning alternatives to campus-based resources and activity. If they are also experienced e-learners, then they will be able to engage with this style of learning from the start of the course. If they have extensive experience of using e-learning, then they can be expected to build on this,

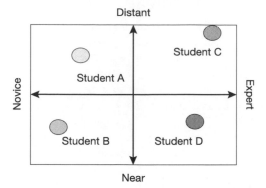

Student A has minimal experience of e-learning and is quite distant from campus – *requires a blend that introduces e-learning gradually; quite dependent on using e-learning.*

Student B is a novice e-learner, learning mainly on-campus – *requires a blend that introduces e-learning gradually; not very dependent on using e-learning, and may use on-campus alternatives.*

Student C is a very experienced e-learner, very distant from campus – *can use e-learning competently without introduction; large distance and high expertise would suit e-learning.*

Student D is highly experienced but able to learn mainly on-campus – *can adapt to extensive use of e-learning from start of course, but also has choice as regards on-campus delivery; the best of both worlds.*

Figure 2.2 Impact of location and experience on e-learning blend

perhaps using a variety of online services to complete assessed work. This relative experience in e-learning is, however, not necessarily dependent on the student's past experience of study, as Figure 2.2 shows.

The four students shown in Figure 2.2 could all be studying the same course. Any, or none, of them could be experienced students in terms of successful completion of conventionally taught courses. There will be other factors, perhaps unrelated to study, that will determine their success on a course which employs e-learning, but what is evident here is that students can approach the same course with differing levels of motivation to use ICT for learning, based on location and differences in their obvious capacity to use it effectively from the start. This is not a problem that is unique to e-learning, but e-learning may offer an effective solution. With moves to create personalized learning and personal electronic learning environments through use of e-learning, we can see that in the future there may be individualized blends, perhaps even a unique blend for each learner. For example, each of the four learners in Figure 2.2 could study the course using different blends of activity and technology to suit their preferences and circumstances.

Informal, work-based and just-in-time blends

There is already very extensive use of the internet for informal learning, whether we think of the research that children might do into their Yu-Gi-Oh heros, the genealogical investigations and other hobby research that many adults undertake online, the sharing of knowledge and resources through specialist discussion boards, or the serendipitous outcomes from following interesting links into unfamiliar areas. Often this informal learning is experienced as part of a loose community, perhaps as a member of a 'community of practice' (Wenger, 1999). Seufert *et al.* (2001) have identified four types of learning communities:

1   Work-orientated communities, such as business communities. Communities of practice (or situated learning communities);
2   Research-orientated communities, such as scientific communities in academia, research and development communities in business;
3   Learning-orientated communities (curricular learning communities), such as class-support communities, virtual learning communities; and
4   Hobby-orientated communities, such as communities of interest and communities of fantasy/gaming.

Many students now entering further and higher education will have prior experience of some of these types of informal learning, either individually or as a member of a learning community. They may supplement the formal materials supplied by the tutor with resources located on the internet. Some tutors will 'formalize' this type of informal use by inviting students to share resources and links as they find them, perhaps even passing these on in edited form to later students. This gives the whole class the opportunity to share useful internet 'finds' and allows the teacher to comment openly on the quality of some of the informal learning material that students are using. We do need, however, to moderate our expectations about the students' readiness to see informal learning as playing a major role in their HE learning (Nicol and Littlejohn, 2005), perhaps because the tutors' expectations and experience (and therefore their course designs) do not support this.

Notwithstanding these reservations, recognition and better understanding of informal learning processes, particularly as these change with use to 'educational' technologies, is increasingly an issue for both institutions and educators. Many students, particularly those in further education, will be studying vocational courses and may be undertaking some of their learning in their workplace. Learning off-campus presents problems in creating effective bridges between practice-based learning on the one hand, and theory- or campus-based learning on the other. Increasingly, electronic communications are used as a means of keeping in touch with students who are on placement, and web-based course resources are often referred to by students as they put theory into practice. For example, a social work student may look to government web sites and their course resources as well as their workplace colleagues for guidance on recent changes in the law. They may engage other students as well as their tutors in online discussion of how to approach work-based problems that are not covered by the course. There is growing recognition in sectors such as healthcare that 'evidence-based practice' requires professionals to develop and use precisely the sort of online information literacy skills that e-learning develops. As those learners move on to become graduates and leave their colleges and universities, they may find that they will continue to access e-learning resources. This could be as part of continual professional development or to update their knowledge on an *ad hoc*, just-in-time basis. Such use recognizes the potential of web-based material to be not only the most up-to-date source but, in some cases, the most authoritative resource available. Example 2.3 is only one of many possible examples.

Example 2.3:

TeachandLearn.net

Described as 'the continuing professional development site for schools', TeachandLearn.net offers accredited courses using e-learning, commissions topical resources by leading educationalists, hosts a virtual staffroom for sharing questions and ideas, and presents reviews of teaching resources. Once a school subscribes, all staff within that school can use the resource, and the site covers a range of staff in primary and secondary schools, from librarians to classroom assistants, from teachers to governors. The emphasis is on topical and practical learning with a strong just-in-time flavour in the examples given – for example, a calendar of significant events tied to themes that could be taken up in school assemblies.

(*Source:* www.teachandlearn.net/)

This type of resource is increasingly in use in other professions, from medicine to mechanical engineering. There are significant barriers to recalling graduates from their employment for regular updating, yet professional bodies now often insist that members undertake accredited continuing professional development in order to retain their professional standing. Blending e-learning offered by universities and colleges with the workplace learning offered by employers is one approach to meeting this need realistically.

There is a bonus for professions in recognizing and supporting the development of 'communities of practice' (Wenger, 1999). Participants can become work- or research-orientated communities (Seufert *et al.*, 2001) and play an active role in developing the knowledge base of their communities, sharing ideas and experiences, reviewing resources and working and learning together.

Is blending bland?

There is a real danger that blending e-learning within a course that has previously worked well with more conventional delivery will be approached on the basis of item-by-item replacement and/or risk containment. Blending can too easily be seen as the conservative approach to e-learning, the least challenging route and one that results in little significant change. You cannot claim to have a blended e-learning approach if you have simply inserted online content into a course without considering the impact on the media blend or the activity blend. If the addition of e-learning activity and resources is based upon some idea of doing least damage, rather than doing most good, its inclusion is unlikely to be valued by either students or staff.

This chapter has introduced some ideas about alternative approaches to blending, including:

- blending informal and formal learning;
- building a bridge between work-based practice and the campus;
- making use of the learning devices in students' pockets alongside institutional resources;
- exploiting changes of format, perhaps wrapping established face-to-face activities around new online resources, or vice versa;
- offering personalized blends for individual students.

These all present challenges and opportunities, and underline that the potential of blended learning is very real. There is a shifting kaleidoscope of e-learning technologies, which with new media formats and new mobile learning opportunities present a constantly changing series of opportunities. A blended approach takes account of the possibility of tailoring a solution to the institution, the course, the tutor, or the student. The move towards increasing personalization and customization in e-learning offers many more opportunities for learner-led blending.

Chapter 3

Devising blended
e-learning activities

We live in a world that increasingly relies upon digital communication devices. We use them socially for play, professionally and socially for work, and increasingly we use them to support our learning. This can either be formal use (as part of the course design) or informal use as part of the experience of being 'connected' in the twenty-first century. Some of these devices support communication. That can be immediate, real-time communication, perhaps using ubiquitous portable devices such as mobile phones. Other communication may take place in convenient but discontinuous asynchronous episodes (e.g. by email). This can create a flexible pattern of conversation between participants who may be located in different time zones.

Teaching is a social process and becoming more so all the time, as the reliance on formal didactic approaches to teaching declines. When we talk about the design of courses and resources, the focus is often on the formal resources and content rather than the communication process that supports them. But we all recognize the importance of feedback from students about the learning activities that they are engaged in and feedback to students to help them to improve and make sense of their learning. Students and tutors need to know how they are doing, and we will look in this chapter at why this is so important in e-learning. New out-of-class modes of communication can help students and tutors *maintain* a dialogue such that feedback is followed by a period of reflection, by action and/or inquiry and so on, allowing space for students to develop their discourse within the course. When we talk about the design of courses and resources we must recognize all the implications of the increasing diversity of media used. It is sometimes easier to see these as contributing only to e-content delivery, without appreciating the opportunities that they afford for communication with and between students. Digital devices may support both informal socialization and more formal learning interaction, with both playing a significant part in effective e-learning.

In conventional teaching and learning environments the social inter-action is often an unstated assumption, expected simply to happen as a matter of course rather than being 'designed in' to the learning activity. Having many curious minds working together on a single topic will often quite naturally generate conversations, questions, ideas and arguments. However, even where there is substantial face-to-face interaction, this should ideally have been planned. Leaving an appropriate space in teaching sessions for student interaction is something that formal lesson planning or storyboarding techniques encourage (see Chapters 4 and 5 for more on this subject). Allocating time for student activity and interactivity is an important part of the learning design and takes account not only of overt activity – such as debate or question and answer – but also the less obvious individual reflective activity that students need in order to learn. Making time to meet students' needs for activity, interactivity and reflection also creates space and opportunity to seek and receive feedback on areas of misunderstanding, to share reflections and understanding with peers and to fully assimilate what has been learned.

When we talk about e-learning activities, we are dealing with an environment where the opportunities for communication around activity needs to be deliberately designed in if we intend the activities to be more than simply *individual* student activity. It is possible to create an e-learning course that offers no interaction with others, either fellow students or even a human tutor. Many of the early computer-based learning courses did just that; the student sat at the computer and interacted with the programs offered, receiving feedback directly from the computer. If there was a human tutor or facilitator, the students did not need to meet or talk with them and there was no direct feedback from one to the other.

For some types of course, and some elements within courses, this type of simple e-learning activity, perhaps leading to a diagnostic or formative test, is still sufficient. However, if e-learning is to be used extensively in higher and further education, it needs to be capable of supporting much more flexible and open-ended conversations between students, and between tutor and students. While some activity will remain individual student activity, most students would benefit from the *opportunity* to interact with peers and tutor as they need to, for example to ask questions or to share understanding.

One of the interesting aspects of online communication is how it can make visible to the whole class conversations that they might not otherwise have been privy to. This can make it a valuable resource for students to refer to. It may also make contributions to the discussion appear more formal than the equivalent, more ephemeral question-and-answer conversation in class. As a result, some students may expend considerable effort on their message posting, refining messages until they 'look' perfect. A further feature of online conversation is that because it is carried out asynchronously, the reader of a message may be finding out about this thread in an ongoing conversation some time after it actually started. However, this need not be a problem as long as students are aware of the opportunities they have to respond and interact online and can take advantage of those within the time set aside for discussion. As learners become more experienced e-learners they will feel more confident about addressing the absent audience, and may happily post messages in the middle of the night when they know that no one else is listening/reading.

These features of e-learning necessitate rather different approaches to the design of learning activity than you may be accustomed to. With large-group, same-place teaching such as lectures the opportunities for interactivity in small groups within the session may be very limited, but against this can be weighed the reassurance that at least those students who are physically present have an equal chance of receiving the same information at the same time and asking questions about it. Online large-group teaching can move into small-group or paired activity without the participants changing physical position. Against this convenience needs to be balanced a concern that the more complicated the navigation within the learning space, the more likely it is that a student may get lost or miss an important part of the online discussion.

Of course, some tutors will blend the two approaches in the ways explored in Chapter 2. They may be using face-to-face sessions for information transmission (reinforced by online publication of handouts and presentation slides on the electronic learning environment). They can also be using online forums to discuss some of the more complex issues, perhaps also using online tools for specialist activity such as collective mind mapping, or polling, capturing opinions and ideas to bring into seminars for face-to-face discussion.

Synchronous or asynchronous?

While synchronous discussion is obviously taking place with involvement of all participants and observers *at the same time*, in its e-learning form it need not necessarily be occurring *at the same place*. Even though the discussion is happening in 'real time' it can be spread over a geographically extensive 'virtual space'. This means that even though we may be more accustomed to the idea and practice of synchronous 'same-place' conversations, there will be differences between this and online synchronous communication (whether using text (chat), audio or video format). Examples of differences include issues such as:

- *Turn taking* – for example, 'How do I know when I can start speaking?'
- *Concern about who is paying attention* – for example, 'I am talking, but how do I know who – out there – is listening?'
- *Time lag* – in audio and video these may be small but significant pauses between the start of the speaking and the moment at which others hear what is being said; in 'chat' text-based synchronous communication this is the space between starting to write and the sending of the message. This effect can lead to overlapping and confusing conversations.
- *Technical difficulties* – although the danger of these occurring is declining with more robust and intuitive applications, and computer-literate students and staff, technical problems with equipment (e.g. audio feedback from microphones) may still occur.
- *Time differences* – where the course is taught internationally, and students are widely distributed, finding one time that is equally convenient for all students to be online may prove very challenging. For example, Mark, an Open University student located in New Zealand, claimed to be the first student to have attended his graduation in his pyjamas, having taken part in the synchronous audioconferenced virtual graduation ceremony held at the Milton Keynes campus. He graduated alongside his fellow students, each of them 'attending' remotely from a variety of locations worldwide.
- *Identity confusion* – although less likely in blended learning, where students will usually already know each other, there is a 'levelling' in electronic discussion whereby it is not automatically obvious what the status of the speaker may be (student or staff member, moderator or participant, expert or novice). There is not usually a front-of-class position that commands attention; rather, the attention is on the current speaker, and at times too much attention (and discussion space) may be paid to speakers who are not talking from a position of strength, particularly if there are no tools to allow anyone to interrupt them.

Various solutions have been developed to overcome these problems. For example, a 'raised hand' icon may be available to indicate that you wish to speak. Options will vary depending on the system used and the medium employed. In a videoconference, where each participant is visible, it is easy to indicate that you wish to speak by raising your own hand. To overcome the time difference problem and other difficulties of same-time teaching it may also be possible to capture the videoconference so that non-participants can view this afterwards and benefit from the discussion. Participants can also use this recording as a memory aid so that they do not feel the need to make extensive notes during the session.

Within a face-to-face conversation or synchronous online discussion, it is possible to be there (present when the conversation takes place), or to be absent (not present). If you are absent, then in order to access what was said you will need to rely upon the memory and goodwill of participants, or some record of the event. You cannot, as someone who was not partic--ipating in the original time-limited discussion, subsequently become a discussant in the original conversation. This is often not the case when a conversation is carried out asynchronously. You can enter actively into a discussion even when others are not there, adding your thoughts, reflections and queries hours, days and sometimes weeks or months after the comment to which you are referring was posted. This is sometimes seen as one of the great benefits of asynchronous communication – that it can occur over a very flexible time-span, allowing participants to make a contribution or catch up on what is happening as and when they are able. It can also make problems for the tutor trying to manage student online participation, or the student planning their workload.

From the point of view of teaching and learning, the use of asyn--chronous discussion, which is almost inevitably text based, allows students and tutors to draw together points made across many messages and refer to these with accuracy. This can lead to some interesting online or blended activities that would not normally be possible during a non-recorded face--to-face discussion. For example, it is possible to keep student groups apart for some stages of the activity and then, at a given time, allow them access to what has happened in other tutor groups so that they can compare *past* discussion. The asynchronous activity can sometimes be blended with face-to-face to act as a lead into, or follow-up to, a synchronous (real-time) discussion. An example of this blending of asynchronous and synchronous tools follows.

Blending asynchronous and synchronous tools to support a debate

A student debate is one approach that tutors may take to introducing, or concluding a controversial topic within a course. Ideally, students will also

---

continued

have had time to prepare evidence and arguments and rehearse these. Conventionally, the audience (or in educational settings the participants) will vote at the end to show which side of the argument they now agree with.

In the MA in online and distance education at the UK Open University the debate has been used several times within different online courses with students located internationally. One format for the debate was wholly asynchronous, with students presenting arguments and counter-arguments in turn, each side meeting deadlines to do so and answering questions placed by fellow students. Another approach to the debate took place using both asynchronous and synchronous tools.

In this instance students were each asked to research a topic (organizational learning and knowledge management) independently drawing initially on resources identified by the course author, but with the expectation that they would search actively beyond these. The students did not at this stage know which side of the debate they would be supporting, although they were briefed on the question that they would be arguing and given an overview of the events and deadlines over the four-week activity. In the next stage the debating teams were identified by the tutor, with each team member then being allocated a role. The roles included those of proposer, seconder, researcher, scribe (to produce a summary of the early discussion) and technical reviewer (to comment on the experience of the technology). In this next stage the students were using asynchronous tools to gather and review the resources that they would use to support their side of the argument in the debate. Towards the end of this stage they obtained access to the asynchronous audioconferencing environment in which the debate would occur. Here they could practise use of the environment and also take advantage of some of the tools such as concept mapping and shared whiteboard to prepare and agree the approach taken in the final presentation of the argument. Although this was a synchronous environment, it was often more convenient at this stage for sub-groups within the debating team to use this, avoiding the need for everyone to be using the space at the same time. The software (Lyceum audioconferencing, a system created at the OU) allowed students to assemble in private rooms that could not be accessed by students from other debating teams. It was therefore possible for several groups to work there concurrently.

The final stage was the debate itself. This took place in real time for all participants, with use of the polling in Lyceum to tally votes at the end. Student scribes and technical reviewers posted their reports after the debate had been closed, so that each group could compare how their approach and use/experience of technology compared.

Although this example is taken from a distance-taught course, it could be adapted to be blended with face-to-face teaching. In that case the students could prepare the debate online asynchronously (and perhaps also synchronously if the appropriate tools were available) and then perform the debate and voting in a face-to-face setting.

The above example is an unusually complex online learning activity, with several stages during which different students took different roles (as actors in a 'Learning Design' sense (Liber and Olivier, 2003)). A formal record of the design of this debate activity using IMS Learning Design methodology would show us exactly how the event is planned – what is happening to who and when. In Chapters 4 and 5 we will look at a less complex approach to learning design using the LD_lite framework. For now you need to recognize that there is usually a more deliberate planning of activities within e-learning, with emphasis on the scheduling of events and the interplay between them. This is particularly the case where there is considerable asynchronous activity over extended periods, or where there are elements of synchronous activity that require all students to be at the same point in their studies at one particular time.

Although the above example is based on an activity that is quite strictly scheduled (each week marks a new phase in the activity), the blend of synchronous with asynchronous activity will often be aimed at extending the dialogue after a class-based activity has occurred, or as a means of allowing students to prepare for a class-based activity. In this form it may become a regular feature of all teaching sessions, particularly those that are aimed at part-time students who may be restricted in the time that they can give to synchronous activities which are campus based.

The synchronous events with which the asynchronous discussion is blended (or around which it is 'wrapped' – see Figure 2.1 in Chapter 2) could be a week-long residential event, or a regular weekly tutorial. Table 3.1 shows examples of the types of activity that could be undertaken in the asynchronous sessions before and after what might be seen as the 'main

Table 3.1 Blending asynchronous and synchronous activities: two examples

	One-week residential or field trip	Regular weekly class
Leading into the synchronous activity	• Revision activities and practice of language skills for overseas residential for some students • Search for information sources relevant to the location and programme of activity during the week (students familiar with 'host' location can contribute links and advice) • Introduction to event and participants (socialization or ice-breaking activity) • Reading lists with links to online resources for review before the trip (students can be asked to share reviews of resources) • Skills training or overview of use of unfamiliar equipment • Diagnostic quizzes with links to appropriate revision packs • Links to previous students' experiences • FAQ list and discussion forum for asking questions	• Reading lists with links to online resources for review before the session (students can be asked to share reviews of resources) • Online small group activity to be presented or commented on in class • Quizzes based on previous sessions – flagging to the tutor common areas of difficulty or misunderstanding • Forum for posting questions for discussion in class • Review of whole-class performance in recent assessed work, highlighting areas of misunderstanding and weakness • Posting slides and handouts and inviting any queries on these
Leading from the synchronous activity	• Feedback on trip from students to tutor and from tutor to students • Posting slides and handouts and inviting any queries on these • Review of the trip, perhaps leading to preparation of resources to help future students, or students who were unable to attend • Continuation of socialization activity between trips	• Feedback on session from students to tutor and from tutor to students • Posting slides and handouts and inviting any queries on these • Identifying topics from session which merit further discussion • Starting discussion activity in preparation for next topic • Sharing information about resources relating to next and last topic, for example topical news stories

event'. In these examples the amount of time allocated to the synchronous activity may be much more modest than that taken by the asynchronous activity. If this is the case, then it is important that the course design take account of the additional student activity. There is a certain irony in designing a very flexible blend of asynchronous and synchronous activity for the benefit of part-time students, only to find that there is now so much activity that they cannot, as part-timers, benefit from it.

'Looking' at student activity

One of the side effects of using e-learning is that it generates a huge quantity of data, not simply the tracking information on student interaction and performance, but also visible, analysable records of student and tutor interaction. When we look at the output from text-based learning and teaching conversations online, we can see a huge number of visible conversations, perhaps hundreds of messages where the course is a large one using course-wide online discussions. Each student and tutor could be aware of and participate in the discussion asynchronously, which will also tend to extend the period of activity, spreading it out and making it feel very time-consuming.

When we think of all the separate individual asynchronous messages that take the place of a single time-limited conversation (e.g. a one-hour tutorial), we can see how the time taken to read and respond to messages can easily be far longer than the hour-long session to which they relate. Although intensive, the tutorial will usually be clearly finished at the end of the session. To refer back to it the students and tutor will need to rely upon memory or notes, which limits the amount of information about the session that they need to *process* once the session is over. If students, or the tutor, miss one of the conversations that was happening, perhaps because several small sub-groups were working on the same problem simultaneously, then this is considered acceptable and, to some extent, unavoidable. However, with asynchronous conversations it is often not so clear what is the end point in the discussion. It may also not be clear to participants to what extent they should involve themselves in discussions in which they were not 'present':

- Should they be participants in every conversation?
- Or should they be aware of every conversation but actively contribute in only one?
- Or should they limit their awareness and participation to a single discussion thread or section?

Neither is it clear at the start how intensive the conversation will be. It is very difficult to estimate how many messages might be generated by a particular open-ended discussion, and one of the problems for online tutors is addressing difficulties that occur when there is insufficient online discussion about a particular topic, or, conversely, where there is so much conversation on one topic that the time required to stay up to date with this is eating into time allocated for other learning activity.

There are many approaches to controlling and organizing online discussions and activity in order to make this more manageable and rewarding for all participants (see Gilly Salmon's work on e-tivities; Salmon, 2002). The following are some of the common tools:

- *Setting clear end dates/times for the discussions* so that those who submit messages before the start or after the end point know in advance that their queries or ideas may not get an audience. You may even decide to close forums at set points; this could make the forum read-only, removing the potential to write new messages to it.
- *Providing some sort of summary of the discussion at key points* – composed by either students or the tutor. The technology will often allow direct links to key messages, so that those referred to within the summary can be easily located by readers. This practice will help all participants to get an overview and is especially helpful to those who are having difficulty keeping up, or experiencing message overload. A skilful summary drawing on (linking to or quoting) messages throughout the discussion is sometimes referred to as 'weaving' because it helps to develop a coherent a structure within the discussion, bringing loose threads together and identifying common strands.
- *Moderating the discussion* – this can range from very active, directive moderation where messages are acknowledged and responded to by a designated person, or could simply focus on making sure that old messages are archived and that new or important messages are clearly displayed, for example by moving misplaced messages.
- *Using off-forum tools to help* – from example, using one-to-one email, telephone or face-to-face discussion to encourage participation by those who may not be very active, or to manage some of the issues raised in the forum. Holding these discussions inside the forum (e.g. 'Why is no one answering me?' or 'Please don't do that again; it upsets other students') may not be productive or appropriate.
- *Modelling productive online discussions* through your own use of online messages. This is particularly useful when you are modelling how new topics might be started (e.g. information subject lines) and how

disagreements might be handled (e.g. acknowledgement and clear stating of differences, with questions to clarify understanding).

- *Using system tools such as alerts* to call students together or to warn about deadlines or the ending of some timed activities. This can also include timely reminders of where certain resources might be found at the points in the course where students are most likely to need them, or to flag up the availability of new resources (e.g. library books, new journal articles, TV programmes or web sites).

- *Organizing the forums so that they each fulfil a different role* – for example, designating particular discussions as social (e.g. the Café) or informational (e.g. a read-only Course Announcements or News area). This makes it easier for students to find what they need and avoid areas that are optional: you would expect every student to read the Course Announcements as a priority, and this would be tutor controlled. Many might choose not to be active, or not to read every message in a student-controlled online 'Café', and the tutor might intentionally avoid this area.

Lurking with intent

'Lurking' is a term that has been used to refer to a particular type of student online activity. It describes the activity of a student (the 'lurker') who is reading messages in an online course discussion but not personally contributing messages. Although this may be considered by other students to be a sign of inactivity, it is not necessarily that at all. The student may well be very busy reading and reflecting on the contributions of others, perhaps carrying out extensive personal research. You could think of these students as readers, with inactive students being 'non-readers'. The work that they may submit for assessment purposes can reflect a deep engagement with the online elements of the course.

The issue for fellow students is that 'lurkers' often appear not to be doing *anything*, and they appear to be benefiting from the contributions of the group while not adding to the stock of messages themselves. This can result in dysfunctional behaviour within the online group:

- Active participants in the conference may decide that they will form a sub-group and find somewhere else to carry on their conversations
- There may be attempts to 'flush out' the lurkers, directly challenging them to 'say something!', perhaps referring to them as 'lurkers' and using this term in a pejorative sense.

- Those who are not participating actively may be made to feel uncomfortable with their place in the group. They may decide to withdraw from the discussion, or even withdraw from the course.

Mason (1994) has suggested that only about one-third of online participants will generally be very active. These students will leave lots of messages and visibly engage in the discussions. A further third will sometimes choose to respond to messages and conduct an online discussion; at other times (perhaps more frequently) they will choose only to read the messages. The remaining third will never willingly contribute to the discussion and may resist all attempts to force them into contributing online. These proportions will of course vary not only with the class composition, but also with the activities set – some of which could *require* participation – and the role played by assessment. The main point is that some students will choose not to visibly participate, and we should expect this. If we relate this to classroom behaviour, we can recognize that this is a common pattern in face-to-face teaching. Some students will be happy to contribute and you would expect them to speak up in class about almost any subject. At the other end of the spectrum, some students will not say a word in class and may be very uncomfortable if they are required to do so. There is no obvious correlation in either offline or online teaching between student performance in assessment and number of words spoken in the class or online discussion.

In considering how active students should be in a forum, we might also reflect on the impact if all students were active online all of the time. There are courses where students are very motivated to post messages in response to most activities, or are required to do so. This can quickly lead to an overload for other students (who then need to read all the messages) and for the tutor who is trying to moderate a complex and lengthy discussion. We can also recognize this problem in other types of online discussion. If a blogger were to receive comments from every person who read their blog, would this mean that the most popular blogs became overloaded with comments, with the blogger spending a disproportionate time reading and responding, and perhaps little time posting new topics?

All teachers know from experience that students attending classes and participating in learning activity are likely to do better in assessment. Attending 'classes' is something that the lurker or reader obviously does, so encouraging further activity is probably unrealistic and unnecessary. A greater problem for the tutor is the student who is skipping classes or discussions altogether. In electronic learning environments their absences can be identified and tracked but it is not easy to contact them.

How am I doing? Providing feedback to students and tutors

In online activities, whether synchronous or asynchronous, the other participants are often not visible to you. You may be aware of them through their contribution to the activity, but if they are 'lurking' you will not necessarily know that they are there at all. You will usually lack visual clues as to whether others are listening to you, ignoring you or engaged elsewhere. Tales are told of students who contribute to an audioconference discussion at the start of the session and then quietly leave for a cigarette break, being found out only if the tutor addresses a question to them by name while they are absent from the room.

Both students and tutor lack some of the familiar tools for making their interest obvious. Except in the case of videoconferencing, there will be none of the body language clues such as head nodding, smiling and murmurs of assent or disagreement. The equivalent of stunned silence in an online conversation is sometimes just silence. It could mean that everyone is listening intently, too immersed in your argument to interrupt. Or it could mean that everyone has logged off and gone home. It could even mean that no one is there, for example because they have not logged on yet, so you have been talking to yourself the whole time. This is a disquieting thought whether you are a student or a tutor, although with an asynchronous discussion it is not necessarily a bad thing as other participants will arrive eventually and that is when the discussion will start up.

It is quite common when using online forums in a course to launch these with some form of ice-breaking activity so that students are required to post a message of some kind. Sometimes this will be an introduction, or it may focus away from the person writing it so that they can concentrate on the process of writing a message online, rather than being concerned about the impression that they are making. This initial online activity not only helps the group to start to work together and gel, just as it would in a face-to-face setting, but also allows group members to become accustomed to using the communication tools for the course, tools that they may not have previously used. It is usual for online ice-breakers to require students to make responses to the messages of others so that they become used to addressing each other online. An example of this style of activity is provided in Example 3.1, but there are many variants.

As a tutor, you will be concerned to ensure that you receive feedback from the students to indicate that they are logging on and keeping up with the e-learning elements of the course. This can be provided through student tracking or through some sort of 'message history' facility (see

Example 3.1:

An online ice-breaker

Getting to know each other
So we can all get to know each other and practise using the tutor group conference, I thought this activity might be fun!

First create a message in our tutor group conference that includes brief information about yourself. You might like to include:

Your name (i.e. the name you like people to use)
What you hope to get out of the course
Your other interests, hobbies etc.
Then add a list of three things about yourself.

What next?
Look for things you have in common with others in the tutor group.
Use the *message reply* option to reply to people, either telling them about something you have in common or perhaps asking about their hobby.
To find out about me, see the next message in this thread.

(*Source*: Open University T171 Tutor's conference)

Chapter 9). You could also use online survey or polling tools. These may initially be the only ways to determine whether a student has actually been online, if that student decides to 'lurk' and not contribute any messages. To obtain more informative qualitative feedback from students you may also wish to devise activities that require them to undertake some sort of visible activity, either visible to the whole group or visible only to you as the tutor. The ice-breaker (Example 3.1) is one example of this style of activity and should make obvious to you which students are already comfortable with this style of communication and which are not.

Another approach to obtaining feedback on how well students are using and understanding the e-learning elements of the course is to allocate a more formal role to online activity. You could use the course assessment to encourage and reward the use of online resources such as databases, tools or e-books, or active engagement with online forums. This approach has the additional benefit of flagging to students that the resources provided online are expected to be helpful and instrumental to their studies, rather than optional 'extras' that they can choose to play with or not. It signals that the tutor is taking e-learning seriously and expects the students to do the same.

Assessing online activity

Once the use of e-learning resources and tools becomes part of the formal assessment of the course, the students recognize that they will need to use these as effectively as possible (or suffer the consequences in their assignment marks). For the institution it also flags that students need to have a robust and reliable system and the skills and technology to use it. For the tutor there is the challenge of how to fairly reward online activity through assessment. There may for example be accessibility concerns (see the section 'Planning for accessibility and usability', later in the chapter).

In terms of the use of resources and tools, these rarely pose a problem in assessment as long as the technical implications are adequately dealt with. In a sense, this is a problem similar to the requirement to use any specific offline tool (e.g. laboratory equipment) or resource (e.g. a library book). The students need to know that they must leave sufficient time to learn to use the tool, allow time to conduct any experiments (perhaps repeating the activity several times to get a good result) and not rely upon the tool being available at the eleventh hour when they, and many of their fellow students, are desperately trying to finish off the work. Online resources, although generally more accessible than their campus library equivalent, may suddenly become unavailable – in this case because of technical problems with accessing a web site rather than because a book has been stolen, misplaced or loaned to someone else.

If you are requiring students to demonstrate engagement with online forums, then there are a variety of approaches that you can use, and some of these are shown in Table 3.2. All of them have different strengths and weaknesses.

Whether or not the assessment rewards engagement with tools, resources or forums, there remains a potential problem connected with the format of the assessment. The students may wish to refer to online resources within their assessment activity, linking to external resources, inserting images and animations, or referencing forum messages through direct links to the source. They may wish to submit as part of a portfolio of assessment a blog or wiki, or some other form of 'connected document'

Table 3.2 Assessment strategies to recognize and reward online activity

Assessment strategy	Strengths	Weaknesses
Allocate a proportion of the marks based on contributions to forums (quantity, quality, length or frequency)	This is likely to boost the online activity of the course and may make the forums more interesting and lively places, with a higher level of participation by all students	Some of the activity that this generates may be not be meaningful. It could simply add to the 'noise' level of the forums, increasing everyone's workload without obvious benefit
Allocate a proportion of the marks based on reference made to the contents of the forum discussions (e.g. quoting from a minimum number of messages)	The students are required to actively engage with the content of the online discussion as they will need to refer to this in their assignment. Even if they do not contribute their own messages, they have an incentive to read and reflect on the messages posted by others	Students may try to boost the arguments that they wish to make in the assignment, by posting messages and arguments that do not reflect any engagement with the body of the discussion. Some students may quote only their own messages, thwarting the tutor's desire for engagement with the work of others
Students may be given tasks to carry out within collective or collaborative online work	Each student has a task to complete and clear indicators of what is required to do this successfully. Some tasks could be designed to be accessible for disabled students	As with any groupwork, the success of the student's own activity will depend upon the willingness of others to play their part. If an overall group mark is awarded, this can create problems if effort was expended unevenly by different group members
Awarding marks for specific individual activities such as acting as moderator, scribe or reviewer for a specific period, or project	This has the potential of allowing the role or responsibility to be matched to the student asked to undertake it	This is unlikely to work well with large groups where the tutor does not know the strengths of each student. The allocation of specific roles may be seen as unfair by some students

that relies upon online access and draws on online resources. This raises interesting issues for the development of an assessment process that can support contributions from students based on e-learning activity.

Social spaces online

Even where students are using online learning environments as part of a blended approach to e-learning, with face-to-face learning and social opportunities on campus, there is an argument for providing social space online within the course. This provision may be formal or informal. The more computer-literate students will probably already use online technologies as part of their socialization tools. For example, they may be using instant messaging to chat to others while working on the course; they may be using mobile technologies and wi-fi to keep up with news, sporting results and social chat while out and about on campus (or even while sitting in lectures). They may use voice-over internet protocols (e.g. Skype) to converse with friends and family abroad, and use FlickR and MySpace to share news and pictures with friends. Some students will already belong to various online communities that share ideas and information around their professional, leisure and special interest activities. The tools that we encourage students to use for formal and informal learning on their courses are also tools which many students are already using for social purposes. Creating specific social spaces within the electronic learning environment, for example by creating a virtual common room or café, provides students with an area for socializing and play which is confined to the course members. Because their personal off-course socialization spaces are 'connected' and online, more ambitious students (or staff) may use social networking tools such as del.icio.us (www.del.icio.us), or a personal blog, to gather and connect different parts of their online lives. Despite the increasing range of tools available from institutions, there is evidence that students are increasingly choosing to communicate using tools within their control (Oblinger, 2004). For social activity around the course they may be attracted to the emerging electronic environments that have been primarily developed as 'social' spaces. These serve as spaces that students can set up and control.

'Social computing' focuses on recreating and even extending social conventions and social contexts online by using email, instant messaging, conferencing or blogs for micro-coordination of study or work-based activities, building communities or maintaining social relationships. Many social computing applications are freely available, and their use is becoming widespread, particularly across specialist communities and among groups of young people. As with 'personal broadcasting environments', there has been a phenomenal escalation in their uptake, and this is having a profound impact on social structures. Examples of these environments include MySpace (www.myspace.com) and YouTube (www.youtube.com). These environments allow users to create their own personalized online spaces. Users are supported in forming communities of 'friends' that coalesce around user-identified topics where they can interact with others as a contributing member. Users are encouraged to create their own profile, post ideas as blogs and comment on the postings of others. Rather than having to view friends' individual blogs, new post-ings are broadcast daily as 'RSS feeds' – or collated versions of updates. Neither are these developments only of interest to students. Staff at colleges and universities may use social spaces to connect with students, past students, researchers and other academics. Figure 3.1 shows an example of staff use of a social computing environment. Here, Glenn Rikowski of the University of Northampton uses MySpace to formulate ideas on education and social class. In this example the online environment is being used to extend ideas generated during face-to-face seminar sessions.

Social computing environments have the potential to shift the locus of control in education. They support the idea of the 'contributing student approach', which involves learners researching one or two topics each, then uploading their findings to an online environment where they can

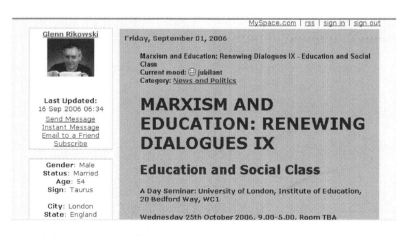

Figure 3.1 Example of staff use of 'social space'

Source: Glenn Rikowski (www.myspace.com/glennrikowski)

share information, comment on the ideas of others and collaboratively generate new knowledge (Collis and Moonen, 2001).

There may be reservations about integrating these tools into a course, because they can require a large time commitment. But where students already have set up personal blogs, etc., these can enrich the social networking within the course. For students who are studying entirely by e-learning, and perhaps also at a distance from each other, having even a modest social space allows the trade of chit-chat and exchange of holiday snaps that would take place on campus in a real common room or café – somewhere where the students feel in control of the environment. Both the real and the virtual social spaces allow students to build relationships with others that will help them to work together more effectively during the course.

Given the easy access to online space beyond the electronic learning environment, course designers should be aware that online social activity between students is likely to happen whether *they* make spaces for it or not. Think of the use that students on-campus make of the social spaces such as local coffee shops or the student canteen.

It is worth considering whether the use of social spaces around e-learning can also serve a valuable function beyond the course. For example, these spaces could remain 'open' between courses, and beyond the final assessment so that students can celebrate their results together, continue to share news and even, as alumni, stay in touch with each other and the institution over a period of several years. Where the students are away from the campus for periods of work-based learning, the support of an established online social networking environment can be very helpful, if only as a space in which to share moans and groans with like-minded individuals.

Planning for accessibility and usability

The conventional teaching methods within campus-based and distance education have been established for decades. In campus-based teaching, students are usually reliant upon lectures, seminars and reading lists as the guide to what they need to learn. For the able-bodied student this may pose few challenges: attending lectures, taking notes, discussing ideas with others, finding, reading and referring to additional resources. For the able-bodied distance learning student the same set of skills is required: reading, attending lectures, taking notes, discussion with others in face-to-face settings and using resources effectively – perhaps with more potential for flexibility and without emphasis on the face-to-face sessions (which may be optional or omitted entirely). Disabled students will need to develop techniques and use tools to access some of the teaching (e.g. a hearing loop for a deaf student or Braille versions of books), but because the teaching methods have changed very little over a long period of time, most institutions will have experience in helping disabled students to access these types of teaching (see Chapter 8). This is not to suggest that the established approaches to teaching are necessarily optimally accessible or usable, but they *are* familiar, with established 'work-arounds' for many of the obvious problems.

That is not the case for e-learning, where there may be an emphasis on multiple media and there will be an emphasis on computer use. As Chapter 1 shows, e-learning is an evolving approach to learning and teaching, and one that we can expect to change still further in the future, both in the type of technologies used and in the uses we will make of them. There is a new challenge here in making e-learning accessible, and the approach is not necessarily the same as that taken in the past. While disabled students may be helped to access inaccessible media by using tools (e.g. the hearing loop) or employing translations (e.g. the Braille or audio book), e-learning also offers assistive technologies in the form of screenreader software or modifiable font sizes and colours. Additionally, it also offers the option of drawing on a wider range of alternatives and substitutes.

The screens within an electronic learning environment are often drawn together from more than one source, perhaps using personalization to ensure that each student is presented with the relevant set of resources based on privileges and permissions. This makes it possible for students with a disability to be given access to a different set of resources, ones that address the same learning outcomes but rely on different modes of access (for example, a very visual resource, inaccessible to a blind person, may be replaced by a text-based audio file). A business student presented with the task of evaluating an advertising campaign could be asked to review a series of poster ads (if sighted) or a radio campaign (if blind). The use of metadata to describe the accessibility implications of each learning activity, or resource, would make it possible for students to choose the most suitable resource or activity for their needs. This also offers interesting potential to help students who are adjusting to a temporary disability and whose needs would not normally be met through the formal support systems.

In Chapters 4 and 5 we go on to look at a learning design framework (LD_lite). For accessible course design purposes it is worth considering what the accessible alternatives might be for each of the activities plotted within that framework.

Blending action and interaction online

We have spent this chapter exploring some familiar and not-so-familiar aspects of designing e-learning activity. It continues some of the discussion of blending from Chapter 2 in highlighting how important it is to offer balance and support flexibility in your designs. There are now many options in terms of how, when, with whom and why we communicate and work together online. Even given the realities of resource constraints in further and higher education, you could be forgiven for thinking that there are now simply *too many* choices. The average tutor can feel quite paralysed by the choices on offer and the unfamiliar aspects of e-learning design.

The following two chapters help provide a framework (LD_lite) for making, recording and revising the important design decisions. One of the more important things about that approach is that it allows for play and experimentation. It allows tutors to develop their confidence in designing for e-learning by facilitating recording of their own practice and that of their peers. It updates the traditional approach to lesson planning to take account of the range of choices that e-learning, particularly blended learning, requires.

Chapter 4

Documenting e-learning blends

Finding the finest blend

Coffees from different origins are blended together to make a coffee that is higher in cup quality than any of the ingredients individually. But the 'blending' of the individual ingredients can have a marked effect on the end result. It is important to know not just what the individual components are, but also, even more importantly, how the blending will result in a better outcome.

If we want to ensure an improved outcome when blending learning, we have to think about what motivates us to blend, and, as we have seen in the previous chapters, the drivers are different for students as compared with tutors. Students are often motivated to use technologies outside class in an informal way, 'blending' different sorts of interaction instinctively. They take risks and experiment. They practise and make mistakes while using these e-tools for a range of different purposes, and then transfer what they learn to their studies. They try things out until their use becomes 'intuitive'.

Students often blend different sorts of interactions across an interface integrating 'face-to-face' and 'virtual' spaces, supplementing face-to-face communications with interactions in virtual environments. They might hold discussions with students in the same room, talking through ideas while collaboratively writing an assignment. On other occasions they may 'SMS' and 'instant message' someone who is in the same room in order to have a private discussion aside from the main conversation. They may choose to interact synchronously, in 'real' time, with fellow students who are geographically dispersed, communicating by phone or by video link. Alternatively, they may work together asynchronously with others at a distance or on 'campus' by contributing ideas to shared online spaces, such as wikis or blogs.

The motivating factors behind choice of blend are different for teachers. Many teachers recognize the advantages of blended learning;

their students may be requesting specific forms of learning. But teachers are subject to a number of constraints, which means that their approach to blending may not be so intuitive or experimental. One constraint relates to control and accountability. When designing courses, teachers may feel that they cannot afford to experiment and get things wrong (Littlejohn *et al.*, 2003). This may reduce their confidence to experiment with e-tools and media to try out a range of blending possibilities. They may be conscious that their students have limited time and that it must be spent productively. A major review of learning activities in UK higher education highlighted tutors' reluctance to experiment with blended learning approaches (Britain and Liber, 2004). Another reason relates to the complexity of learning and teaching processes. Learning involves a number of interrelated processes that need to be blended. These processes change according to the learners' context. Changing one variable may have a huge impact; for example, if students cannot meet at the same time, the dynamics of the whole course will change.

Overall, each blend involves consideration of a range of factors from both the tutors' and the students' perspective. Different teachers and support staff will favour different blends. There is no one perfect blend for a specific context, just as there is no one perfect blend of coffee for a particular occasion. There are good, very good, interesting and excellent blends. There are even 'inspired' and innovative blends. Successful blending requires careful thinking through of the ways in which each of the individual components affect one another.

Factors affecting blending

To make sure blending results in an improved course or learning activity, we need to consider the dynamics that may affect blending. There are at least three interrelated factors (MacDonald, 2006). The first aspect is *the purpose of the learning*, which depends on the learning objectives or outcomes. The second factor is *the context of learning*, which takes into account how specific characteristics of the learners will influence the optimal blend. These include aspects such as students' previous educational and work experiences and where they are learning. The context in which the learner is learning is relevant not only in terms of the discipline and level, but also in terms of the proximity or distance from the teacher and teaching resources (mentioned in Chapter 2), and the resources learners may have available in particular environments (e.g. a workplace with supportive work colleagues). The third factor focuses around tutors' and students' preferred *approaches to teaching and learning*. These preferences may be affected by access to resources and services, experiences with particular approaches, personal style and time available. To find the best blend, we must consider all these individual aspects and the ways in which each will impact upon the others. This means that the blend will be slightly different as each factor changes.

Factor 1: the purpose of learning

Different media can be blended to suit particular learning objectives or outcomes. Students might learn to critique a play through reading the script, discussing the central concepts of the play and synthesizing their ideas through writing a review. Languages can also be learned through reading, writing and discussion. However, if we want to learn a conversational language, we might concentrate on discussion, which requires interaction with others. Some skills-based learning objectives or outcomes, such as learning to fly, require an approach and blend of media that allow students to learn the skills necessary for flying, realistically but without risk. This can be done through a blend of simulations and real-world tasks.

So, the choices when selecting a blend of communication tools and means of interaction will be influenced by the learning objectives or outcomes. Another influential factor is the context of learning.

Factor 2: the context of learning

Just as students are becoming more diverse, so are the different contexts in which they learn. We can no longer assume the 'standard' student in a 'common format' classroom or lecture hall setting. The 'full-time' attendance of even residential students cannot be guaranteed; over 40 per cent of students in higher education in the United Kingdom are now studying part-time: 30 per cent of undergraduates and over 60 per cent of all postgraduates (Universities UK, 2006). This rapid growth in part-time education is reflected in other countries around the world. Part-time students may not be able to meet at the same time outside the scheduled lectures and tutorials.

There are many reasons why students are studying part time. They may have jobs to fund their education. They may live some distance from campus. They may be distance learners. They may be learning in the workplace. Technology can help bridge the divide between work and study. For example, if students cannot meet face to face, technology can be used to help discussion continue between scheduled classes, but there are many other ways technology can be used. Between timetabled classes you might ask students to download a course reading from an electronic learning environment and discuss concepts using an online discussion tool. In this case, all interactions will take place asynchronously, online. This has the advantage that the learners can contribute at times that are convenient for them rather than at a time determined by the teacher. However, the choice of interaction does not depend only on whether learners can discuss face to face. Even if students can meet, there may be reasons relating to the learning goals why you might ask them to upload their ideas online and reflect on the postings of other students prior to meetings or classroom sessions. This can free up time in face-to-face discussion or in class to interact and give feedback, preserving this scarce resource for activities that make best use of it.

Now imagine teaching the same course within a different context: your students cannot meet in a single location, but can interact at the same time. In this case students might prefer a different blend. Synchronous communication technologies support the 'immediacy' of free-flowing conversation. These sorts of technologies include telephoning (with a land line, mobile or internet phone) or videoconferencing (using a webcam with a variety of free software). Depending on the concept and the context, synchronous communication might not be the most suitable form of interaction. Synchronous communication can present difficulties, since some students may prefer to read and reflect upon postings from other students before responding. They may value being able to generate a record of their discussion and use this as a self-generated learning resource. It can be difficult to participate in, or even to follow, a synchronous discussion involving more than a few other students, although the opportunity to ask for immediate clarification is there. So, even though learners are able to interact in real time, they may sometimes choose other options.

Now think of the same course in a third context. In this case the students are able to meet easily at the same time in a single location. The most effective means of communication may then be face-to-face discussion. These discussions could take place in a classroom, 'breakout' room or a coffee house. When the students have reached a consensus, and within an agreed time-frame, the views of the group can be reported back conventionally through a face-to-face presentation to the class. This need not be the only option. Group reports could be drawn together and posted to an online forum. Students might then review and reflect upon the postings of others over an extended period. Using e-tools alongside the face-to-face discussion, students may share ideas, views, articles and work-in-progress documents in an electronic learning environment or other online space.

In summary, the 'blend' will be influenced by the learners' context. Getting the blend right requires insight into individual characteristics of learners and their diverse contexts. In turn, these factors will shape your approach to teaching and support.

Factor 3: approaches to learning and teaching

Teaching can be a very personal experience, and every teacher has a set of preferred teaching methods. The approach to teaching will have a significant impact on the blend. The blend of e-tools will also depend on the ways this approach is supported by the institution. The institution may have invested in a particular range of systems, which could affect the choice of e-tools; for example, it might support a particular electronic learning environment. Institutional support will have an impact on what is in the blend, and this is investigated further in Chapter 8.

Similarly, the blend will be influenced by students' favoured learning styles, as these will impact on the choice of software, e-tools and learning resources. Studies have shown that students in different disciplines have favoured methods of learning and choice of learning resources (Littlejohn et al., 2007; Beetham, 2004). These different approaches mean that students make use of different media and e-tools in different ways. Some will prefer to learn using visual resources, such as texts or diagrams, while others favour aural stimuli. Some will have prior skills in using certain media, acquired through previous study.

In addition, students' prior experience will influence their selection of learning resources and e-tools. Students of languages may have experience of using e-tools to allow them to view videos, or listen to audio, or for verbal communication. However, they may not have access to the e-tools or skills necessary to adapt video or audio content. Students of film and TV studies, however, will usually have access to software that allows them to edit digital video and audio. Their course will probably also provide them with the skills and support to do this.

Students who have no experience with computers will generally require more support in e-learning or blended learning than those who have strong ICT skills – although, as noted in Chapter 2, specific ICT skills and previous online practices may not translate directly into e-learning. This, in turn, may be related to the discipline. Students of computing or engineering may have stronger information technology (IT) skills than social scientists; journalism students may have better communications (C) skills than students of more technical subjects.

Students, particularly those studying at higher levels, will value some level of autonomy and choice as to how they will interact. Giving students choice within a supportive environment (that is, making sure they have access to appropriate technologies and the skills to use them) is also important. Having access to an experienced tutor who can support them will further increase their motivation and level of engagement in learning activities.

What is in the blend?

We have already seen that there are a variety of individual components involved in blending: different types of media resources, learner tasks, learning environments and even various time zones. It is important to unravel these different components in order to know why certain blends will result in a different outcome. Changing each of these components will have different implications for tutors and students:

From the student's perspective:

- *The space blend* depends on whether students can meet up and interact face to face or whether they have to use technology-mediated communication.
- *The time blend* is also influenced by learners' ability to meet at the same time, which depends not only on their geographical location, but also on their availability. This factor will determine whether they carry out tasks in 'real time' (synchronously) or in delayed time (asynchronously).
- *The media blend* is affected by the types of e-tools and resources students can access. If they have access to the internet, they may communicate via text using online forums or instant messaging. On the other hand, they may choose to hold discussions by phone if this mode of communication is available and more expedient. They will use resources in a variety of formats: as supplied, in an edited form or even as created by themselves, using specific e-tools (e.g. mind-mapping software).
- *The activity blend* may be largely determined by the teacher or can be led and facilitated by students, working individually or in groups. Approaches such as problem-based learning give students autonomy over setting their own learning objectives and tasks. This will be further explored in Chapter 6.

From the tutor's perspective:

- *The space blend* is influenced by whether students can meet face to face, but it also depends on the types of learning environments available.

These could be virtual or physical spaces. The lack of a suitable physical space for some activities may foster exploration of online alternatives. This is explored in Chapter 7.

- *The time blend* depends largely on learners' ability to meet during a single time slot (are students distributed across different time zones?) and on curricular constraints (does the course take place over a whole year, or in one intensive day?).
- *The media blend* is reliant on available resources and e-tools, and is likely to vary from one discipline to another. Mathematicians will use a different range of software and file formats from those used by graphic design students. We have already cited examples of blending media, ranging from students downloading lecture notes and PowerPoint slides from an electronic learning environment to schoolchildren collecting and integrating resources (see the 'Mudlarking' case study in Chapter 2 (Example 2.1)).
- *The activity blend* is predictably influenced by the tutor's orchestration of a number of different learning activities to create a learning design. Different approaches to teaching may place this orchestration to some extent in the hands of the learners.

Mayes and de Freitas (2004) have written a comprehensive review on approaches to learning and teaching which concludes that different activities can be supported using different media and that the components outlined in this chapter affect one another. The overall blend has to be one that the tutor – and the students – feel comfortable with. This requires effective orchestration of the individual components.

Orchestrating the blend: blending different approaches to teaching

We have already established that our choice of where, when and what to blend is influenced by at least three major factors, including the tutors' preferred approach to teaching. In *How Do People Learn?*, Reynolds *et al.* (2002) outline four distinct perspectives on teaching. Each of these may require different blends:

1   *Learning as behaviour*, or skills training, focuses on skills-based competences. Examples include learning how to drive a car. The student first learns driving theory and becomes accustomed to using the controls in a stationary vehicle. Then they progress to learning how to steer, then to how to use the gears and clutch. Eventually the learner acquires the

necessary skills, and driving becomes 'intuitive'. This type of learning often requires 'real-time' interaction, though it does not necessarily mean that learners have to be in one particular location, or use the services of only one teacher. Sometimes skills training can be supported through simulation software, such as flight simulators. The role of the tutor can be carried out by colleagues, experienced peers or workplace mentors. What is distinctive about skills training is that the learner will need to practise their skill in an 'authentic' way at some point.

2   *Learning as understanding concepts* is based on the idea that students learn through discussing ideas with others. During discussions, students receive feedback from tutors and/or other learners, allowing them to self-assess how well they understand each concept. When using technology, the ability to take part in a discussion is largely independent of location, so learners could be geographically dispersed. For example, synchronous audio discussion can occur using a land line telephone, a mobile or the internet. Although we are accustomed to thinking that discussion is about audio-based dialogue, it need not be. There are a variety of other tools that can support text-based discussion, including instant messaging, blogs and online forums or mailing lists. Some of these allow discussions to take place in 'real time' (synchronously) or over a period of time without all participants being present at the same time (asynchronously). The decision whether to discuss in synchronous or in asynchronous mode depends on whether students are all available at the same time and require time for reflection before responding. Of course, it also assumes that students will have the right skills and good access to appropriate technology that allows them to carry out electronic discussion.

3   *Learning as knowledge construction* is based on the idea that learners 'build' knowledge by constructing artefacts, such as project-based assignments. It is sometimes referred to in educational literature as 'constructivist learning'. There are a wide variety of learning activities that focus on knowledge construction, ranging from tutorial questions to designing or scripting a play or problem solving through design and/or product development. Students might build knowledge individually or in groups. A by-product of these activities may be 'work-in-progress' artefacts. In the previous examples these might be tutorial answer sheets or scripted plays. These artefacts do not always present the full story about learning; even if students fail to create a play, they may still have learned something in the process. However, the artefact can give an indication of how well the students are learning and can be used as a means of assessment.

Knowledge construction can be planned to be independent of location (space) and time. In other words, students may carry out activities of this type face to face in real time, or asynchronously and distributed over various locations supported by technology. While assembling assignments and other artefacts, students can integrate resources from a variety of sources, so the blend of media will be strongly influenced by the student.

4   *Learning as social practice* involves learners operating as part of a community of practice. According to Wenger (1999), each learner may be initially at the edge of a learning community, but as their skills and knowledge increase, they will integrate within that community. All of us are part of many different communities at any given moment in time. Community members may interact independently of space and time, but they often use a range of media that is appropriate to the community type. For example, tutors and students on music courses are likely to use media in audio formats, whereas those on statistics courses may be using large, complex datasets.

When we design courses, we 'blend' different combinations of these teaching approaches. Then we integrate different media, e-tools, and so on. The end result can be complex, particularly for those new to blending. Therefore, it is important to document how we intend to blend individual components – akin to 'scoring' a play or piece of music.

Knowing the score: documenting learning and teaching practice

Blending a number of learning activities, media and e-tools can be compared with orchestrating a stage performance (Liber and Olivier, 2003). It is helpful to have different types of information about the performance at different levels. As a starting point, it is useful to have access to a short synopsis, of the kind you would read in an announcement or on a poster or in a directory. Its purpose is to outline the ideas and abstract the pattern behind the activity. For blended learning, this sort of information is useful for tutors other than the author of the learning activities, since it gives them sufficient information to choose between one 'performance' and another.

If the synopsis seems of interest, then you might want to find out more detail about the individual learning activities. This greater level of detail is akin to that in a script or screenplay. It gives information on what happened during an activity sequence, providing details of each learning activity to tutors who were not there at the time. For others, who are part of the 'performance' (tutors and students), it indicates what to do at each stage. The screenplay is usually presented as a detailed, linear document about a set of events happening in one space as a continuous flow. For blended learning, this information is often presented as a 'lesson plan'.

Unlike a play, learning activities might not take place sequentially. Depending on the complexity of the sequencing, it may be essential to have an overall mapping of the learning activities. In blended learning, this is a 'learning design sequence' that can be viewed as akin to the 'director's working document'. It is a schematic of the technical performance with stage directions (choreography) and parallel processes (lighting, stage directions, etc.) included. Unless you wanted to host the performance or adapt it yourself, you might not want to look at this level of information.

These diverse ways of representing a stage performance serve different purposes. No single representation can convey the whole story at every level. The same situation exists when planning learning and teaching; there are a wide variety of ways that tutors document their practice (Beetham, 2001, 2004).

Documenting teaching practice is not a new idea. You probably already use a number of different planning frameworks to document and describe your teaching (Sharpe *et al.*, 2004). We have been working with tutors from a variety of different UK universities and colleges teaching a range of subjects to find out the ways they plan and document the teaching of their courses. This study was part of an initiative funded by the UK Joint Information Systems Committees: the Mod4L (Falconer and Littlejohn, 2007; www.academy.gcal.ac.uk/mod4l/). What we have discovered is that tutors use a range of different approaches and planning tools to document teaching and learning activities. These frameworks operate at a variety of degrees of 'granularity': from a whole course down to an individual learning activity. When we asked a sample group of tutors which sort of framework was most useful to them, their response was that it depended on what the framework was going to be used for and who was using it. Some of these frameworks are listed in Table 4.1.

From our study we know there is significant enthusiasm among tutors towards developing a common way of describing teaching practice that will allow them to share ideas and learn from one another. Tutors sometimes form beneficial informal networks to share information about teaching approaches online. The Personal Repositories Online: Wiki Environments (PROWE) project, a Joint Information Systems Committee (JISC)-funded initiative in the United Kingdom, is looking at ways in which e-tools can support individuals within a part-time tutoring community to share ideas about practice. Similarly, the Australian based LAMS community

Table 4.1   Frameworks used by tutors to plan and document teaching

Framework	Description	Usefulness	Target users
Module plan or master folder	Text-based overview of the module. Usually available as a Word document or in paper form	Essential for quality assurance procedures such as external assessment	Tutors Programme leaders External examiners
Case study	A narrative overview of a teaching and learning situation – ranging from an entire module to a single classroom activity	Case studies are used to communicate ideas about teaching practice. They are most useful when they outline specifics about what went wrong as well as positive outcomes	Tutors Course developers
Briefing document	A narrative overview of a teaching and learning situation, focusing on class management issues	The briefing document is similar to the case study, but has more of an emphasis on class management issues, such as resourcing and timing	Tutors Programme leaders External examiners
Pattern overview	A rich, narrative description of a learning activity or set of activities	Useful for communicating teaching ideas to other tutors. The 'pattern' abstracts information about the teaching approach. It gives more concise information than the case study. Its intention is to provide an overview at a glance	Tutors Course developers
Contents table	A list of contents of a module or a single class	Useful for communicating an overview of a course (or class) to other tutors. The 'contents table' focuses less on the teaching approach and more on the subject matter. Students can use such a list as a course overview	Tutors Students

Table 4.1 (continued)

Framework	Description	Usefulness	Target users
Concept map	A mapping of concepts and/or learning activities	The concept map can be used to communicate ideas on learning activities and teaching approaches. It can be used by students to help them understand the ways in which concepts and/or activities fit together	Tutors Students Course/audio-visual resource developers
Learning design sequence	A sequence of learning activities	The learning design sequence is similar to the concept map. Its purpose is to orchestrate learning activities. This is fairly straightforward where learning activities are sequential, but becomes more complex with learner-centred approaches, such as problem-based learning	Tutors Students
Storyboard	A mapping of concepts and/or learning activities	The storyboard is similar to the concept map, but usually has more detail. It can be used to communicate ideas about instantiation of specific teaching scenarios to tutors, but may be too detailed for students	Tutors Course/audio-visual resource developers
Lesson plan	A mapping of concepts and/or learning activities	Lesson plans map learning activities with resources. They are highly contextualized, but do not give information on the effectiveness of teaching approaches – what works and what does not work in practice	Tutors

is sharing ideas on course design. However, this information is often buried in extensive online collections of archived messages and is hard for new tutors to find. Even when the information is located, it will usually not support easy side-by-side comparison. This is partly because such a variety of frameworks are used. Another problem is that the information is often written for personal use and may be recorded in incomplete and inconsistent notation. To address these problems, we decided to develop an integrated planning tool that would draw on the strengths of some of these individual frameworks. We have termed this planning tool 'LD_lite'.

The central idea of the LD_lite tool is that it allows tutors to document learning activities for reuse and re-implementation by others. The tool was developed from a series of case studies of teaching activities where a process similar to LD_lite was used to help tutors plan and implement blended learning activities. These case studies were collected and developed during the period 2004–2006 from case authors in Europe, Asia, Australasia and the United States.

The following sections outline the thinking behind the LD_lite planning tool and how it might be used to reflect upon, design and map activities with e-tools and resources to suit specific teaching contexts. LD_lite can also help you anticipate some of the generic technical support or implementation problems that you may encounter. The framework will not, on its own, address the insecurity that you or your students may feel in using e-tools for the first time. Its main purpose is to help you to think through how to blend media, activities and e-tools across environments and give timely feedback to students.

The LD_lite planning tool: three into one

LD_lite is derived from several international studies: a process for tutors to document learning activities, developed in the late 1990s by Allison Littlejohn and David Nicol at the University of Strathclyde in Scotland (Littlejohn, 2003); a system for documenting effective practice developed by Helen Beetham for the UK Joint Information Systems Committee (JISC, 2005); a method of sequencing activities developed by Ron Oliver and colleagues on the Australian Universities Teaching Committee (Oliver *et al.*, 2002); a means of abstracting patterns of activities, developed by Peter Goodyear at the University of Sydney, Patrick McAndrew at the UK Open University and others (McAndrew *et al.*, 2005); and a simplified interpretation of an international notational sequence that underpins many educational learning environments and tools, IMS Learning Design (IMS LD) – hence the title 'LD_lite'.

The LD_lite tool integrates three types of frameworks that capture the details of a course at three different levels. The three parts of the LD_lite framework can all be created and reused independently, or they can be used as a three-stage process in planning blended learning. This approach reflects the preferences of the Mod4L tutors, who felt that the framework most helpful in supporting reuse of practice would combine elements of familiar frameworks, reflecting an overview of the teaching scenario as well as the details of implementation (Falconer and Littlejohn, 2007). Our investigations examined different framework combinations, the most popular being 'lesson planning'.

The lesson plan

While developing the LD_lite tool, we wanted to start from a position that would be familiar to many tutors. While supporting tutors developing blended learning courses at the University of Strathclyde, we found that the lesson plan methodology helped tutors to think through their course design (Littlejohn, 2003). The lesson plan framework used at Strathclyde drew upon specific elements from IMS Learning Design (IMS LD), a notational sequence being developed by the international standards organization IMS to underpin the development of learning technology software. IMS LD was initially based on an analysis of a large number of e-learning scenarios by colleagues at the Open University of the Netherlands (OUNL). All these scenarios could be summarized in a single statement: '*People* engage in *activities* with *resources*' (Koper, 2003, 2004; Koper and Olivier, 2004; Britain, 2004). Therefore, key elements of the IMS LD are:

- The activities or tasks that students complete to attain one or more learning objective(s) or outcome(s). During these activities, students receive *feedback* from a variety of sources (such as peers or tutors).
- People (what IMS LD calls 'actors'), including *students* and *tutors*, who are assigned roles within these activities (moderator, group summarizer, etc.).
- Resources including *content materials* and *software supports* (discussion boards, groupware, etc.) required to carry out the activities.

The LD_lite framework considers the context of learning focusing on these key elements: tutor role, student roles, content resources, services resources (e.g. e-tools such as discussion software) and feedback, as illustrated in Figure 4.1. This documents a simple online learning activity

Time	Mode	Tutor roles	Student roles	Resources (content)	Resources (courseware)	Feedback and assessment
Days 1 and 2	Online	Divide students into groups; introduce students to task and article	Read task and download article	Online article – link to university library (.pdf file)	Electronic learning environment	
Days 3 to 6	Online:	Moderate discussion; offer feedback and encouragement to students	Group discussion online; one group member to summarize discussion	Summary generated by students	Online conferencing discussion board	Online summaries are assessed by the tutor; feedback from peers and tutor

Figure 4.1 A lesson plan for a simple online learning activity

designed for a class of distance learning students. To carry out this activity, students are divided into small groups of four. Each group downloads course readings from an electronic learning environment. Students share and compile ideas within an online forum, so all interactions take place online. This type of lesson plan can be used by tutors to think through benefits and drawbacks of using particular learning approaches, resources and e-tools – for example, why use online communication instead of face-to-face discussions? The online forum may be useful in allowing learners to review ideas posted by other students. But although this approach may be useful for learners, it may be difficult to manage.

We saw earlier in this chapter that if students can meet in a single location, it may seem unnatural for them to use an online forum. They may prefer spontaneous, face-to-face conversation that allows them to formulate ideas rapidly. The activity documented above could be redesigned to allow students to discuss ideas face to face and then post group summaries online. This new scenario is documented in Figure 4.2. In this scenario, student groups meet in an mutually acceptable location, to discuss, collate and post their ideas to an online forum. Each group of students can review and reflect upon the postings of other groups and debate issues online, allowing further development of ideas beyond the end of their meeting. This blend of face-to-face with online interaction means that students can put together ideas rapidly through free-flow discussion and, at the same time, can benefit from reflection upon other online postings.

Is lesson planning like this a useful method for documenting teaching practice? We have held trials of this approach with hundreds of tutors of different disciplines in several countries. They tell us that indeed it is a useful framework for documenting specific learning tasks and reflecting upon how to blend specific activities. Some tutors have used lesson plans as 'work-in-progress' representations that help them think through how to blend a range of factors important to blended learning. Other tutors have used lesson plans to try to communicate ideas and actions that are often 'hidden'. This tacit information is often the true essence of good teaching. It is difficult to embed this sort of information in a lesson plan, so tutors may make it available as a text narrative, sound file or video clip appended to the lesson plan.

Like all methods of representing teaching practice, these lesson plans have several limitations. First, while the matrix structure is useful for orchestrating linear sequences of activities, it is limited in the way it can document the coordination of non-linear tasks, and is not always useful for orchestrating non-sequential learning activities. An example of a set of

Time	Mode	Tutor roles	Student roles	Resources (content)	Resources (courseware)	Feedback and assessment
Day 1	Online	Divide students into groups; introduce students to task and article	Review task and download article	Online article – link to university library (.pdf file)	Electronic learning environment	
Day 2	Face to face	Moderate discussion; offer feedback and encouragement to students	Group discussion face to face; one group member summarizes discussion online		Online conferencing discussion board	Feedback from peers within the group
Days 3–6	Online	Comment on summaries; post feedback to discussion board	Submit summary to discussion board. Group should comment on summaries of two other groups	Summaries generated by each group (.doc); feedback comments from tutor can be reused across student groups	Online conferencing discussion board	Group summaries are formatively assessed. Feedback from peers and tutor

Figure 4.2 **Revised lesson plan linking online and face-to-face activities**

non-linear activities could be problem-based learning, where students are asked to design a product. Problem-solving tasks can usually be subdivided into smaller activities that might take place simultaneously or iteratively. Second, the lesson plan does not provide a quick overview of the lesson. Therefore, it may not be enough to allow reuse or review of a particularly complex iteration of activities. Third, it does not give full consideration to the context of the learners. For more ideas as to how to think through and plan for different learning contexts, it may be useful to read *Effective Practice in e-learning* guide (JISC, 2005).

If you plan to use only *one* framework to think through your course design or to communicate it to others, we recommend that you use the lesson plan. Nevertheless, as illustrated in Figure 4.1, there are other types of planning frameworks that may be more useful for documenting the synchronization of tasks.

The pattern

A pattern is a quick overview of the teaching scenario that allows us to get a flavour of a particular teaching and learning scenario (McAndrew, 2004). The pattern focuses on the purpose of learning, giving information on the learning goals (aims and objectives or outcomes). It examines specific problems in learning and teaching, and offers solutions. This is a good starting point when planning blended learning. Most educational developers would recommend starting out by defining learning goals and/or assessment criteria before selecting content resources or topics.

Patterns are not entirely new. Many course or module descriptors have a broad outline of the course in a 'master folder'. McAndrew *et al.* (2005). have used patterns of this type to abstract teaching processes and document them as 'blueprints' that can be used and reused across a variety of teaching situations within a range of disciplines. Figure 4.3 is an example of a pattern.

If you want to communicate broad ideas and perspectives on your blended learning courses, we recommend that you use the pattern framework. However, patterns are limited. Although the pattern is a useful way of gaining a snapshot of a learning scenario and outlining specific objectives, it does not give comprehensive information on learning activities. This requires the more detailed LD_lite lesson plan outlined earlier in this chapter.

Pattern: Discussion and reflection on principles of course design

Overview of problem:

A group of students need to develop their ideas about a concept or issue in collaboration with other members of the group. Students can learn from others through discussion, review and reflection. They can debate issues, promoting further development of ideas. However, there is a tension between the potential benefits of an online discussion where tutor and students can review all postings, and the spontaneity of face-to-face conversations that allow students to share ideas rapidly.

Solution:

A balance of offline and online discussions enables students groups to discuss ideas face to face and then post group summaries online. Discussions take place offline. When a consensus is reached, the views of each group are collated by a group member and posted online. Each group of students can then review and reflect upon the postings of other groups (online) and debate issues (offline).

Aim:

To outline key principles of designing an online course

Objectives:

By the end of this lesson, you will be able to:

- describe three theoretical models of learning;
- illustrate each of these models with specific examples;
- outline key similarities and differences.

Apply these models to specific learning scenarios.

Figure 4.3 A pattern documenting the same scenario as in Figure 4.2

Blending space and time: the learning design sequence map

Learning tasks may take place in a linear, sequential order. On the other hand, different models of learning, such as problem-based learning, involve students carrying out activities in parallel or in iterative sequences. Orchestrating complex series of tasks requires a sequencing tool, such as the learning design framework developed by the Australian Universities Teaching Committee (Oliver *et al.*, 2002). This type of learning design sequence has already been used by tutors in several universities across Australia to orchestrate learning tasks and map them to resources and support services. An example is illustrated in Figure 4.4, and more examples of these sorts of learning designs can be found at www.learning designs.uow.edu.au.

A major feature of these learning designs is that each sequence focuses on the learning and teaching perspective. Some perspectives have linear sequences of tasks, while others involve non-sequential, iterative tasks. If you want to communicate information on the integration and sequencing of learning activities, we recommend that you use this type of learning design framework.

Learning design sequence maps are becoming more widespread in their use. Colleagues at Macquarie University in Australia have set up a community to share and swap learning design sequences as reusable learning designs (Dalziel, 2003). These maps can be interlinked with narrative patterns and lesson plans, providing a useful combination of perspectives.

Which of the three levels of LD_lite is most useful for describing and documenting practice and can most easily be reused? We presented this question to sample groups of tutors. Their response was that since all three types of descriptions serve different purposes and would be useful to different people at different times, they each provide a useful aid to thinking through potential issues and designing blended learning. However, while lesson plans are useful frameworks for planning blending activities, resources and space, they do not take account of the complexities of sequencing learning activities. Sequencing requires a 'timeline', such as the LD_lite learning design sequence map, which outlines how activities, resources and support services might be integrated (Figure 4.4). The complete LD_lite framework provides too much detail if you wish to share a broad outline of your course design. For that, you need something closer to the broad, narrative overview of the course that we show in our LD_lite 'pattern' (Figure 4.3). So, each part of the framework serves a different purpose. This is why the LD_lite framework interlinks all three types of description.

Problems with blending

While gathering the case studies that underpinned the development of the LD_lite framework, we asked colleagues what sorts of problems they experienced in planning blended learning. Our aim was to develop the

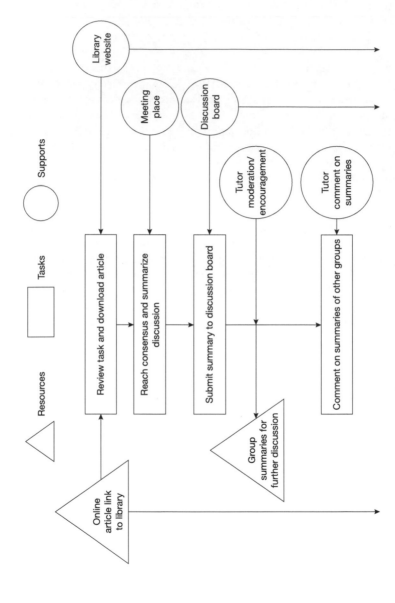

Resources ◁   Tasks ▢   Supports ◯

Online article link to library

Review task and download article

Reach consensus and summarize discussion

Submit summary to discussion board

Group summaries for further discussion

Comment on summaries of other groups

Library website

Meeting place

Discussion board

Tutor moderation/ encouragement

Tutor comment on summaries

Figure 4.4 A learning design sequence map documenting the same scenario as in Figure 4.2

LD_lite framework to help overcome these difficulties. The problems they expressed include:

1 *Difficulties in deciding where activities should take place and whether communication should be synchronous or asynchronous.* When students can meet in the same location, it can be difficult to decide on the best forms of interaction. Earlier we illustrated an example where it may be difficult to choose between fast-flowing face-to-face chat or technology-mediated interaction. The free flow of face-to-face, synchronous communication may be an effective way of expressing ideas and getting fast feedback. On the other hand, asynchronous technologies allow time for reflection and can mean that students are more likely to receive better-considered feedback from tutors and peers. These concerns are not straightforward even if students are learning at a distance, as there are a range of affordable technologies that can support synchronous communications. New e-tools are constantly appearing and existing tools are being extended or altered. It has become impossible for most institutions to keep up with the pace of change. A potential solution is to map learning activities against e-tools that can support them and, at the same time, place learners in control and allow them to choose the technologies they use. As illustrated in this chapter, the LD_lite lesson planning framework helps overcome this problem by providing a 'matrix mapping' of activities and e-tools.

2 *Difficulties in designing and blending learning activities, particularly those that encourage students to participate in a meaningful way.* Unless you are planning a course that uses only distance learning, deciding whether learning activities are best performed face to face or mediated by technology is sometimes a difficult choice. A major factor influencing this decision is how the purpose and usefulness of the activity are valued by the participant – that is, learner motivation. Online socialization is most successful when participants are motivated by carrying out authentic tasks that are meaningful and valuable to them, and that can directly benefit from connections with others. Regrettably, current e-learning is frequently designed to showcase e-tools, rather than support learning processes and the needs of the learners or learning community. By highlighting learning activities, rather than the e-tools that support them, the LD_lite framework can help shift the focus of design from e-tools towards learning processes.

3 *The time required to plan and implement blended learning methods.* A great challenge for teachers in colleges and universities in the twenty-first

century is to offer learners flexibility and choice in the ways they interact and communicate while, at the same time, structuring student learning. This requires careful effective planning of teaching methodologies. In our evaluations we have established that the LD_lite framework can reduce the time spent planning, developing and implementing blended learning activities.

4   *Problems with blending different media and e-tools.* Choosing the best technology tool and set of resources to support each learning activity is complex. Earlier we cited a review of the use of electronic learning environments in UK higher education by Britain and Liber (2004) which confirmed that lecturers do not have the time or confidence to try out a range of blending possibilities. e-Tools are almost always used to distribute class information or course materials. That is not to say that delivering content is bad practice; it simply does not draw upon the full potential of the communication technologies available. A more recent study discovered that in almost all online learning activities, students are requested to use one tool: an online conferencing system or online forum (Conole *et al.*, 2005). The range of e-tools used is often limited. This may happen because 'e-learning' often involves technology being retro-fitted on to existing practices and courses, resulting in course designs that may be ineffective and that do not provide motivation for students. There are major qualitative differences in communication afforded by different types of technology. One tool may be more appropriate to a particular learning situation (Laurillard, 2001). In the case of an online forum discussion this may *appear* similar to a classroom discussion, because both involve some sort of dialogue. There are, however, qualitative differences between the two: online discussion may be structured differently, it may be asynchronous, and it requires different skills. For campus-based learning situations, students may prefer spontaneous, face-to-face interactions (Meyer, 2003; Weinberger, 2002). The way forward sometimes requires radical redesign of learning tasks – rethinking which e-tools and media will support individual learning activities. LD_lite matrix mapping allows for consideration of different e-tools. It can help you decide on the most appropriate tool for a specific set of learning goals within a particular context. This will be illustrated further in Chapter 5.

Framing the problem

Blending is a complex business, but the LD_lite tool can help you deal with the complexities of blending. LD_lite integrates a number of frameworks that view a lesson from different perspectives: teaching and learning 'patterns', individual learning activities and learning activity sequences. Are these frameworks useful? On the one hand, they may help you plan blended learning courses efficiently. On the other hand, each framework is limited, so there are benefits to using combinations of them. Combined, they can help support your thinking on how to orchestrate a blend of media, e-tools and learning activities across a range of learning environments. But how can you make sure you are planning the finest blend? That is the topic of the next chapter. There we illustrate other, more complex scenarios and illustrate ways in which non-linear relationships across learning activities can be documented. We will seek the finest blend.

Chapter 5

Choosing e-tools for blended activities

An abundance of activities?

For effective learning it is important that students are actively involved and are motivated by what they are asked to do. This can best be achieved if we design courses in which students are engaged in shaping their own learning through carrying out a range of learning activities. There is no one standard approach or activity. Different types of activities and approaches will suit different learning objectives or outcomes and contexts. Although in theory a wide variety of learning activities are potentially usable in blended learning, this is not what is happening in practice. A recent scoping of the full range of different types of e- and blended learning activities being used by tutors across the United Kingdom revealed that most tutors design the same sorts of learning tasks (Conole *et al.*, 2005), selecting from a narrow range of activity types and approaches. The same is likely to be true in other countries. Many tutors may be using the same approaches again and again, with little variation. This means that the vast majority of the available activity types are not being used and are probably not even being considered. An analogy could be made to the use of washing machines and the like, where there are typically dozens of settings that could be used, yet the average user will select the two or three that they are most familiar with. Some features will never be used, perhaps because the owner of the appliance has forgotten that they are available or does not know when and how to use them.

The most common activity types implemented by tutors reflect the most familiar e-learning activities: *assimilative and information handling*. An example of an *assimilative* activity would be where a group of students are required to read an online article or access PowerPoint slides, then discuss key concepts. The students conclude by uploading their ideas to an online forum or participating in a face-to-face discussion. Another popular activity involves *information handling*, where students in small groups are asked to research a topic, locating online information resources and structuring and reviewing these within a shared virtual space, such as an online forum, presentation wiki or blog. Free online social spaces such as MySpace (www.myspace.com), and electronic learning environments such as Elgg (elgg.net), are useful for these sorts of interactions. We explore these online spaces in more detail later, in Chapter 6.

As part of the development of the LD_lite framework we asked a sample of teachers what was limiting the range of activities they implemented. Their responses focused around the e-tools they were using. These responses highlight a problem in designing blended learning: that focus often shifts from learning processes to the tools that support these practices. This is why we believe it is important to use a planning framework that focuses on learning and teaching practice, rather than the e-tools.

Problems identified by the tutors included difficulties in integrating into the curriculum the diverse range of popular e-tools, such as phones (land line, mobile, voice-over internet protocols), iPods, DVDs, and so on, and software systems, such as blogs and wikis. Students and staff may be using incompatible tools, and the technical and other support facilities within the institution may not allow deviation from a narrow range of 'approved' systems. This may account for tutors' preferences for a restricted range of e-tools. These may be e-tools with which they are themselves already familiar, or those that are best-supported within the institution. Typically the e-tools used will be those that are embedded within their institutional electronic learning environment, or commonly used software tools such as Microsoft PowerPoint and Microsoft Word. This chapter explores examples of practice, outlining the reasons influencing tutors' choice of tools. In some cases tutors have selected tools supported by the institution; in other examples, tutors have chosen tools that are commonly used by students.

For many institutions the current commitment to e-learning will be restricted to lecturers creating, and then making available online, teaching resources created using presentation or word processing software, with or without embedded links. As you will by now have realized, we see the challenges – and opportunities – of e-learning as extending far beyond 'everyday software such as PowerPoint and Word'. These e-tools do have an important part to play, not least because they are familiar and well supported within most institutions. It is, however, the blend of these and other e-tools and e-resources with e-activities that present the way forward for e-learning. There needs to be a rich and considered balance if e-learning is to offer a valuable, new and different teaching approach – blended or otherwise – rather than simply be an adjunct to, or straight replacement of, segments within conventional teaching.

In Chapter 3 we established the importance of basing the design of learning activities on student needs and learning goals, rather than on the availability of e-tools. By understanding the types of interactions that can be supported by e-tools, we can switch our focus away from the tool itself towards the learning goals they can support.

Mapping tasks with tools

An important consideration is not what tool to use, but how to use it. The success – or otherwise – of a learning activity depends on the choice of tools or resources used to support that task as much as it does on the *use* of the tools and resources (Littlejohn, 2004). We know that online discussion forums can allow students to share and develop ideas. However, these learning tasks will be successful only if the discussion is perceived by students as relevant and timely, if the forum is structured and managed, and if the learners are given adequate support (Conole *et al.*, 2004).

One strategy to retain focus on students' learning needs is to start by planning learning tasks, then map the range of tools that might support each task. Colleagues from the University of Southampton have developed a matrix taxonomy that allows a mapping of different sorts of learning activities to the types of tools that might support these tasks (Conole and Fill, 2005). This matrix is illustrated in Table 5.1.

The matrix is based on five broad learning activity 'techniques' derived from Laurillard's Conversational Model (Laurillard, 2001).

- An *assimilative information* handling activity is one in which students process 'narrative' media. An example is when students receive information by attending lectures, watching DVDs or reading texts, then manage and structure this information.
- An *adaptive* activity utilizes an environment that changes according to learners' input. Examples include online simulations or computer games.
- *Communicative* activities are focused around discussion. Examples are 'ice-breaker' discussion sessions or debates.
- *Productive* activities involve students producing something, for example the construction of an assignment artefact. Examples are essay writing, video production, and so on.
- *Experiential*, or 'interactive', activities are those that focus around problem solving. These include field trip simulations and role-play exercises.

Table 5.1 The Dialog Plus mapping of learning tasks and tools

Type (what)

Assimilative
Reading, Viewing , Listening

Information handling
Gathering, Ordering, Classifying, Selecting, Analysing, Manipulating

Adaptive
Modelling, Simulation

Communicative
Discussing, Presenting, Debating, Critiquing

Productive
Creating, Producing, Writing, Drawing, Composing, Synthesizing, Remixing

Experiential
Practising, Applying, Mimicking, Experiencing, Exploring, Investigating, Performing

Technique (how)

Assimilative

Information handling
Concept mapping, Brainstorming, Buzzwords, Crosswords, Defining, Mind maps, Web search

Adaptive
Modelling

Communicative
Articulate reasoning, Arguing, Coaching, Debate, Discussion, Fishbowl, Ice-breaker, Interview, Negotiation, On-the-spot questioning, Pair dialogues, Panel discussion, Peer exchange, Performance, Question and answer, Rounds, Scaffolding, Socratic instruction, Short answer, Snowball, Structured debate

Productive
Artefact, Assignment, Book report, Dissertation/thesis, Drill and practice, Essay, Exercise, Journalling, Presentation, Literature review, Multi-choice questions, Puzzles, Portfolio, Product, Report/paper, Test, Voting

Experiential
Case study, Experiment, Field trip, Game, Role play, Scavenger hunt, Simulation

Interaction (who)

Individual, One to one, One to many, Group based, Class based

continued

Roles (which)

Individual learner, Group leader, Coach, Group participant, Mentor, Supervisor, Rapporteur, Facilitator, Deliverer, Pair person, Presenter, Peer assessor, Moderator

Tools and resources

Assimilative
Word processor, Text, image, audio or video viewer

Information handling
Spreadsheet, Database, Statistics package, Bibliographic software, Microsoft exchange, PDAs, Project manager, Digital image manipulation software, Mind-mapping software, Search engines, Libraries

Adaptive
Virtual worlds, Models, Simulation, Modelling

Communicative
Electronic whiteboards, Email, Discussion boards, Chat, Instant messaging, Voice-over internet protocols, Video conferencing, Access grid, Blogs , Wikis

Productive
Computer-aided assessment tools, Electronic learning environments

---

Source: G. Conole, 'Describing learning activities and tools and resources to guide practice', in H. Beetham and R. Sharpe (eds) *Rethinking Pedagogy for a Digital Age: Designing and Delivering e-Learning*, London: Routledge, 2007 (reformatted)

The matrix lists a wide variety of possible types of activities. These range from tasks in which students assimilate information by reading, viewing and listening, or information handling, to tasks where students gather and structure information, through to operational activities such as experimentation.

Each activity type can be supported by more than one tool. In Chapter 4 we saw that the choice of tool depends largely on the learning objective or outcome, although it will also be influenced by the learning context and on students' and tutors' preferences for learning and teaching. There is no one perfect or universally applicable choice of tool. While carrying out an 'information handling' activity, students on one course might structure information using spreadsheet software such as Excel. On another course, or the same course with a different tutor or different students, information handling might be conducted using concept mapping techniques.

If students are carrying out an assimilative task to help them write an essay, they are likely to use a text-based word processing tool. On the other hand, video or DVDs are better tools for assimilating the information needed to learn a dance. Tool selection is also influenced by the context of learning, therefore learners with impaired vision may prefer to combine audio tools with text-based tools, to assimilate information for an essay assignment. The taxonomy given in Table 5.1 can help you to identify the different tool options for various types of tasks.

The tools listed in this taxonomy are a mixture of software and hardware maintained by institutions or national organizations, along with widely available tools belonging to students. This provides another way to consider e-tool choices.

Types of e-tools

The choice of e-tools for blended learning is growing rapidly. Students are no longer restricted to the tools made available by universities and colleges. As home, mobile and wireless technologies become widespread, many students have ready access to their own sets of e-tools. Aside from hardware tools, such as mobile phones, MP3 players and the like, there is an array of ubiquitous software tools, such as Microsoft Office software. Alongside these pervasive software tools is a range of freely available social software: blogs, wikis and forums.

Widely available hardware tools are the sorts of tools now commonly used every day. These include 'hardware' devices such as land line, mobile or internet phones, digital cameras, MP3 players, computer gaming devices, DVDs, desktop computers and, increasingly, laptops and PDAs. Many of these hardware tools are becoming more portable and multi-purpose. For example, many mobile phones now can take photos, capture video and allow internet access.

Commonly used software tools are often those supplied in 'Office' packages. These include word processing and presentation software as well as databases and spreadsheets. Because it is now often possible to 'connect' electronic documents using hyperlinks, it has become more possible to publish documents online and link them within web sites. There are now many new applications that are outside the standard Office tools and that focus on use for social purposes. These include wikis, blogs, social bookmarking, online discussion forums and polling software. Use of these is becoming more common in educational settings, often in combination. Some institutions have integrated these tools into the software learning environments that they maintain.

Institutional software tools are the sorts of e-tools maintained and supported by universities and colleges. These are increasingly provided within a single electronic learning environment. This environment may integrate student record systems with e-tools such as online discussion forums, shared workspaces, online quiz tools and RSS feeds. At their simplest, these sorts of environments can provide links for students to electronic learning resources. At their most complex they can be highly sophisticated online spaces offering a range of learning and support options and used by most courses within the institution. Using an electronic learning environment provides tutors with a means of securely publishing online material to specific student groups and cohorts.

WAP and wireless technologies open up opportunities to access educational opportunities regardless of location. They move us towards 'ubiquitous' computing, or, coupled with broadband access, 'always on' computing. This lends itself to possibilities for more spontaneous use of e-tools, as they are near to hand and can be used wherever the student is. These technologies provide easier and more convenient access to both 'everyday' and 'institutional' software tools. More and more wireless spaces are emerging in cities across the world, making it possible for some students to access materials and participate in the course online when away from campus and away from their desktop. For example, New York has created numerous wireless spaces within public parks, while in London the number of internet cafés is decreasing as wireless spaces become available in ordinary cafés and other public spaces, and Tokyo has a number of high-tech, hands-on play areas within the city. Access to wireless networks and broadband is still limited, however, in other, particularly rural, areas.

Many institutions are encouraging individuals to purchase and own mobile devices. In the Netherlands the government has been providing students with low-cost home access to broadband for many years (SURF, www.surf.nl). Some Dutch institutions provide very low-cost mobile phone services. Many institutions in the United States, United Kingdom and other countries have set up 'laptop schemes' that enable students to purchase portable computers (usually wireless enabled) for use both within and outside institutional networks. While universities retain ownership of a number of specialist hardware and software e-tools, such as engineering or scientific software applications, the trend is that ownership of e-tools is shifting towards the individual learner.

Trends in the use of e-tools

Current trends in dynamic knowledge creation combined with increasing availability of mobile technologies extend the potential of blended learning activities and the uses of emerging and existing e-tools. Emerging technology landscapes are reviewed in regular 'Horizon Reports' (www.nmc.net/horizon/).

Assimilative information handling activities that involve students sourcing materials online are often popular with students who are familiar with the art of 'Googling'. The students will need support in critically assessing a range of educational resources and also in evaluating online content that may not have an 'educational provenance'. Web publishing of text-based documents is now much easier, and the range is expanding all the time. Moreover, the types of self-published online resources available to students are becoming more diverse. Increasing availability of tools that support personal broadcasting, such as digital voice and video capture tools, along with devices for video and audio broadcasting (MP3 recorders and mobile phones), not only extends the pool of information but also makes use of a different range of e-tools.

For example, the San Francisco Museum of Modern Art sends out monthly 'podcasts' as downloadable audio broadcasts featuring the voices of artists and curators discussing new works and exhibitions. The podcast format means that these recordings can be listened to on a range of devices, from desktop computers to ultra-portable MP3 players. The latter allow students to access the recordings anywhere: at home, in class, on the move or in the museum itself. They can form the basis of class discussions, which could themselves be podcast audio comments. More information is available from www.sfmoma.org/podcasts/.

Audio files have long been used to teach music, but are also useful for teaching aural skills. North Carolina Schools for the Arts use podcasts to help drama students learn accent and drama. The students can investigate and record different accents themselves, building their own resource library. However, free, informal personal broadcasting technology sites such as Google Video (www.video.google.co.uk) are extending the potential of audio and video podcasting, as these sites are used by students to build media resource banks with others across the world.

Economics tutors at the University of Sydney have carried out assimilative information handling tasks, using SMS messaging to conduct classroom-based experiments that help students learn theoretical concepts. Students in class carry out individual calculations, but they have to share this information with others in the class to complete further tasks.

Information sharing is supported by texting to a central telephone number. This allows information to be pooled and displayed on a screen.

An example of the way in which *adaptive activities* have been transformed is through online gaming, particularly when games are developed by the students themselves. Playing computer games requires an understanding of the rules. Creating a game, however, necessitates a deeper level of understanding: appreciation of key concepts and the rules that interlink them. History scholars at the University of British Columbia in Canada are working with colleagues at Oxford University in England to develop collaboratively an online game representing the cultures of antiquity. Content, created from archaeological data, is peer-reviewed before being added to the game. The end result will be an online multi-player game grounded in current research, but available to anyone interested in informal learning in this increasingly popular area.

Simulation-based adaptive activities are increasingly being used in nursing, medicine and dentistry. Two international organizations have been collecting and developing these types of simulations from medical schools around the world. Based at the University of Dundee in Scotland, IVIMEDS (www.ivimeds.org/) and IVINURS (www.ivinurs.org/) are collections of educational resources for medicine used in several countries.

Communicative activities tend to fall into two categories: synchronous or asynchronous. Conventional, classroom-based communicative activities tend to be synchronous, focusing around free-flowing face-to-face discussion. Conventional technology-supported communicative activities are often based around the use of asynchronous online forums. Emerging e-tools in the social sphere, such as blogs, wikis, audio and video phones and messaging tools, have increased the potential of communicative learning activities. They now support learning activity that would not have been possible within traditional boundaries.

One example of synchronous social computing is 'World Jam', a global initiative involving IBM employees around the world. For seventy-two hours these employees used a variety of technologies to carry out collaborative community-based educational activities. This was a one-off pilot study, but its success has led to a number of organizations considering setting up educational social computing events.

Asynchronous social computing is being also being taken forward through a number of educational community blogs. For example, at the University of North Carolina in the United States the Interdisciplinary Center for eLearning maintains a blog that allows students and tutors to discuss technical issues of importance to the community (www.icenotes.blgspot.com). One of the best-known examples of an asynchronous communicative activity is Wikipedia, a free-content multilingual encyclopedia written collaboratively by contributors around the world (www. wikipedia.org/). Anyone can edit and add to an article. Wikipedia has transformed our thinking on how information is gathered, shaped and shared. Controversial issues can be discussed within the wiki, reflecting multiple ways of thinking and many perspectives.

There are a number of examples of wikis being used to support *productive activities*. For example, at Trinity College in Dublin, students of anthropology investigate sociological issues in virtual worlds using a variety of qualitative and quantitative research methods. Each student investigates a unique question, but their findings are collaboratively pooled using a classroom-based wiki. The wiki offers a convenient platform that can be accessed easily and edited by any student at any time, whether or not they are able to meet up. However, while wikis offer a quick information resource and a way of collectively sharing knowledge, there is a danger that readers may assume that the content is quality-assured. In reality, the entries in a wiki may not be accurate and could even be libellous. This emphasizes the argument that students and tutors require skills in evaluating the suitability and accuracy of online resource materials.

Other types of productive activities are based around the production of simulations. For example, maths students at the University of Illinois at Urbana-Champaign have collaboratively developed software that can simulate three-dimensional worlds using a mathematically based open-source gaming engine. The collaborative development of the software engine allowed the students to develop a deep understanding of the underlying principles of gaming as well as the interrelationships between concepts.

Experiential activities focus around acquiring experience in real-world problems. One example takes place at the University of Melbourne and Macquarie University in Australia, exploring Middle Eastern politics. Students, in groups of two to three individuals, are each allocated the role of a prominent Middle Eastern figure. Each group develops a detailed profile of the role they are playing, which they post on the web for other students to view. Once the profiles have been completed, the tutor releases a scenario in which the groups role-play, using asynchronous technologies. At the end of the course, students discuss emergent issues in a video-conference.

All of these different activity types can be documented using LD_lite. Examples of each type are presented in the next section.

Documenting activities using LD_lite

We invited hundreds of tutors from colleges and universities across several countries to construct examples of their own teaching practice using the LD_lite framework. We have selected one example of each type of activity presented in the previous section: information handling, adaptive, communicative, productive and experiential. Our criteria for the selection of examples for this book were:

- *Affordability* – each case study had to have been implemented without the need for project funding, with one industry-based exception.
- *Relevance to student learning* – each example identifies a problem that students are experiencing, then sets out to provide an alternative solution.
- *Simplicity* – each case is relatively easy to implement and could be part of an ongoing programme of change within the curriculum.
- *Granularity* – each example has a high level of granularity. In other words, it represents a small chunk of learning, rather than a whole course or module. Small fragments of courses are easier to document. In Chapter 6 we explore the complexities of documenting larger course segments.

Example 5.1:

An information handling activity: personal broadcasting of ideas about swing dancing

This unusual example of an information handling activity was created by Matthew Riddle from the University of Melbourne in Australia. It focuses around personal broadcasting, drawing upon widely available technologies to allow students to create and share their own video and audio materials. These technologies have recently become widespread, through the adoption of video and digital cameras an d low-cost mobile phones that can capture still images, video and audio.

This example illustrates a growing phenomenon: the increasing number of informal, hobby-based communities that want to 'formalize' learning about their hobby. Matthew is a keen swing dancer and a course designer. He realized that many swing dancers in his local area wanted to extend their understanding of the underlying social and historical significance of the dance. They wanted to combine their informal dance classes with a more structured form of learning, and so Matthew acted as their tutor. His central idea was to provide dancers with opportunities to learn collaboratively about the history of the dance from the twentieth century. Swing dance communities are using informal online environments such as YouTube (www.youtube.com) to share this sort of information. (Informal online environments are discussed further in Chapter 6.)

Matthew set out for each student an activity in which they explored a range of social and historical topics in chronological order over the course of a semester. While carrying out this activity, each student chose a unique topic. They then spent a couple of weeks gathering resources. Each student presented their topic in class, integrating dance demonstrations with video clips and music to seed class discussion. This teaching scenario is documented in Figure 5.1a (the pattern) and Figure 5.1b (the lesson plan). In this scenario the student group comprised a community of swing dancing enthusiasts who had no other reason for meeting up. They were not necessarily even local to each other (unlike on-campus students). Matthew had to redraft the scenario to enable students to learn at a distance (see Figure 5.1c). Planning the distributed scenario allowed him to think through how he could make use of communication tools such as voice-over internet protocol, internet relay chat and videoconferencing to maintain contact and carry the distributed discussion.

A learning design sequence map for the swing dance scenario is presented in Figure 5.1d.

There are many examples of 'hobby-orientated' communities that take part in this sort of informal learning every day. Tutors will be aware that the free-flowing dynamics of these informal communities can be severely constrained when interactions are placed within a formal framework. So, the design needs to be extremely flexible and responsive to the needs of the group, which may be very different from that of a more conventional class.

Pattern of an information handling activity

Problem:

Hobby-based students would like to learn about the historical and social context of their hobby. Students meet face to face to learn dance, but have limited time to discuss social and historical aspects.

Solution:

Students research the historical and social context by gathering information resources and sharing them online with a hobby-based community.

Aim:

To have an awareness of the social and historical contexts in the twentieth century

Objective:

By the end of the course you will be able to outline a range of social and historical aspects of swing dancing in question area uploaded to a shared online area.

Figure 5.1a A narrative pattern of an information handling activity

Time	Mode	Tutor roles	Student roles	Resources (content)	Resources (courseware)	Feedback and assessment
Week 1	Online	Post topic readings online; ensure each student has access to online space	Read topic summaries	Topic list and readings for each topic	Online repository or database (possibly within an electronic learning environment)	
Weeks 2–3	Classroom-based, then self-study	Facilitate discussion	Research one topic in detail to present in class (may include dance demonstration)	Range of resources sourced by students (e.g. video clips, photos, music, DVDs)	Online repository or database; DVD and CD players	Students and tutor provide comments
Week 4	Online	Moderate online discussion	Students post presentation notes. Other students discuss the topic		Online bulletin board (possibly within an electronic learning environment)	Students and tutor provide comments
End of week 4	Online		Students post summary of discussion		Online bulletin board	Feedback from tutor on the summary

Figure 5.1b A lesson plan of an information handling activity

Mode	Tutor roles	Community member (student) roles	Resources (content)	Resources (courseware)	Feedback and assessment
Online	Post topic readings online	Community members must ensure their own access to the online space; read topic summaries	Topic list and readings for each topic	Online community repository or database	
Online	Set time for synchronous meeting and facilitate discussion	Research one topic in detail to present to class (may include dance demonstration)	Range of resources sourced and shared by the community	Skype, MSN Messenger and webcams	Community members provide comments using MSN Messenger
Online	Set time for synchronous meeting and facilitate discussion	Community members discuss each topic		Skype, MSN Messenger and webcams	
Online		Community groups post summary of discussions		Online bulletin board	Feedback from members of the community

Figure 5.1c A lesson plan of an information handling activity for geographically dispersed students

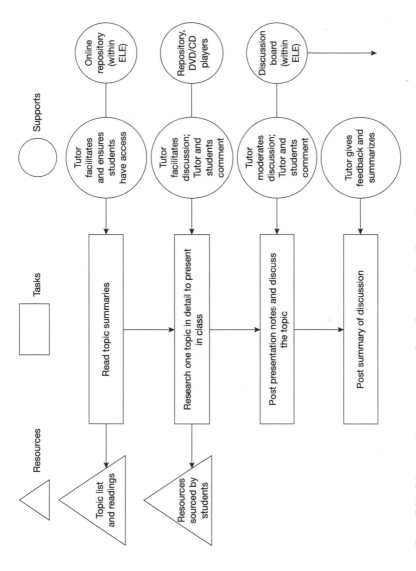

Supports

Tasks

Resources

Online repository (within ELE)

Repository, DVD/CD players

Discussion board (within ELE)

Tutor facilitates and ensures students have access

Tutor facilitates discussion; Tutor and students comment

Tutor moderates discussion; Tutor and students comment

Tutor gives feedback and summarizes

Read topic summaries

Research one topic in detail to present in class

Post presentation notes and discuss the topic

Post summary of discussion

Topic list and readings

Resources sourced by students

Figure 5.1d A learning design sequence of an information handling task

Example 5.2:

An adaptive activity: chemistry virtual experiments

This example was developed by two chemistry tutors in the United States: Professor Loretta Jones of the University of Northern Colorado, and Professor Stanley Smith of the University of Illinois at Urbana-Champaign. In their chemistry classes, students often had difficulty connecting the concepts learned in lectures to the procedures in the laboratory. They also had difficulty learning the laboratory techniques themselves.

Loretta and Stan realized that students needed two kinds of laboratory skills: intellectual and physical. Intellectual skills were those that involved the use of chemical knowledge to make decisions in the laboratory, while physical skills represented the ability to carry out a procedure and use equipment properly and safely. The students were very much distracted in the laboratory by the need to learn new physical skills while at the same time trying to apply chemistry concepts to solve problems.

Stan and Loretta decided that physical skills had to be developed through hands-on use of equipment, but that intellectual skills could be taught through simulations. They designed a series of video-based virtual experiments that would help students to learn laboratory techniques while at the same time reinforcing the concepts of chemistry. A screenshot from a virtual experiment that helps students learn how to balance equations is shown in Figure 5.2a. Students could use this set of virtual experiments ('Exploring Chemistry') to select reagents and see what happens when they react. The feedback to the students 'adapts' according to the students' selections. This method is more effective than working in a laboratory situation for two reasons. First, students are not 'distracted' by the laboratory setting and can be guided by the Exploring Chemistry software in linking chemical theory and practice. Second, these reactants are too dangerous for the students to use in the laboratory.

The narrative pattern drawn up by Loretta Jones is illustrated in Figure 5.2b. This pattern illustrates the general form of these activities that can be used in many scientific fields.

When they developed the multimedia lessons they called 'Exploring Chemistry', Stan and Loretta wrote learning goals for each lesson and analysed each target concept and laboratory technique, breaking them down into individual learning steps. They set certain criteria for the lessons:

- Students must have the opportunity to make experimental decisions.
- Students must predict the outcome of the experiments they designed.
- Feedback must always come from viewing the outcome of their choices, not from a written or oral statement.
- Students must interact with the simulated equipment in a manner as close to the actual operation as possible.
- Video sequences to be used in the lessons must always be shot from the viewpoint of the student, as if the student were actually working at a laboratory bench.

These criteria helped them devise the learning activities illustrated in Figures 5.2c and 5.2d. These adaptive activities have supported students learning chemistry in universities across the USA.

This approach illustrates an effective way of blending theory and practice. Prior to carrying out each experiment, students are posed a series of questions on theory. Their responses trigger video clips and animations of illustrating the consequences of their choices. The system 'adapts' and gives feedback depending on the learner's rationale and choices. Thinking through concepts prior to carrying out 'hands on' practical activities gives the learner a better grounding in the underlying theory. This method helps the students develop intellectual skills and conceptual models alongside practical, physical skills.

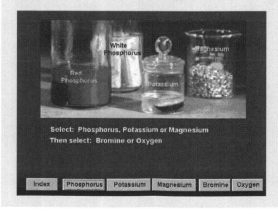

Figure 5.2a
The 'Exploring Chemistry' lesson on balancing equations

Pattern of an adaptive activity

Overview of problem:

Students find it difficult to connect scientific concepts with laboratory practice. They also must learn many laboratory skills in a short time and often fail to learn them well.

Solution:

Students complete simulated virtual laboratory lessons that help them to connect concepts and laboratory practice. Feedback on their choices received from the courseware also helps to train students in laboratory technique.

Aim:

To learn the conceptual and physical laboratory skills required to operate a spectrometer and carry out a titration

Objective:

By the end of the course you will be able to explain the nature and operation of a spectrometer and be able to predict the outcome of a titration. You will also be able to use these techniques in the laboratory.

Figure 5.2b A narrative pattern of an adaptive task

Time	Mode	Tutor roles	Student roles	Resources (content)	Resources (courseware)	Feedback and assessment
Week 1	Offline	Introduce students to the laboratory and courseware	Complete activity	Hands-on laboratory activity		Feedback from other students and tutor
Week 2	Online	Monitor student use of the courseware	Student performs simulation and uses the data collected to answer questions on the worksheet	Worksheet with adjunct questions	Exploring Chemistry lesson on spectroscopy	Feedback on predictions and choices in the multimedia lesson
Week 3	Offline	Supervise student laboratory activity	Students carry out a spectroscopic analysis using the skills gained from the simulation	Hands-on laboratory activity		Feedback from other students and tutor
Week 4	Online	Monitor student use of the courseware	Student performs simulation and uses the data collected to answer questions on the worksheet	Worksheet with adjunct quest	Exploring Chemistry lesson on titrations	Feedback on predictions and choices in the multimedia lesson

Figure 5.2c **A lesson plan of an adaptive activity**

continued

Figure 5.2c (continued)

Time	Mode	Tutor roles	Student roles	Resources (content)	Resources (courseware)	Feedback and assessment
Week 5	Offline	Supervise student laboratory activity	Students use the information and practice gained in the simulation to carry out a hands-on titration	Hands-on titration in the laboratory		Feedback from other students and tutor
Week 6	Online	Monitor student use of the courseware	Student performs simulation and uses the data collected to answer questions on the worksheet	Worksheet with adjunct quest	Exploring Chemistry lesson on oxidation–reduction reactions	Feedback on predictions and choices in the multimedia lesson. Randomly generated computer quiz

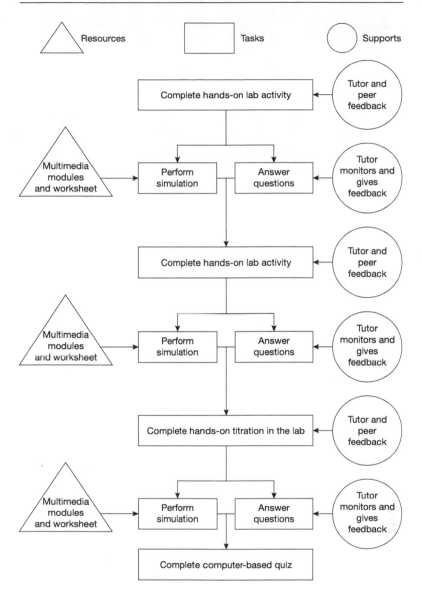

Figure 5.2d A learning design sequence of an adaptive activity

Example 5.3:

A communicative activity: supporting student reflections in engineering

This example of a communicative activity was developed by Professor Lorraine Stefani from the University of Auckland, New Zealand. It illustrates a growing trend in learning and teaching: the use of social computing to support student reflections. There are a variety of software tools available for this purpose, including wikis (web pages that can be edited and extended by multiple users), blogs (online 'personal diaries' to which authors can add a variety of media such as text, video and audio that can be commented upon by readers) and vlogs (similar to a blog, but video based).

While working with groups carrying out projects in mechanical engineering, Lorraine recognized that the students were not making good use of their tutors' comments. As part of the solution, each student group was asked to provide periodical 'work in progress' reports to their tutors, using an online wiki. The tutors provided weekly feedback on the learners' progress using a series of wiki pages. These wikis could easily be edited by any tutor offering feedback to the students; it was a convenient way to record feedback and make it available to every member of the student group. Each group would meet together to read and reflect upon this feedback. They would integrate their ideas into an action plan, which would be uploaded to their group wiki. Wikis were used by the student group because they were a useful way of being able to collaborate and share information and ideas. Figure 5.3a illustrates a 'pattern' of this scenario.

While developing the lesson plan, Figure 5.3b, Lorraine suggested that student groups might meet face to face every week to reflect upon their tutor's feedback. Synchronous communication was selected to complement the asynchronicity of their reflections. Groups could choose to communicate using any form of synchronous technology available to them. Some groups chose to meet using groupware (MSN Messenger), while others used videoconferencing. Figure 5.3c, the learning activity sequence, illustrates these weekly iterations. The LD_lite planning process allowed Lorraine to choose the most appropriate e-tools for this learning context. It also allowed her to monitor new resources generated through each iteration. It allowed easy identification of resources sourced or created by students as well as those supplied by the tutor.

Pattern of a communicative activity

Problem:

Students do not make optimal use of feedback from tutors

Solution:

A group of students reflect and act upon feedback provided by the tutor. The online environment supports reflection. Students can read tutor feedback and debate face to face how to act upon this feedback. Discussions take place offline. When a consensus is reached, an action plan is uploaded to a shared online area.

Aim:

To reflect upon tutor feedback

Objectives:

By the end of the course, learners will be able to:

* reflect upon the tutor's feedback;
* use this feedback to construct an action plan;
* implement the action plan and reflect upon the outcomes.

Figure 5.3a A narrative pattern of a communicative activity

Time	Mode	Tutor roles	Student roles	Resources (content)	Resources (services)	Feedback and assessment
Day 1: one-hour lecture	Offline	Lecture on mechanics	Take part in lecture	PowerPoint slides		
Day 1	Online	Encourage students to access wiki; ensure each student has access	Access the wiki	Mechanics e-book (.pdf)	Wiki	
Days 2–3	Offline	Meet with students if required	Assign roles to team members; plan project task; monitor and reflect on progress; make decision on future goals			Feedback from peers and (if required) tutor
Day 4	Online	Monitor student progress; provide weekly feedback; ask relevant questions to stimulate debate; encourage submission of reflective reports	Provide weekly progress report in wiki; highlight future tasks and goals	Uploaded resources shared across groups	Wiki	Formative assessment of project tasks by tutor; feedback from tutor, peers

Time	Mode	Tutor roles	Student roles	Resources (content)	Resources (services)	Feedback and assessment
Day 5 Process repeated each week	Offline	View student presentation; agree assessment criteria with students; assimilate and distribute criteria; cross-check peer assessment	Students present group project; group presentations are uploaded to wiki for use with subsequent student groups	Final presentations generated by student groups		Summative assessment of presentation by peer groups

Figure 5.3b A lesson plan of a communicative activity

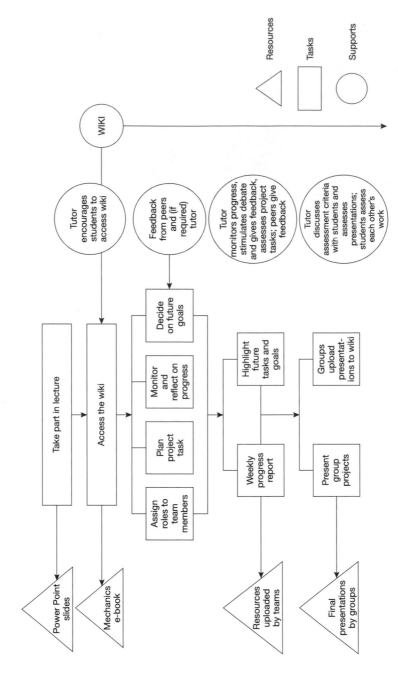

Figure 5.3c A learning design sequence of a communicative activity

Example 5.4:

A productive activity: collaborative construction of a glossary of terms in genetics

Productive activities are those in which students learn through 'producing' an end product. This example of a productive activity was developed by Jane Tobias, a lecturer at Bell College of Further and Higher Education in Scotland. It illustrates an emergent phenomenon in social and community-based networking: the collaborative development of ideas and definitions. A well-known example, Wikipedia, was highlighted earlier in this chapter. This example is on a much smaller scale, but is based on a similar principle.

Jane identified that her students experienced difficulties in understanding the meanings of terms. The conventional method of tackling this problem is to provide paper-based or online glossaries of terms. The problem is that the language within the definitions was not always easily understood by students.

Jane devised an alternative solution in which her students collaboratively constructed their own definitions of terms and documented these using a wiki. Students were encouraged to post terms they were unsure of to the wiki. Fellow students could 'translate' listed terms by providing a definition. If other students disagreed with the definition, they could offer an alternative, seeding discussion and debate around each term. The narrative pattern, illustrated in Figure 5.4a, communicates a general overview to other tutors from a variety of subjects who may experience a similar problem in their teaching. The pattern is deliberately 'discipline agnostic' and institutionally independent, making it as widely applicable as possible.

In developing this LD_lite plan, Jane constructed a mapping of the activity with the supporting tools and resources, illustrated in Figure 5.4b. Appropriate e-tools had to be selected to suit the context of implementation. The students could meet face to face, so they could 'blend' class-based discussions with collaborative online editing of a vocabulary. Jane selected a 'wiki' tool to support the development of the glossary. The wiki allowed students to contribute their ideas collaboratively in an easy and accessible manner. An alternative e-tool might have been 'social bookmarking' software that would have allowed students to share links to terms and definitions. These bookmarking e-tools are good for creating a view of how terms are related and being used.

Jane also had to think through how she might integrate face-to-face and online activities. By constructing the learning design sequence illustrated in Figure 5.4c, she was able to document new content resources generated as outputs from the learning activities. This included glossaries of terms written in language accessible to the students. Each glossary was a resource that could be reused by subsequent cohorts of students. There are further benefits in students constructing their own 'translation boards' and comparing their ideas against exemplars from other student groups.

In this case, the glossary of terms was constructed using a wiki. The main reason for selection of this tool was that it was supported by the college and could easily be accessed by the students. Other tools that could potentially have supported this task include blogs. At the time blogs were not supported by Jane's institution but students could have used social blogging software, such as My Space (www.myspace.com).

Pattern of a productive activity

Problem:

Students have problems understanding the meaning of terms

Solution:

Students construct their own vocabulary through 'translation' of terms. Students can flag any terms they have problems understanding using an appropriate online tool. Other students will 'translate' this term by writing a definition. Debate can take place online, then, when a consensus is reached, the definition is agreed.

Aim:

To construct a vocabulary of terms

Objective:

By the end of the course you will be able to define a range of terms associated with 'evolution'.

Figure 5.4a A narrative pattern of a productive activity

Time	Mode	Tutor roles	Student roles	Resources (content)	Resources (services)	Feedback and assessment
Semester 1	Offline	Divide students into groups; introduce students to task				
Semester 1	Online	Initiate a 'translation' list on a wiki. Place some words and translations as exemplars (online). Moderate stage 1 discussion (online)	Each student group investigates one piece of evidence for evolution; students upload terms they are unsure about into a 'translation'; board – then respond to others by providing definitions in their own words	'Evolution and early development' article (.doc)	Wiki site for translation	Formative assessment: the meanings of terms; peer feedback on meanings of terms; tutor feedback when terminology is misunderstood
Semester 1	Offline	Give feedback re translations and encourage continued use	Group discussions offline (in class) about evidence. Group agrees on a summary and group summary writer posts this to the wiki	Translations created by students	Wiki	Feedback from peers during group discussion

continued

Figure 5.4b A lesson plan of a productive activity

Figure 5.4b (continued)

Time	Mode	Tutor roles	Student roles	Resources (content)	Resources (services)	Feedback and assessment
Semester I		Monitor wikis, ask relevant questions to stimulate discussion	Post initial group summary; read postings from other groups	Translations created by student groups	Wiki	Feedback from student groups to other groups. Overview from tutor – summary of main issues articulated by student groups
Semester I		Monitor wiki	Determine what the common themes are across groups (by accessing wikis and holding face-to-face group discussions); post ideas to wiki		Wiki	Formative assessment: determining common themes. Feedback from other students and tutor
Last week of semester I		Summarize glossary of terms and post summary to wiki	Read final glossary		Wiki	

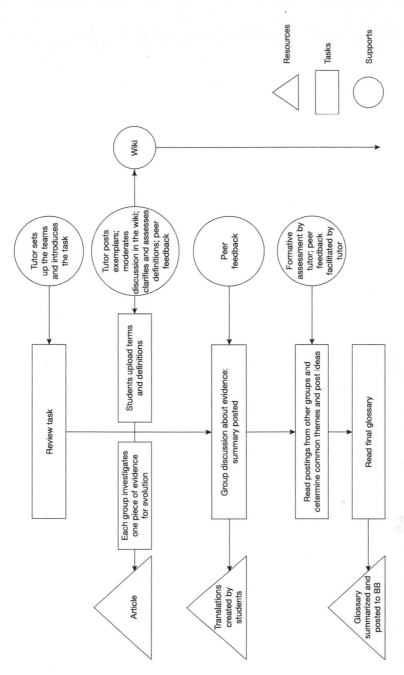

Resources

Tasks

Supports

Wiki

Tutor sets up the teams and introduces the task

Tutor posts exemplars; moderates discussion in the wiki; clarifies and assesses definitions; peer feedback

Peer feedback

Formative assessment by tutor; peer feedback facilitated by tutor

Review task

Students upload terms and definitions

Each group investigates one piece of evidence for evolution

Group discussion about evidence; summary posted

Read postings from other groups and determine common themes and post ideas

Read final glossary

Article

Translations created by students

Glossary summarized and posted to BB

Figure 5.4c A learning design sequence of a productive activity

Example 5.5:

An experiential activity: collaborative problem solving and knowledge sharing in a work-based setting

Good examples of experiential activities are solving 'real-world' problems. This example of an experiential activity is from a corporate learning context, illustrating how learners around the world might collaboratively solve workplace problems. This example is from a course on production systems optimization designed by Burney Waring, Learning and Development Leader at the Learning Centre of Shell Exploration and Production (EP) in the Netherlands. At Shell EP, Learning and Development Leaders are course directors who have extensive subject matter and field experience. Each course director spends four to five years developing and teaching courses at the Learning Centre. This course had originally been designed to run over a two-week period in a classroom-based format. However, changes in the company meant that the course had to be redesigned. The rationale behind the redesign of this course is underlined by the fact that the company will experience a major 'crew change' over the next ten years. Experienced engineers will retire and new staff will come from much more varied backgrounds than is currently the case. To prepare for this shift, experienced professionals need to share their knowledge and skills with less experienced colleagues. This problem can partly be overcome by teaching new staff real-world problem solving through coaching from experienced staff.

Since staff are geographically dispersed, the best way to link them together is by online or blended learning. Burney redesigned the course as a blend of three parts: pre-work (online), a classroom event (offline) and post-work (online). The aim of the pre-work session is to help learners to develop a common understanding even though they represent a variety of specializations. The classroom-based session is a one-week face-to-face event, during which student teams build upon their submissions from the first portion of the course. The post-work session focuses on applying newly learned skills and knowledge in the workplace.

In the initial online session, students prepare a 'Moments of Discovery' presentation on how they overcame a production systems optimization problem in their own work context. The students upload their presentations to an electronic learning environment, where Burney can assess each submission and give feedback. These initial submissions are further developed during classroom sessions. The students are divided into groups of four to present and discuss their 'Moments of Discovery'. Feedback from peers allows the students to rethink their ideas and re-present these in the online environment. A narrative pattern of these activities is illustrated in Figure 5.5a.

This narrative provides an overview of how an experiential approach might be useful in solving real world problems and is a useful means of disseminating general ideas about this approach. But the LD_Lite matrix in Figure 5.5b provides a better illustration of how the experimental approach works in practice. The matrix defines the ways in which tutors and students interact as well as the sorts of resources and e-tools they require for collaboration. The mechanism by which learners solve real world problems may seem rather unstructured, but the Figure 5.5c illustrates that there is a logical sequence of activities. Learning design sequences can provide students (and tutors) with a useful overview of how they might structure tasks. This could be particularly useful for novice learners.

Pattern of an experiential activity

Problem:

Engineers in a multinational company need to share experiences and knowledge related to aspects of optimization of oil production systems located in diverse geographical areas worldwide.

Solution:

Learners submit reports on solutions to novel problems from their workplace. They share knowledge on the implementation of these solutions with their peers.

Aim:

To enable peer learning, collaborative problem solving and knowledge sharing

Objectives:

By the end of the course, learners will be able to:

* identify novel solutions developed and implemented in other parts of the company that will be of relevance to their own workplace
* communicate effectively with peers worldwide and contribute to the ongoing development of a community of practice in their discipline.

Figure 5.5a A narrative pattern of an experiential activity

Time	Mode	Tutor roles	Student roles	Resources (content)	Resources (services)	Feedback and assessment
Weeks 1–3	Online (from workplace)	Sends the URL and password for the course web environment to the students	Log in to the course web environment	Interactive presentation of the blended learning concept	TeleTOP electronic learning environment	Tutor supports students in familiarizing themselves with the course and the electronic environment
		Posts a welcome message introducing the course activities, timelines, expectations, objectives	Familiarize themselves with the features, requirements, etc.	Introduction to the electronic learning environment		
		Invites participants to complete task I, 'Moments of Discovery'	Carry out 'Moments of Discovery' task; prepare a presentation on a real-world workplace problem and solution	Guidelines on completing the task and exemplars from previous cohorts of students		Tutor gives feedback on clarity of problem formulations and solutions; suggests revisions; marks submissions
		Invites participants to study peers' submissions, identify those of most relevance to their own workplace and prepare questions for classroom discussion	Study other participants' submissions and identify those relevant to their own workplace context	Assignments submitted by peers in the course		Tutor marks submissions based on a set of criteria
			Prepare questions to the proposers of the relevant problem and submit to the course environment			

continued

Figure 5.5b A lesson plan of an experiential activity

Figure 5.5b (continued)

Time	Mode	Tutor roles	Student roles	Resources (content)	Resources (services)	Feedback and assessment
Week 4	Classroom	Facilitates presentation and discussion of problem solutions	Present individual 'moments of discovery' in groups in a poster session. Participants rotate through presentations and ask questions to the presenters	Posters based on submissions in pre-work portion of the course Assignments submitted by peers in the course A summary list of 'moments of discovery' collated by the tutor	TeleTOP	Participants share knowledge and experiences; tutor facilitates presentation and discussion of ideas
Weeks 5–7	Online (from workplace)	Posts instructions and guidelines on completing the last master assignment of the course	Participants analyse their own oil fields and submit an extensive report and action plan relating to their own workplace problem. Activity concludes with a presentation on solution and outcomes to the participant's workplace supervisor	Relevant resources available in participants' workplace (manuals, guidelines, reports, documentation), supervisors and coaches, course and workplace peers; course resources	TeleTOP	Tutor provides support and feedback on each step of the master assignment; supervisors and tutors jointly give feedback on and assess the final activity

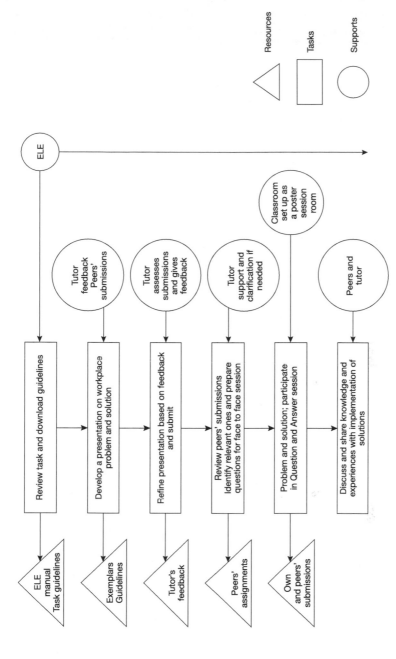

Figure 5.5c A learning design sequence of the experiential activity

Blending old and new

The designs described in the cases above show the importance of visualizing all the elements that will impact on effective learning design – not simply the e-tools, resources and activities but the balance of activity across the range of actors: tutors, students, content, services and assessment. Using this method of analysing and displaying the design allows course designers to understand what role the online elements will play. It also allows designers to question – where there is both face-to-face and online teaching – why certain tools are used and to see whether there may be further opportunities for more migration to e-tools and e-activities. This framework encourages articulation of design decisions about inter-activity so as to judge better how meaningful participation may be. It also encourages identification of the tools in a way that makes it easier to judge whether alternatives might be possible.

Documenting resources and services will provide stretched departments, and those for which e-learning is new, with a means of identifying a range of essential resources required to support new learning designs. Where the design is being reused, it gives good information about what the resource and service implications might be, and how the approach might be adapted to fit particular institutional contexts. It also identifies what the training implications for staff may be. In short, documenting course design will help with planning essential support requirements.

Getting up to speed with blended learning

In this chapter we have illustrated how planning frameworks can be used to help think through design decisions. The time invested in using such frameworks to plan and document blended learning activities can lead to more effective courses. These frameworks can help us reflect on why we are setting particular learning tasks for students. They can aid selection of the most appropriate sorts of e-tools to fit the task across different learning contexts. This approach reflects our belief that the design of e-learning should not be led, or unduly shaped, by technology tools. It can otherwise be tempting to start by choosing from a 'shopping list' of e-tools available, possibly selecting tools that are not appropriate for specific activities.

The development of electronic learning environments that integrate a range of e-tools together in one 'virtual space' has vastly reduced the time investment required to get up to speed with e-learning. However, there can be a temptation to design activities that use these e-tools, rather than thinking through the ways in which these environments might be used to support learning tasks. This dilemma is the focus of the next chapter.

Chapter 6

Environments to integrate activity blends

Problem-based learning: a case for complex blending

The types of learning activities that are motivating and meaningful for students are those that are as near as possible to complex, real-life problems. These types of 'authentic' learning activities often require students to work together in groups to solve a problem. Students think through how they will approach the problem, divide up tasks and regulate their own progress. 'Problem-based learning' is one method that embodies this approach.

Problem-based learning usually begins with an open-ended problem around which student groups organize their studies. The students discuss the problem and work together towards a solution by sourcing and using learning resources. Rather than drawing upon a single learning activity, problem-based learning is based around sets of activities that can take place sequentially or concurrently and sometimes iteratively. These activities are reflective and constructive, raising students' awareness and skills in solving complex problems.

Medical schools across the world have transformed their curricula into problem-based blended learning. For example, the St George's Medical School in London uses problem-based learning within its graduate programme. In this programme, students learn 'key topics' by investigating and offering solutions to a problem. The students define their own learning objectives and construct a framework (within a Word document) outlining the tasks they will carry out to solve the problem that they have identified. Next, the students carry out these tasks by sourcing resources and contacting 'experts' who can help them solve the problem. Electronic learning resources, such as interviews with actors posing as patients, scanned images of medical histories and prescriptions, and reference works, are made available to students to download and incorporate into their final assignment. Students also have the option to create their own resources and integrate these into their final assignment. The final assignment is reviewed by a medical expert, who cross-checks the assignment against the learning objective framework. A number of international organizations are advancing other implementations of problem-based learning in medicine. One such organization is IVIMEDS, which provides high-quality electronic learning resources to partners in Europe, Australia, Asia and the United States (www.ivimeds.org). Let us develop the St George's Medical School example further to illustrate different stages within the learning process:

• The initial planning stage involves students defining their own learning objectives and setting tasks. This stage could be supported using e-tools that support iterative project planning. These project planning tools would enhance collaborative planning, since all students would have access to project plans at all times.

• While developing solutions, students could create their own resources and integrate these self-generated materials with those provided. This process is best supported by content management tools, such as databases or repository tools, which are essentially central storage spaces.

• During the final testing and evaluating stages, peer discussion and reflection may help evaluate the effectiveness of the solution. These discussions could take place face to face or could be supported by communications tools.

The strength of this approach is not simply the access to high-quality learning resources, but that it encourages students to reflect upon their learning at different stages. John Cowan (1998) defines these stages of reflection as 'before action', 'during action' and 'after action'. In terms of the student activity above, 'before action' is when the student is devising key objectives and tasks, 'during action' is when sourcing resources and talking with experts, and 'after action' is while assembling resources to create the final assignment document. An important question is, which e-tools can best be used to support each of these stages? Table 6.1 illustrates different sorts of tools that can support each stage of problem-based learning. The left-hand column shows where in the problem-based learning process reflective activities occur. The right-hand column illustrates a variety of e-tools that might support these activities (Nicol and Littlejohn, 2005; Oliver, 2001).

Table 6.1 Stages of problem-based learning

Stages in problem solving	Types of reflection (Cowan, 1998)	Blended learning activities	e-Tools that can support blended learning activities
Problem definition	Initial setting up of groups	1 Authentic task presented, usually based on real-life scenario. Deadlines and milestones set	Complex problems can be presented as text using a web page, wiki or blog. Problems may be presented as videos or using a variety of media
			Online calendar can be used to indicate deadlines
			Reference list links to relevant reading
		2 Students divided into groups or work individually	Learners can set up their own groups using student home page (web pages) or discussion tools
			Tutors can set groups using student registration tools in electronic learning environments
	Reflection for action	3 Problem discussed. Students identify what is known, what resources are needed and plan who will carry out specific tasks	Students can use a variety of workflow management tools
			Workflow management could be presented using course calendars, concept maps, PowerPoint slides or images drawn on a whiteboard
Developing solutions	Reflection in action	4 Individuals or groups research different issues, gather resources relating to problem	These activities can be supported by web pages, wikis or blogs with links to external resources. Alternatively, more

Table 6.1 (continued)

Stages in problem solving	Types of reflection (Cowan, 1998)	Blended learning activities	e-Tools that can support blended learning activities
Developing solutions (cont.)		and check for gaps in information	dynamic tools are available, such as 'repository' or knowledge management tools
	Reflection on action	5 Resources discussed and evaluated (individually or in groups) in relation to problem	This task can be carried out face to face or supported using conferencing, e-mail or chat tools
		6 Above cycle repeated 3–5 until the problem has been framed adequately and a solution has been developed	
Testing solution		7 Solution tested. If solution is not appropriate, stages 3–5 are repeated	Depending on the problem, this task may be carried out face to face or supported using technology tools
Evaluation solution		8 Solution is evaluated. Possible actions, recommendations, solutions generated	Actions can be collated using web pages, wikis, blogs or conferencing tools

In Chapter 5 we saw that lesson planning matrices are too linear to document the complex iterative processes involved in problem-based learning. One way to develop a record of a problem-based approach is to construct a narrative pattern alongside a learning design sequence based around the four stages of problem-based learning. Examples of these will be illustrated later in the chapter. First, let's look at the sorts of tools and electronic learning environments that can support complex learning.

Electronic learning environments: who is in control?

Problem-based learning activity sequences cannot be supported by a single e-tool; they require a range of different, integrated e-tools. e-Tools such as real-time chat or conferencing are useful in allowing students to negotiate solutions to problems. Other e-tools such as shared workspaces, or databases, may make the sharing of resources easier across members of a group. Many colleges and universities maintain electronic learning environments that have a number of these sorts of e-tools integrated within a single system. The advantage of having one standard system is that the institution can concentrate technical and staff support on one system. Also, whichever resources the individual lecturer deposits can be made available to others, either to share good practice or to benefit a wider range of students than those for whom the resources were created.

An electronic learning environment is a collection of tools that support learning processes. These tools generally include online discussion fora (through bulletin boards or chat facilities); tools for submission of group work; assessment tools (such as computer-marked tests, computer-managed submission of essays, or e-portfolios); access to teaching resources (for example, course notes, handouts or simulations); and administrative course information. Most systems have simple interfaces that support tutors' design and development of 'blended' courses. This enables tutors to concentrate on course design issues rather than worrying about technical issues – a factor that dominated earlier online course developments (Littlejohn and Peacock, 2003).

Electronic learning environment tools

Electronic learning environments provide a range of inbuilt e-tools to support students in carrying out learning tasks. Most systems will include e-tools for asynchronous (delayed time) interaction, such as:

- class discussion areas with information on assignments and so on;
- shared workspaces;
- content management systems, which can publish material instantly or at a set time or date in the future;
- e-portfolios, which can link to resources from many sources and periods of the students' development;
- newsfeeds, which allow learners to be updated on any changes in the submissions within an environment – particularly important where information is dynamic and rapidly changing.

There are also e-tools for synchronous (real time) interaction, such as:

- audio and videoconferencing, instant messaging and text-based discussion tools;
- shared whiteboards and drawing tools that support the collaborative creation of images and diagrams;
- online formative assessment tools, such as quiz tools that can give students instant feedback.

Most systems have a range of administration tools, including:

- 'drop boxes' where students can upload assignments;
- student and tutor access to records of past performance;
- contact information and other personal information on individual students (usually visible only to specified users).

Some environments include other tools for learning and social interaction, including recommender systems, blogs and wikis.

Electronic learning environment systems offer a quick and simple way of using e-tools for online or blended learning. They offer different advantages and rewards to tutors and students. For tutors, they support different types of activities, including content management and administration, besides supporting teaching. Content management is fairly simple. Most systems allow tutors to upload learning activities and resources to a central, online storage environment, making them available to students within a class. Materials can be given a unique identification that allows them to be easily sourced by students and staff with relevant access permissions. Essentially this means that the same set of resources can be reused elsewhere within a course, or even shared across several courses. Many environments also have tools that allow easy course administration. For example, there are tools that allow personalized dissemination of course information and assignment results to students, perhaps through an email alert. All electronic learning environments have a range of communication tools that can be used to support the learning activities illustrated in the examples in Chapter 5. These tools can be useful in guiding students through learning tasks and for offering feedback.

Electronic learning environments can offer students personalized course information and access to learning resources. Personalized information may include assignment outcomes or individualized tutor feedback. The sorts of learning resources that students can access through these systems range from library resources to materials created by tutors or even by other students. They also provide students with access to e-tools that allow students to carry out the sorts of collaborative learning tasks illustrated later in this chapter. Some systems allow resources and activities to be released to students or groups at specific times.

While these systems offer many advantages, they also have some limitations. It is useful to have a range of different e-tools integrated within a single system, as this serves as a 'Swiss army knife'-style mix of tools. A tool will be at hand, ready for you if you need to use it. However, this will not always be the best tool for the job. Another problem is that, in setting up an environment that will serve the needs of multiple types of users, such as tutors, students and administrators, the system might not perform well for any single user group. A variety of different systems are available, placing emphasis on particular system uses or user groups, but your institution is likely to have already chosen one or other of these for you.

Despite the widespread availability of electronic learning environment systems, the limitations associated with them are having an impact on the ways in which these systems are being used.

Most tutors find it difficult to use the electronic learning environments to support active learning. The main use of these systems in the United Kingdom is to 'deliver' lecture materials and slides to students (Britain and Liber, 2004). This is hardly surprising, since the early electronic learning environment systems, developed in the mid-1990s, were designed around the lecture–tutorial model of teaching. Within these systems was an inbuilt assumption that lecturers will follow a common design pattern in creating courses. These systems offered limited opportunity to experiment and play with designs to find out what might happen. Using these environments to support complex forms of learning, such as problem-based learning, required great imagination and skill. Moreover, the technical 'overhead' to set up a new course design for each course was considerable.

Some systems are still based on the lecture–tutorial model of teaching. However, some commercial and open source systems are supporting more active forms of learning and are aiming to cut overhead costs by enabling course designs to be reused. Later in this chapter we will illustrate how reusable course designs may support automatic creation of courses in the future. Next-generation electronic learning environments focus on the design and implementation of individual learning activities as well as activity sequences or 'blends'. The new wave of environments allows students to actively negotiate assessments, develop and upload their own learning resources, set up online interactions via conferencing, blogs or wikis, and even support open, collaborative socialization and personal broadcasting outside the institutional environment.

We can view electronic learning environment systems as lying in one of three categories. Some are 'commercial'; in other words, the software has been created by a company. Others are 'open source' and are freely available for downloading and programming by software specialists. A third group are freely available online environments designed for personal use by individuals.

Many institutions struggle in their decision as to which system to implement. Using an open source rather than a commercial system means that institutions can potentially avoid 'vendor lock-in', where the company sets the tone and development priorities of the system. Alternatively, implementation of commercial systems means that institutions do not have to employ software developers. However, it may be students who have the last word. It is highly probable that the rapid growth in personal online spaces will have an impact on the sorts of systems supported by institutions.

Commercial electronic learning environment systems

In the late 1990s, dozens of commercial electronic learning environment (ELE) systems were created in the race to make money from the growing online and blended learning environment market. In the United Kingdom, several universities developed their in-house systems to create commercialized versions of electronic learning environments (ELEs) such as COSE (www.staffs.ac.uk/COSE/), COLLOQUIA (www.colloquia.net/) and Bodington (www.bodington.org/). Wikipedia has an interesting overview of the development of these sorts of learning environments (en.wikipedia. org/wiki/History_of_virtual_learning_ environments).

At the time of writing, the most commonly used commercial system is the Blackboard Learning System (www.blackboard. com), which originated from the University of British Columbia in Canada and in 2006 merged with WebCT (another leading ELE). Blackboard has been popular because it provides tutors and students with a one-stop online place for a range of services including course news and information, learning materials, personalized course information and assignment upload. The effect on its popularity of its recent attempts to claim intellectual property rights in many common aspects of ELEs remains to be seen.

An example of a course on learning technology within Blackboard is illustrated in Figure 6.1. This example is from Carol Higgison of the University of Bradford. The course is based around a series of activities and learning resources presented to students as web pages and course documents. Students can access these activities and use a range of in-built

Figure 6.1   Blackboard at the University of Bradford

Source: Carol Higgison, University of Bradford

tools to carry out these tasks. Tools include conferencing and chat systems, shared whiteboards, assignment drop boxes, and so on. A course 'announcement' system keeps students up to date with the latest news. Carol, as the course tutor, has access to a wide range of course development tools not available to students. These tools allow tutors to upload materials to the central database, set learning tasks, and so on. Figure 6.2 illustrates a software tool that can be used by tutors or students to upload documents, images, animations and other sorts of resources to an electronic learning environment system.

Most commercial systems have software licences that ensure tutors have control over the learning spaces. This means that conferencing tools are usually set up by the tutor or an administrator and are usually restricted access, with access most often being confined to the students studying the course and specific staff who support them. This may limit the way students wish to work, since they may wish to contact experts and peers outside their own institution.

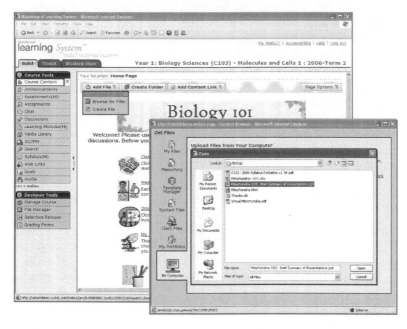

Figure 6.2 A tool to upload resources to an electronic learning environment
Source: Blackboard

Open source electronic learning environment systems

Open source systems are freely available to download and adapt to suit the specific needs of an institution. Moodle (www.moodle.org/) is an example of a popular open source environment that is becoming increasingly widely adopted. Some open source systems, like Moodle, allow students better control over theirlearning. These systems offer students greater freedom in deciding which groups or activities they would like to participate in and how that participation will occur. Increasing sophistication of electronic learning environments can support greater degrees of variation in the teaching or tutor-defined *or* learner-defined groups.

With the interest in greater variety of learning design within online activity and, perhaps, more willingness to try out new activities and approaches, it becomes more important for course designers to have some view on what the course will look like and feel like within the learning environment.

Interest in more flexible and dynamic creation, and ongoing alteration, of e-learning designs has led to developments such as the Learning Activity Model System (LAMS) at the Maquarie E-Learning Centre of Excellence (MELCOE, www.melcoe.mq.edu.au) in Australia (Dalziel, 2003). LAMS is open-source software that takes a different approach to designing e-learning courses as compared with that of many commercial electronic learning environments. It is based upon linking sequences of learning activities. LAMS provides the tutor with a highly visual authoring environment for the development of activity sequences, together with a learner run-time environment (to see what the learner will see) and a system for monitoring student progress (Dalziel, 2003).

LAMS moves away from the 'create-a-list' and 'select-from-list' design interface of many other electronic learning environments, where the emphasis is on learning content management rather than activity management. Each course is designed by a tutor as a set of learning activities using the 'toolbox' options to the left of the screen. Each of these tools allows automatic creation of one or more learning activities. Tools include 'grouping' (i.e. setting up student groups), reflective polling (a voting system), instant text-based chat, assignment submission, question and answer, noticeboard, chat and scribe, resources and forum, polling, share resources, forum, reflective question and answer, reflective chat and scribe, multiple choice, notebook (public). The tutor can quickly set up activities by dragging and dropping the relevant icons on to the 'authoring area' and arranging (and rearranging) them in that space. Although these tools are similar to those found in other electronic learning environments, the emphasis here is on learning activities with active student participation. For example, the resources (publication) option is 'resources and forum'. This challenges assumptions about the electronic learning environments as a simple digital storehouse with emphasis on e-content and e-delivery.

Using the LAMS interface, the tutor is essentially constructing a 'storyboard' or 'learning design' of the course with dependencies, prerequisites and supporting activities shown within the flow of learning activity. The tutor connects the various activities to guide the students through the course. Figure 6.3 illustrates a learning design with a fairly linear course sequence. This design could be reused and repurposed to be made less linear – as illustrated in Figure 6.4. In this example the design purpose is the same but has been repurposed to divide the class into small groups. Each group is asked to summarize ideas and share relevant resources. Readings and posting of ideas are offered as optional activities (located at the right-hand side of the screen). Relating this to the planning frameworks

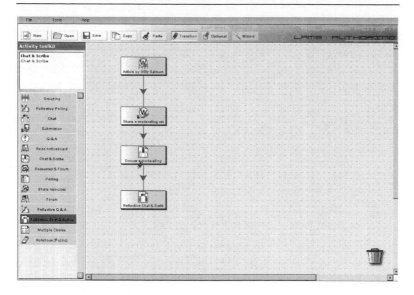

Figure 6.3 The LAMS visual authoring environment

Source: LAMS, www.lamsfoundation.org

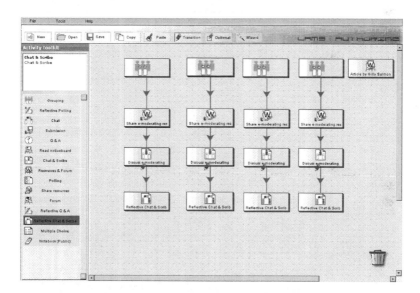

Figure 6.4 A LAMS learning design with non-sequential activities

Source: LAMS, www.lamsfoundation.org

introduced in Chapters 4 and 5, the overall purpose or learning design (the pattern template) remains the same for Figures 6.3 and 6.4, but the lesson plans are different.

One of the most appealing things about systems like LAMS is that the system allows content, activities and designs to be developed and transported from this system into other electronic learning environment systems that are 'standards compliant'. This means that course designs and resources can be used within a variety of contexts – across different levels, disciplines and institutions.

Examples of complex blending

In this section we present two examples of authentic learning tasks. We illustrate two different electronic learning environments that have been used to support students in carrying out authentic tasks using problem based learning. In the first example the tutors have used an 'off-the-shelf', commercial system, while the second example illustrates use of an open source system.

Example 6.1:

Electronic environments for technology-supported learning

Like most higher education institutions across the world, the University of Twente in the Netherlands has had to cope with an increasingly diverse student population. One way of addressing this challenge is by providing flexible forms of learning that can be made more relevant to a range of student needs and situations. This example and the associated LD_lite framework were provided by a tutor from the programme, Dr Anoush Margaryan. The example illustrates ways in which Anoush could offer flexible, problem-based learning to part-time, working students using an electronic learning environment. In this case the learning environment was a commercially available system initially developed at Twente: TeleTOP (www.teletop.nl).

The postgraduate programme within the Faculty of Behavioural Sciences, Technology Applications for Education and Training (TAET), aims to prepare students for professional careers in e-learning in both the public and the private sectors. A module within this programme provides a theoretical and practical background on research methods used in the design and use of technology supported learning. Students select, apply and describe appropriate research methodologies for specific research applications (personal communication from Drs Joachim Wetterling, Manuela Bianco and Anoush Margaryan, 2005). A screenshot of the course environment is shown in Figure 6.5.

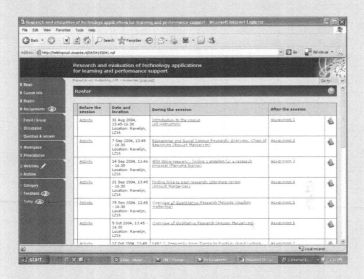

Figure 6.5 The TAET course environment in TeleTOP

Source: University of Twente, the Netherlands

The student cohort is diverse at three levels: professionally, ethnically and in mode of study. In terms of their professional experience, students represent a range of professional contexts, including teachers, educational developers, educational managers, policy makers, consultants and educational software developers. Some are recent graduates with backgrounds in a range of disciplines. The second aspect of their diversity is their ethnic background: the student group is international in scope. The third diverse level is mode of study, with a mixture of part-time as well as full-time students.

The programme was designed using a 'blended learning' model in order to accommodate the three levels of diversity and ensure that the course design was as flexible as possible (Collis and Margaryan, 2005). Students attended weekly class sessions, supplemented by individual and group-based self-study. Collaborative, problem-based learning assignments were designed to be as close as possible to real problems faced by the learners. To allow maximum flexibility, face-to-face sessions were reduced as much as possible, and learner interactions were supported via TeleTOP. Individual students submitted these assignments to the electronic learning environment so that feedback could be offered from both tutors and peers.

Course assignments were developed incrementally, leading to the development of research proposals for a Master's degree. These integrated assignments had four key components: formulation of the research problem; identification of the research methodology; identification of the instruments required to carry out the methodology; and piloting of the approach.

The students used the classroom sessions to carry out collaborative case studies by exchanging ideas and experiences and critiquing others' submissions. Part-time students who could not attend face-to-face meetings joined in by videoconference. Outputs from these group sessions were captured and made available via the electronic learning environment system, so that students who were unable to attend still had the opportunity to catch up and contribute ideas to the online discussion forum within TeleTOP. Between the face-to-face sessions, students worked on their individual proposals. These developing proposals were then uploaded to TeleTOP, where they could be discussed and critiqued by tutors and peers.

For the final assessment, students submitted a research proposal to an online portfolio. Individual proposals were presented to a panel of tutors and mentors. Part-time students who could not attend the university had the opportunity to present their ideas dynamically, using conferencing systems.

Despite the complexity of this example, each stage can be documented using LD_lite. The narrative pattern (Figure 6.6) gives a useful overview of the scenario, while the lesson plan (Figure 6.7) documents the detail of each learning activity. The learning design sequence map (Figure 6.8) could be the most useful element of the LD_lite framework to tutors who want an overview of this fairly complex scenario, since it presents a useful outline of the ways in which the range of learning activities interrelate.

Pattern of research and evaluation of technology applications course

Problem:

Accommodating needs and workplace situations of a diverse group of students

Solution:

Use a virtual learning environment to offer a blended learning course, the main features of which are flexibility, learning collaboratively in small groups, problem-based activities and direct application of course experiences to students' own situations

Aim:

To enable a flexible learning provision giving students the choices with respect to what, when and how they learn

Objectives:

By the end of the course you will be able to:

- identify an appropriate research or evaluation methodology for a given problem relating to technology applications for learning and indicate how the method will be applied in a particular situation;
- appropriately carry out a user-orientated or an impact-orientated research or evaluation related to your own ongoing project;
- professionally report about a specific research or evaluation process;
- find, evaluate, manage and use appropriate scientific information during all the steps in a research or evaluation process.

Figure 6.6 Narrative pattern of a flexible problem-based learning activity

Figure 6.7 **A lesson plan of a flexible, problem-based learning activity**

Time	Tutor roles	Student roles	Resources (content)	Resources (courseware)	Feedback and assessment
Day 1: classroom	Introduce the course objectives, topics, activities and expectations	In groups, share previous research experiences, articulate expectations and topics of special interest with regards to subject matter of the course (part-time students participate via videoconference)		TeleTOP and a videoconferencing system	Information and facilitation from tutors in class
		Summarize results of groups activity and submit to course environment			
Weeks 1–3: online and face to face	Provide an overview of the topic, answer questions and give feedback; assign students for peer review	In groups, analyse a case study related to a research problem definition; identify strengths and weaknesses, and propose alternative problem statements	Textbook; examples of research proposals contributed by the tutors or sourced by the students	TeleTOP; videoconferencing	Feedback from tutors and peers; assessment from tutor
		Summarize results of group activity and submit the summary to the course environment			
		Work on problem formulation for own research proposal and submit			
		Review peer submissions and provide comments			

Weeks 4–6; online and face to face	Interacts with student groups, offering feedback on group and individual activities; assign students for peer review	Find links to past research in relation to own research problem by reviewing literature and web-based resources	Textbook; student-generated resources	TeleTOP	Feedback from tutor and peers on the relevance of the resources.
		Summarize key resources, seminal publications and key authors in relation to the research problem		World Wide Web	Tutors and peers contribute and share resources from their own collections.
		Integrate the summary within the research proposal and submit		University library catalogue	Assessment from tutors
		Review peer submissions and comment			
Weeks 7–9; face to face and online	Tutor interacts with student groups, in class and via TeleTOP, and assigns students for peer review	In groups, analyse a case study related to selecting a methodology and tools; identify strengths and weaknesses, and propose alternative methodologies justifying the choices	Textbook; examples of research proposals contributed by the tutors or sourced by the students	TeleTOP	Feedback from peers and tutor; assessment from tutors
		Summarize results of group activity and submit the summary to the course environment			
		Select and justify an appropriate methodology and instrumentation for own project			
		Integrate methodology and instrumentation within the research proposal and submit			
		Review peer submissions and comment			

continued

Figure 6.7 (continued)

Time	Tutor roles	Student roles	Resources (content)	Resources (courseware)	Feedback and assessmen
Weeks 10–13: face to face and online	Tutor interacts with student groups, in class and via TeleTOP. Tutor gives formative feedback on the development of the research proposal	Pilot methodology and instrumentation and develop an implementation plan Integrate findings within the research proposal and submit Review peer submissions and comment	Course materials; exemplars contributed by tutors and students	TeleTOP	Feedback from peers and tutor; assessment from tutor
Week 14: classroom	Tutor assesses presentations and gives summative feedback	Present the final proposal, justify the decisions, and outline potential impact and added value for the stakeholders	Course materials	TeleTOP; videoconferencing	Feedback from peers and the panel
Week 15: online	Tutor monitors and provides clarifications if needed	Reflect on course experience, main learning points, competences acquired and impact on personal development plan Submit a summary into the TeleTOP site as well as into the personal e-portfolio	Course materials	TeleTOP; e-portfolio	Feedback from peers and the panel; final assessment from tutors

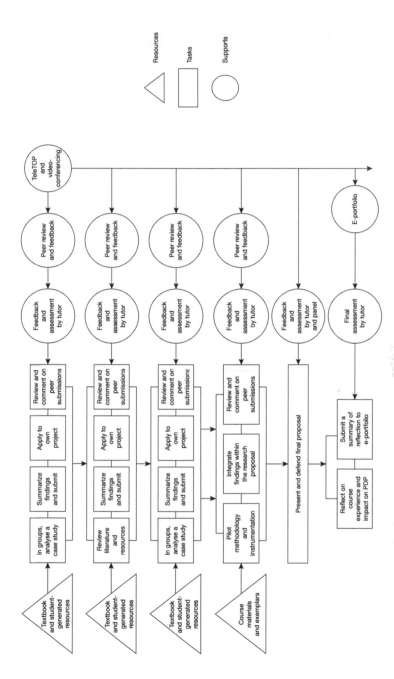

Resources

Tasks

Supports

Figure 6.8 A learning design sequence of a flexible, problem-based learning activity

Example 6.2:

Workspace wikis in engineering

A common problem in group design projects is the sourcing, storing and sharing of resources that inform the design. Shared workspace systems allow storage and distribution of a variety of materials useful to collaborative group projects. This example was provided by course developers from University of Strathclyde (in Scotland) and Stanford University (in the United States) to illustrate how students might use wiki-based electronic learning environment systems to support collaborative knowledge construction. The learning environment used in this scenario, Laulima, is an open source system, illustrated in Figure 6.9 (McGill et al., 2005).

Figure 6.9 A wiki-based learning environment
Source: University of Strathclyde

The students using Laulima were studying design, manufacturing and engineering management. Each student was given a brief for a product design, in this case a domestic can-crushing device or a breadmaker. The class was divided into small groups of four students and each group was given one aspect of the design process for initial investigation. Aspects included ergonomics and mechanics. Each group of students sourced and evaluated a wide variety of resources covering their specific area (texts, images, technical data, etc.) before uploading the materials to a shared workspace. The students arranged their own resources into an informal shared workspace so they could be accessed, repurposed, reflected upon and reused by other groups. Figure 6.10 illustrates a 'file gallery' area that students used to search or browse for useful information. Students discussed the information from these resources both face to face and using electronic communication tools such as phones and instant messaging.

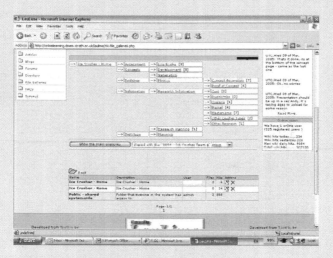

Figure 6.10 A file gallery where students store and share learning materials

Source: University of Strathclyde

After two weeks of initial resource collection, each group drew up a product design. This involved sifting through and evaluating information collected by all the other groups. Each group was required collaboratively to construct a concept map that justified its design decisions. Some groups chose to meet face to face to draw up this concept map and to discuss its structure and meaning. Geographically dispersed groups communicated using

continued

tools such as shared whiteboards along with instant messaging tools or voice-over internet protocols. An example of a hyperlinked concept map is shown in Figure 6.11. The students populated these maps with information resources illustrating the *process* by which their ideas were developed, capturing unwritten thoughts and courses of action as appended notes.

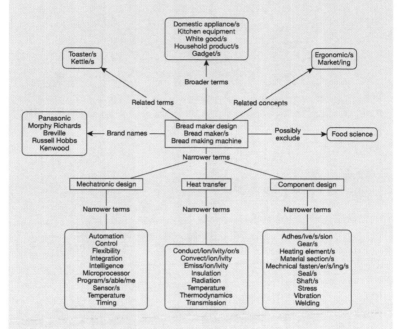

Figure 6.11 A concept map illustrating the design process

While defining the problem, students met face to face to agree how solutions might be developed and who would carry out what tasks. The assignment was communicated face to face, though a range of tools were available to allow students to communicate this information, for example a 'shout box' texting tool (to the right of the screenshot in Figure 6.9). Some groups of students chose not to use these tools, because they could meet face to face. However, project documentation was available via the 'file gallery' file database system. While developing a solution to the problem, students collected resources from external sources and integrated these with self-generated materials. This process was supported using a database 'file gallery' system along with a wiki tool that was used to construct project assignments (see Figure 6.12). Students built, tested and evaluated the prototype design face to face, with feedback from their tutors either face to face or via the wiki tool.

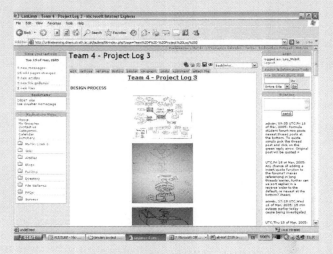

Figure 6.12   **Wiki-based project assignment linking learning resources to the wiki tool**

Source: University of Strathclyde

Evaluations of this learning scenario revealed that the shared online environment gave students a 'space' to think through ideas, linking information to create new knowledge. The main problem for the students was rooted in the level of information literacy skills required to work effectively in this sort of environment. Students had to source information, then decide which information sources were most reliable. The students also had to learn about organizing information, versioning, and so on. It was important that they understood why the sharing and interlinking of information resources was useful for their learning. The team leading this initiative built learning literacy skills training into the core of the module (Littlejohn, 2005). This was the most effective way to support students in collaborative knowledge construction (Nicol et al., 2005).

continued

The narrative pattern of this complex scenario is shown in Figure 6.13, the lesson plan is summarized in Figure 6.14 and the learning design sequence is shown in Figure 6.15.

Despite its complexity, the learning design sequence is a useful tool that can be used to reflect on the interplay of the range of learning activities.

Pattern of a product design activity supported by wiki tools

Problem:

Student teams working on a design project need to be able to source, store and share resources that inform the design in a well-structured and easily accessible way

Solution:

Use a workspace wiki-based learning environment that allows students to store and distribute a variety of materials useful to collaborative group projects

Aim:

To support sourcing, structured storage, sharing and reuse of resources

Objectives:

By the end of the course you will be able to:

- collaboratively design, develop and test a working prototype domestic device;
- source, evaluate and use resources supporting the product design process;
- document the design process in a structured and reusable way;
- improve your skills in collaborative design and working with others;
- improve your information literacy skills.

Figure 6.13 A narrative pattern of the collaborative product design scenario

Figure 6.14 A lesson plan of the collaborative product design scenario

Time	Tutor roles	Student roles	Resources (content)	Resources (services)	Feedback and assessment
Day 1: Classroom	Gives class a brief for product design; divides class into groups of 4 students	Study the design brief	Design brief for design of a domestic product		Information and feedback from tutor in class; information specialist available in class to support students in information management
Weeks 1–2: online and face to face	Assigns an aspect of the design process for initial investigation	Collaboratively source and evaluate resources covering each group's specific area	Student-generated resources	Laulima; wiki-shared workspaces; communication tools within Laulima; e-mail, phones, instant messaging	Feedback from tutor and peers
		Upload materials to a shared workspace in a structured way			
		Reflect upon and discuss collected information with team members			
		Review and evaluate resources submitted by other groups			

continued

Figure 6.14 (continued)

Time	Tutor roles	Student roles	Resources (content)	Resources (services)	Feedback and assessment
Weeks 3–4: online and face to face	Interacts with student groups, offering feedback on selected resources and on the concept maps Tutor also contributes additional information resources	Draw up a product design Design a concept map documenting the design process and justifying design decisions	Student-generated resources	Shared whiteboards, instant messaging, voice-over internet protocols	Feedback from peers, tutor and information specialist. Tutor feedback focused on the relevance of the resources and the construction of the concept map. Information specialist feedback on sourcing, selecting and managing resources as well as constructing concept maps
Weeks 5–6: face to face and online	Tutor interacts with student groups, in class and via Laulima, and gives feedback on potential solutions	Develop solution Plan implementation of solutions and division of roles within team	Student-generated resources	Communication tools within Laulima; file gallery database system within Laulima; wiki	Feedback from peers and tutor; tutor feedback focused on proof of concept prototype

Weeks 6–12: face to face and online	Tutor interacts with student groups, in class and via Laulima and gives formative feedback on the development of a prototype	Collect resources and integrate within the existing resources Build, test and evaluate the prototype design	Wiki	Final assessment is via the online wiki plus a face-to-face presentation and working demonstration of the prototype model

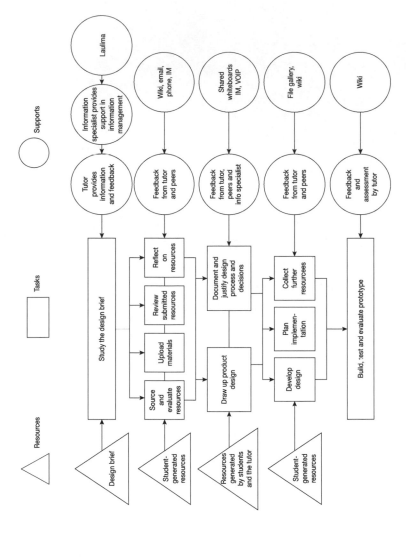

Figure 6.15 Learning design sequence map of the collaborative product design scenario

Documenting complex blends

Complex learning tasks are more difficult to document than the simple examples illustrated in Chapter 5. Approaches to learning that involve a number of non-sequential tasks, for example problem-based learning, are particularly difficult to document. Yet tutors who become more skilled in designing and developing blended learning are more likely to plan these sorts of complex scenarios. The complexity is partly due to the 'granularity' factor. More complex models of learning usually involve a number of related learning activities, as compared with the individual activities illustrated in the case studies in Chapter 5.

Furthermore, the case studies in this chapter have highlighted the interplay between the usefulness of the final product versus the process of designing blended leaning. The *process* of preparing of a documented learning design, rather than the end *product*, may be more useful for the tutor. This depends to a certain extent on the 'granularity' of the learning design (Falconer and Littlejohn, 2007). The process of documenting the sorts of highly aggregated learning designs presented in these case studies (i.e. those involving a number of interrelated tasks) may be of more benefit than the representations themselves. Whereas with individual learning activities, like those illustrated in the case studies in Chapter 5, the products may be very useful.

The electronic learning environment system illustrated in the second case study was developed specifically for the problem-based learning scenarios outlined in this section. However, bespoke systems are not usually a realistic option for courses on limited budgets. Instead, many colleges and universities will use the 'off-the-peg' systems that are already available. These may be part of an existing electronic learning environment. As they are not tailored to a specific learning situation, they may not as easily fit the learning tasks required. Nevertheless, with some careful design and planning, they can offer a platform for problem-based learning. For many courses the most effective use of these systems is when they are 'blended' with physical learning environments.

Blending physical and virtual learning spaces

For the successful implementation of blended learning, adaptable physical learning environments are as important as flexible electronic learning environments. The sorts of conventional teaching spaces found in many institutions were not designed to allow students to carry out the sorts of tasks involved in problem-based, collaborative work. These interactions include sourcing information, discussing ideas and collaborative knowledge construction. As is mentioned in Chapter 1, some institutions are beginning to recognize the importance of providing flexible learning spaces that can support use of technology in physical spaces. Some are experimenting with different kinds of physical learning spaces, including design studios and wireless interactive classrooms. Others have introduced learning cafés, where students can meet in a social environment to discuss learning issues over a cup of coffee. Most of these cafés have wireless access, linking the informal physical space with online learning environments. These sorts of spaces can support a variety of learning exchanges, including the sorts of group work outlined in this chapter. We can think of the physical environment as one of the tools of blended and e-learning, as the example of Glasgow Caledonian's Saltire Centre (Example 6.3) shows.

Open-plan teaching spaces offer more 'controlled' environments for learning. While they do not allow students the same degree of flexibility in their learning as do open learning spaces such as the Saltire, they are generally less noisy and easier for teaching. Open-plan classrooms often have a 'teaching' space at one end and an open seating area at the other with a series of computer terminals, or a wireless environment. Some design studios have a library section, a 'workshop' or even a 'laboratory' area. Virtual design studios may have large screens connected to computers, allowing students to experiment with virtual design. These virtual studios are especially popular in design-orientated disciplines, such as architecture, where students can design buildings using software models and then view their designs on large, cinema-style screens. These screens are useful for testing light levels or wheelchair accessibility in a newly designed space.

The real innovation in open teaching spaces is how they are used to support teaching. Rather than holding a one-hour lecture, tutors are moving towards short briefing sessions, after which students can work collaboratively, moving around from one space to another as required. These open teaching spaces are designed to neatly integrate students' use of physical and online environments.

Another form of teaching space is the 'wireless interactive classroom'. These range from lecture theatres with in-built voting systems to classrooms with a range of virtual interfaces through large screens (shown in Figure 6.17 in use at Strathclyde University). Classroom-based voting systems are an effective way of getting students actively involved in lectures. During a lecture the tutor can present multiple-choice questions at regular intervals, polling the students for their answers. Students could be encouraged to discuss concepts and ideas prior to answering. This

Example 6.3:

Glasgow Caledonian: Saltire Centre

Some institutions are moving a step further in the creation of open flexible spaces that integrate physical and virtual learning environments and provide students with a full range of student services. One example is the Saltire Centre at Glasgow Caledonian University (Figure 6.16). The Saltire is essentially a place where students meet, interact and study in an informal way. It integrates the university's learning café, library and student services. The library is adjacent to an open social space with a café and wireless facilities, while a central reception area allows students access to services such as academic counselling and health services. Students can browse journals and books within the library, read and discuss books in an informal, social space with a café area, and access online resources and learning spaces using terminals and kiosks available throughout the building or, alternatively, their own wireless devices. Student services, such as support with study skills, academic or personal counselling, can be accessed from a single area within the Saltire (called 'the base'). Guidelines on developing flexible learning spaces is available from JISCInfonet www.jiscinfonet.ac.uk/infokits/learning-space-design.

Figure 6.16 The Saltire Centre at Glasgow Caledonian University

Figure 6.17 Hand-held
polling device

methodology offers a 'stepping stone' between conventional teaching and
the use of e-tools, having been used to transform large lectures in several
countries across Europe, Australasia, America and Asia.

Electrifying or encumbering environments?

This chapter has explored ways in which electronic learning environments
can help you to implement e-learning within a course – from recording
reusable learning designs through to storing, describing and sharing electronic resources. There has been emphasis here on sharing learning designs
and content within the institution using the electronic learning environment as repository and also identifying suitable external resources that you
could reuse, adapt or be influenced by in populating your e-learning
course. The development of e-learning tools and environments is continuing and will offer even more in the future – both for blended and for
fully online courses. Electronic learning environments are being developed
that will allow students even greater flexibility in managing and sharing

their own content to suit their individual preferences and needs, and incorporating their choice of tools. This is a move towards the personal learning environments referred to in Chapter 2 (Downes, 2006). The use of these sorts of systems will allow a far greater degree of individualization for students – a massive change from the undifferentiated, Fordist one-size-fits-all teaching approach that has traditionally been the basis of further and higher education.

We have seen here the advantages of sharing and learning from learning designs. Designing activities and resources that can be reused or repurposed is becoming essential if you want to ensure that the design of your course can easily be updated or scaled up. Colleges and universities often struggle to find suitable resources and activities that they can use, and having made these for one course may find them hard to reuse within another. We need to design courses using activities and content that can be easily scaled up, updated and repurposed for new learning contexts. In the next chapter we explore a range of approaches to blended and e-learning that will support sustainability.

Chapter 7

Sustainable blended e-learning designs

We have spent some time exploring blended learning and e-learning, in particular how to plan, develop and refine an optimal blend. Although we have been concentrating on decisions about how to approach e-learning regardless of cost, you should have already realized that implementing blended learning can require considerable investment in e-tools and e-resources. Sourcing and creating suitable learning materials is a significant part of that cost because it usually relies upon staff time – one of the costliest resources within educational institutions. As mentioned previously, in e-learning, resources are often used in different ways from the way that we might use apparently similar resources within more traditional forms of teaching. Even resources that sound as though they should be the same will be different from their physical counterparts. For example, a 'virtual microscope' may vary in design from a physical microscope. In some cases the resources are so different that there is no physical equivalent. Within blended learning you will probably be using resources that are different from those you might have used before – for example, you might use resources in different formats. You may be using these in conjunction with more familiar resources, but they may well affect the way in which you use *those* resources. Chapter 6 explored some of the interplay of e-resources and e-tools in complex blends.

The introduction of e-resources and e-tools may also have some less obvious effects on how students view the teaching. There is a more obvious requirement to keep online and computer-based materials up to date. This is not only because the internet lends itself to 'comparison shopping' by students – the finding of alternative resources and reviews to the ones that you have chosen. There is also a sense in which out-of-date resources have more impact and are more obvious to users. A book to which you refer students will not be obviously out of date, while a web site may be suffering from 'link rot' or have ceased to exist entirely. This is something that we need to bear in mind when we consider the cost of e-resources.

As we pointed out in Chapter 1, research evidence shows that the transition to blended or e-learning is unlikely to save an institution or organization money. It takes time and resources to get it right, and this is not a one-off investment. For most teachers this level of time investment is impossible to sustain when courses are scaled up from pilot phase to large-scale implementation. Any cost savings or benefits are likely to be offset by the need to invest in resources and support services (see Chapter 8). This will mean that you need to find a cost-effective approach to the design and implementation of blended learning, one that takes account of the need to invest in e-resources (creation and updating); to adapt learning designs to exploit new e-tools; and to invest in ongoing professional development for staff.

Since digital resources are automatically more shareable and reusable than traditional physical resources, an obvious way to cut costs is to reuse existing resources as much as possible. By 'reuse' we mean that the resource can be used 'as is' on future presentation of that or other courses with minimal resource requirements. A second way to ensure cost-effectiveness is to make sure that learning resources are easily adaptable (repurposable) so that they can be changed to suit different purposes. Easy reuse and repurposing of resources both rely on deliberate actions in the design of those resources. In Chapter 1 we saw that resource generation may become cost-effective only when learning materials can be altered to suit different cohorts of learners in a range of contexts. Therefore, we need to create resource materials that are easy to reuse and repurpose, so that courses can be designed to allow for easy and rapid updating.

One of the most effective ways in which we can do this is by designing courses using a modular approach, so that each element that might be used is designed as a small chunk of learning. In Chapter 4 we illustrated ways in which you can plan courses around 'learning design' patterns (i.e. learning activities with associated resources). These can quickly be updated by replacing one type of resource with another, or shifting the position of resources and activities within the course. Later in this chapter we will consider how small the chunks within a course may be.

Finally, we need to remember that the changes to e-learning and the skill to create optimal blends will not be obtainable without change in the institution and in the teaching and support staff. One way to support and disseminate good teaching practice on blended and online environments is by sharing practice. In Chapter 5 we demonstrated how LD_lite can be used to share good design ideas with colleagues. This approach to the design and documentation of courses allows the templates to be reused across a range of courses.

Another aspect of professional development will be to offer courses and development opportunities so that staff can 'skill up' to use the new tools. Within limits, a teacher may be able to create e-resources independently of in-house experts. Even if they prefer to use technical experts, the teacher will get better results if they can 'speak the language' of the developer and make an informed choice from the options available. Gaining the skills to create or commission e-resources can be surprisingly beneficial. Even simple changes of format can provide advantages. For example, broadcasting course content via the streaming of video lectures and/or podcasts can allow you to use face-to-face teaching time to discuss ideas with students and answer their questions. However, this does not fundamentally change the approach to teaching and the additional professional development required to support reskilling will have cost implications.

In this chapter we will consider a range of tactics that help you develop a strategic approach to sustainable and scalable blended learning.

Tactic 1: Sourcing and reusing existing materials

The most obvious way to increase efficiency when planning blended learning and e-learning is to cut down the staff time required to create learning materials by using existing material. You will already have experience in sourcing, repurposing, evaluating and reusing conventional learning materials for your teaching. You probably regularly search for materials within the library, ask colleagues for useful resources or reuse material created by previous classes of students. Many of the resources that you may wish to reuse on a blended learning course will be e-content – electronic forms of resources that you have used in the past. Using these in digital form makes them relatively easy to repurpose (or edit) for a specific class, although this depends on the resource format. For example, text-based resources in standard formats (e.g. doc files) can be quickly and easily repurposed or updated. Other, more specialist formats, such as Latex (maths notation) files, may be more complex to amend, and multimedia files will often require a level of skill and resource that is unavailable to you. If you have insufficient time to repurpose a resource, you may decide to seek alternatives. You can take advantage of the wide variety of options now available online, using these as an end product or drawing on them as inspiration.

Migrating 'offline' resources for reuse in blended learning usually requires some time to be invested in repurposing. Most course authors write for a specific audience in an effort to be as learner centred as possible. The content of the resources that they produce will therefore tend to be quite context specific. For example, a resource on simple pathology which appears to be reusable by paramedics, doctors and nurses could take a view of the subject (that of the doctor) which is found to be inappropriate to paramedics within the same institution (Thomas, 2005). Unless you have changed institutions during your career it can be difficult to appreciate how diverse or similar the approaches of different institutions may be and what their teaching contexts are. The materials released through the Open Content Initiatives across the world offer a fascinating insight into a range of approaches across a range of institutions, as well as providing a source of teaching resources. These include the Open University in the United Kingdom (www.openlearn.open.ac.uk/) and Massachusetts Institute of Technology (MIT) in the United States (www.ocw.mit.edu/). As you might expect, these two initiatives have adopted different strategies, with one set producing resources aimed at teaching students who are remote from the institution, while the other uses many resources based on being in class with students.

While MIT has made a range of materials openly available, it has not invested in designing or redesigning these resources so they can easily be repurposed. It is interesting in sharing what happens in MIT rather than making this adaptable for other institutions. Since many of these materials were not developed for use in e-learning, it would require considerable effort to repurpose them for this purpose. Some are so specific to the particular course or context that it is very difficult to reuse them elsewhere, although they could provide ideas and inspiration. You may find that many of your own teaching resources were also written with a specific teaching context in mind and that these would need some adaptation before they could be transferred even into other courses which you are teaching.

The Open University (OU), on the other hand, has a history of publishing resources with consciousness that they might be reused externally. Many non-OU courses have reused its printed units, readers and audiovisual resources within their own institutions. For its OpenLearn Initiative the OU has gone a step further in selecting material that is more granular (smaller chunks) and particularly suited to recontextualization. In some cases it has needed to 'transform' these resources to improve the reuse potential. Across the OU, there has been increasing concern to make as much material as possible reusable. This strategy pays off over a longer term, since the costs of updating courses are reduced and there is more potential to offer versions of existing courses which can be adjusted for a new market, or even personalized for specific student groups. The requirement for social work education material tailored to suit the regional context of the student (i.e. whether working in England, Scotland, Wales or Northern Ireland) is an example of where this was necessary. You may wish to consider reuse when you start to design your own teaching and learning materials, making them suitable for repurposing from the outset.

Many tutors start collecting resources by looking for sources of 'formal' teaching and learning materials. A relatively unproblematic route is to provide links to online journal articles. This exchanges a list of references that require a visit to the physical library, for one which allows use of a virtual library instead. The resources used are facsimiles of the print version, very formal and subject to familiar quality assurance mechanisms.

Below, we offer some further suggestions for strategies in sourcing and selecting materials.

Sourcing resources: where to look

Where are the best places to look for digital learning resources? Try using Google or other search engines and you may find useful resources. However, despite investment around the world in creating reusable resources, there are three major problems. First, online resources are not all reliable in terms of their 'durability' (how likely they are to remain online in the form that you have selected). Second, online resources are frequently not quality-assured. Third, it can be difficult to find the resource that fits your learning objective, which means that you may have to repurpose the resources. However, these materials may be difficult to repurpose. To improve the efficiency of your searches you may wish to try:

The library

A good place to start looking for resources is through your institution's library. Most universities and colleges now have access to e-books and e-journals, which means that your students will be able to use these resources online and the number of physical copies need not be a restriction on use (as it would have been with print books or journals). Your library may also subscribe to commercial databases such as Proquest (www.proquest.com/) that allow you to search across a range of journal titles. Librarians are often the best people to point you to new resources that you might not otherwise have discovered, and explain how you can get access for yourself, or your students, to restricted or subscription-only resources.

Publishers

Sometimes resources will come to you! Publishers are increasingly interested in creating e-resources and encouraging lecturers to use these in their teaching. Some of these resources may already be familiar to you in other non-e formats. Remaking or recreating these learning resources in digital form has meant that their life has been extended. Resources that you may have once rejected as not available or accessible to students may now be worth reconsidering. Many publishers are also encouraging course text authors to design learning activities for use with those texts. You will often find that there are digital resources to supplement those texts freely available online. The content of these book sites can be very helpful even if you are creating your own teaching materials. For example, they may include digital copies of figures and tables or illustrations used in the book, allowing you to build these into your own presentations. These resources are usually accessible online, sometimes password-protected. Where the resources are particularly extensive they may be available for purchase as materials to be directly uploaded to your electronic learning environment. For example, several publishers now create 'e-pack' materials for use within commercial electronic learning environment systems such as Blackboard, Lotus or TeleTOP. These resources are created specifically for quick uploading into a course within a proprietary system. The packs can include lecture notes, glossaries, animations, video clips and test banks, and are designed so that they can be repurposed or customized to suit the requirements of an individual course or context.

Organizations

There is an interesting trend for educational resources to be created and disseminated online by organizations such as galleries, museums, research institutes and professional bodies (for example, the NASA space images at www.nasa.gov/). Extending the potential 'publishers' list further are organizations whose primary purpose is not education, but who make available potentially significant educational resources. One of these is Google Earth (www.earth.google.com/); another is the BBC's personalized newsfeed service (www.bbc.co.uk/). Organizations such as Amazon, from which you might purchase learning resources (e.g. books, DVDs, etc.), provide reviews so that you can check how prior purchasers of these resources rated them and how they may have used them.

National collections

Some countries have educational strategies that specifically encourage online sharing of digital resources. In those countries, government funding may have been made available to support the development and sharing of content. For example, in the United Kingdom there is the National Learning Network (showcasing and supporting reuse of resources for use in further education) and JORUM (www.jorum.ac.uk a national repository launched by JISC in 2006 for storing and sharing resources within further and higher education). MERLOT is a national repository of resources based in Canada (www.merlot.org). Both these national repositories hold a wide range of reusable resources that are specifically geared to use in post-16 education. There is now also a trend to requiring government-funded projects involving the development of learning resources to make these available beyond the life of the project – ensuring the 'durability' and national availability of resources that have been commissioned using central funding sources. Interntional collections are also emerging, such as IVIMEDS (www.ivimeds.org), an international collection of resources for medical education, illustrated later in Figure 7.1.

Discipline-specific collections

Although the national resources mentioned above will include discipline-specific resources like IVIMEDS, the development and dissemination of resources within discipline-specific groups is often a separate venture. Discipline-specific resources may be identified through libraries, external publishers and national organizations. They are the most likely resources to be shared across organizations, perhaps through national and international conferences. In the United Kingdom the Higher Education Academy (www.heacademy.ac.uk) is 'home' to the twenty-four subject centres. Their web sites not only provide resources specific to discipline areas from religious studies to hospitality management, but also offer reviews and advice on using third-party resources within electronic learning environments.

Students

Your students are a great source of resources! They often locate and create their own digital materials as part of the learning activity of the course. Reusing these within a cohort (allowing students to see each other's work) or retaining the best for future students is easy to do where your electronic learning environment supports shared workplaces. Where you are using e-portfolios the students' material may be comprehensive and of high quality. If so, making such material accessible to future cohorts can prove motivational as well as informative. Some institutions are allowing students to create and manage their own collections of resources, giving them access to a wider pool of learning resources than simply those chosen by the teacher. So, you might consider reusing your students' learning resources, having obtained their permission to do so (the copyright in their work will usually be theirs and not yours). This is not a new tactic; tutors have been disseminating exemplar assignments for hundreds of years.

Colleagues

Your colleagues may be willing to share, or even 'swap', compilations of resources such as course notes, slides, student activities, and so on. You may choose to tap into formal resource collections such as digital, online libraries or national collections of resources stored within 'repository' tools, which are, essentially, a store for digital learning resources. We will illustrate examples of repository systems later in this chapter. Some tutors now use 'personal repository systems' to manage digital resources. Personal repositories are often 'database'-type systems within institutional electronic learning environments. These systems allow individuals to manage resources, by sourcing, sharing, accessing, recombining and reusing learning materials within and across a series of online courses. This means that time that might otherwise have been required to create new resources can be devoted to interacting with and giving feedback to students.

Sourcing resources: what characteristics to look for

1   *Search for 'small' resources.* You may be searching for large resources that fulfil several objectives, rather than integrating a number of smaller resources. Try to search for small resources, each fulfilling or contributing to only one learning objective.

2   *Search in places where copyright is not an issue or where you know you will be able to reuse under existing licences.* You are likely to feel under more scrutiny with regard to copyright of materials distributed to students online, as compared with the distribution of paper-based

---

resources. Unfortunately, the copyright position of online materials is not always clear. Even when the copyright position is known, it can take weeks and considerable effort to clear rights. You may prefer to start your search within sources where you know the rights issue has already been resolved.

3   *Choose resources that are well maintained and managed.* You may have concerns over the durability of some online resources. If a resource is contained within a repository or digital library, rather than an informal web site, it is likely to be more robust (that is, it will continue to function) and it is more likely still to be available when you need it. For example, libraries and repositories will often automatically check the links within resources to which you refer, and may offer an instant alert when those links change or cease to work. The desire to choose sites that are regularly updated does need to be balanced against the problems that can occur. A site that changes its content on a regular basis may be up to date, but could suddenly replace resources that you particularly wished to refer to and that – for your purposes – were more appropriate.

4   *Seek out resources from reputable sources.* You may be sceptical about the quality of online materials. It is easy for an insubstantial operation to appear authoritative online. Many tutors share concerns about quality assurance in e-learning. Although some repositories do have quality assurance measures in place, many do not. One project that has implemented a peer review process within communities of practice is MERLOT, 'Multimedia Educational Resource for Learning and Online Teaching' (www.merlot.org). In MERLOT, peer review comments are generated within web-based worksites and attached to each resource (Schell and Burns, 2002). Key factors in evaluating the usefulness of a resource include accessibility, relevance, writing style and language, durability, quality assurance, copyright and ease of customization (Littlejohn et al., 2003).

If you become familiar with a variety of places where you can reliably locate resources, both offline and online, you will discover where there are materials that can easily be repurposed for the kind of contexts you deal with. Remember that the sources do not need to be formal educational sources. Finally, another useful tactic is to share your own 'informal' learning materials, used across a number of courses that you teach.

Tactic 2: Making your own resources

When you begin reusing learning materials you may quickly discover that there is an inverse relationship between the 'educational value' and the 'reusability' of a resource. In theory, the smaller a resource, the greater the possibility of its being reused in other educational contexts. For example, an individual image is likely to be more readily reused than an entire course. However, it may be less time-consuming to reuse a larger resource, such as a learning activity, than to construct a course from its most basic components. Therefore, larger resources often have greater educational value. The optimal size for learning resources is a fine balance between the educational and reusability factors. It is likely to include a number of learning resources linked to a student learning activity (Thorpe *et al.*, 2003).

It is useful to create resources that do not contain any context-specific material, although this may not always be easy. It means keeping segments of materials that need regular updating in separate sections of the resource. An example is grouping all web site addresses together in one place, rather than distributing them through a text. This makes them easy to find when updating. It is well known that web site addresses may change between course updates as the content moves or is deleted – an effect called 'link rot'.

This process of creating and repurposing resources may seem counter-intuitive as compared with the way you might normally modify and adapt non-digital materials to fit specific teaching situations. To create materials that are as reusable as possible, they should be decontextualized. This does not mean that there will be no contextual information for the student (this can be added by the teacher in face-to-face discussions, or as a narrative or study guide). You will, however, need to consider when writing whether you have options other than to make contextual information an integral part of a resource. You need to challenge your own assumptions about the way in which this resource may be used. For example, you might be creating a section on diseases of the circulatory system within a course where this happens to be the sixth section within the course. During study of this topic you might wish to refer students to an earlier section on veins and arteries, suggesting that students should have covered this previously, perhaps mentioning a specific location, date or teacher. Ask yourself whether you need to embed this information within the resource. Could it be a separate section, called something like 'Preparation for studying circulatory diseases'? Doing this would allow a small 'preparation' section, rather than the whole resource, to be updated if the course and section numbers later change. Instead of saying 'As you saw in Section 4 . . .' you might name the topic (veins and arteries) so that students who have studied that topic in another context will recognize it. In a different context, if you are teaching students about the history of Van Gogh's painting *Sunflowers*, you might wish to keep the image and text as separate files, that are assembled within a web page but not tied to each other otherwise. This means that the image of the painting could be reused across a variety of disciplines. It could be used in a popular culture quiz on records for artworks auctions. It could illustrate a lecture on the propagation of flowers. It could provide an illustration for explaining oil technique, or an art history tutor could attach information to it about Dutch painting, and so on. The image in this way becomes very reusable, and the contextual information can also become a reusable resource. For example, within the quiz a different image could be used to illustrate the information about plant propagation.

To design online courses in a cost-efficient and sustainable way you should plan to reuse as many resources, activities and course designs as possible. This means that when you create resources for yourself you also need to be mindful that they could be useful to others or could be used in different contexts. You need to consider what will make your course context independent, or too context specific to use elsewhere. Is this necessary for learning? Sometimes it will be, and you can consider whether you can structure this contextual information so that it is easy to identify and change. On other occasions there will be alternatives to the way in which you provide the contextual information. For example, you may decide to add contextual information in discussions (either face to face or online) and not within the resource.

What you will usually be doing, when designing reusable materials, is creating courses which are designed as a series of learning activities with associated resource materials that can quickly and easily be updated or adapted. You can use the LD_lite framework to help you think through how you will do this. You are aiming to create learning resources in such a way as to make them reusable over a range of teaching and learning contexts. You should also configure any electronic learning environment that you use to allow resource sharing either across a number of your own courses or with colleagues and their students.

Tactic 3: Repurposing resource materials

You probably already share your own paper-based learning materials – not least with yourself. So, the first place to look for materials to repurpose and reuse is within your own courses. Perhaps you have a paper-based portfolio of articles, diagrams or questions and activities you like to reuse in a number of classes. Digital resources, by their very nature, should be much easier to reuse. They could be sourced and adapted without having to physically 'photocopy, cut and paste'. The trick is to design learning materials with reuse in mind and to manage them in a cost-effective way.

Reusing resources need not be difficult or intimidating. However, it does require some planning to make sure learning materials are available for reuse across a range of contexts. To increase their reusability, resources (activities or content) should not contain information specific to a particular subject discipline, course or class (Naeve, 1999). Therefore, to understand the ways in which we might prepare materials for reuse, it may be useful to think about our motivations.

Reasons for repurposing

What are the main motivating factors that encourage us to repurpose materials? Colleagues at the Open University in the United Kingdom have identified ten key factors and have developed strategies for adapting resources around each of these aspects. The LD_lite framework can be used to support all ten strategies:

1 *Updating* materials that have already been used within an earlier version of the same course, or another course. In this case materials are only slightly adapted, usually by updating the content.

2 *Reshaping* involves more radical adaptation of materials, often to improve the effectiveness of a course. In this case the structure or themes of the course materials are altered without changing the overall size of the resources themselves.

3 *Resizing* usually means that resources are either broken down into a number of smaller materials or merged to produce larger resources.

4 *Transnational repurposing* involves preparing materials for reuse in courses in other countries. This requires attention to cultural sensitivities around course content.

5 *Sectoral repurposing* means altering materials to fit a specific constituency such as a discipline, educational sector or workplace.

6 *Level adaptation* involves adapting course materials for use at a different level within a curriculum or qualifications framework.

7 *Framework repurposing* focuses on the reuse of the structural framework or 'learning design' of a course.

8 *Cross-media redesign* is useful when course materials need to be adapted for presentation through a different medium (for example, if materials originally designed for CD-ROMs are repurposed for the web). Use of cross-media redesign in this way may require rethinking as to how learners might interact through web-based communication.

9 *Generic adaptation* is the production of materials that are not context specific and may be reused across a range of scenarios.

10 *Preversioning* involves designing courses that are easy to version in one or more of these ten ways. Use of LD_lite will support preversioning.

Adapted from Thorpe and Thorpe (2005) describing the approach of the CURVE (CoUrse Reuse and VEsioning) project. Retrieved on 6 June 2006 from http://kn.open.ac.uk/public/index.cfm?wpid=5392.

Tactic 4: Designing courses in small, reusable chunks

One of the lures of blended learning is that, in theory, it should provide an economical way of scaling up courses. Once a resource has been created, it can be reused many times with different groups of students, offering cost-effective benefits to teachers, learners and the institution. However, as outlined in Chapter 1, scaling courses through blended or e-learning is not the straightforward cost-saving device that some institutional or organizational administrators would like to believe. Designing courses in small, reusable chunks may seem intuitive if you already reuse and repackage paper-based content from several different sources into a single course. On the other hand, assembling a course from a large number of individual reusable resources may seem daunting.

Some of the best examples of e-learning and blended learning have been assembled in this way and the case studies in Chapter 6 provide good examples. Both these case studies illustrate courses based around learning tasks. Each task is, essentially, an independent learning resource. Many tasks will have content resources associated with them: course readings, illustrations, links to web sites, and the like. Each of these content resources could be used in other courses. And, of course, the resources created by the students themselves – the materials they source from libraries and the internet as well as the outputs from their assignments – become reusable resources themselves. The 'glue' that holds it all together is the 'learning design' which exemplifies the way these activities and resources are linked with the e-tools within the learning environment.

Designing courses in small chunks can help us to personalize the learning experience. Students can be offered a menu of topics to select from. Alternatively, they could choose a personal navigation route through a course on the basis of prior experience, diagnostic tests or their performance and preferences as they follow the course. Allowing choice and selection improves the potential of courses to address learner diversity. However, it requires course resources to be, to a large extent, independent of each other as well as independent of the context of the course.

This approach can also help improve accessibility. If students are offered a choice of learning resources in a variety of formats (video, text, etc.), they can choose a format that is in the most suitable form for them. For example, a student might choose an offline activity if they do not have broadband access. A student who has dyslexia might choose an activity that requires face-to-face discussion and argument rather than writing. A student with mobility problems might value a virtual alternative to a field trip.

Sizing up learning objects

Creating your own materials is a great way of ensuring that your learning resources address your needs. The problem is that resource creation is time-consuming. We have already seen that the most cost-effective approach to resource creation is to make sure the resources you create are as reusable as possible. A problem with reusing resources is to do with the 'fit' across different courses. The 'larger' the resource, the less likely it is to fit in with the objectives of a number of different courses. Until recently, digital learning materials have largely been designed as large, monolithic blocks of resources (Downes, 2000). These materials are not cost-effective, since they cannot easily be reused. A more economical approach is to design learning materials in small chunks. Each 'chunk' may comprise learning activities with associated content resources. If the activities are kept separate from, though linked to, the resource materials, courses can be easily updated or scaled up. Both the activity resources and the learning materials can be repurposed and rearranged for use across a wide range of learning contexts. These reusable chunks of materials are known as 'learning objects' (or sometimes reusable learning objects (RLOs)) and are discussed in detail in Chapter 5.

There are many definitions of 'learning objects' (LOs). Some are very wide, including non-digital, non-educational material. Others make no mention of reuse. In our view, LOs need to be digital, focused on learning and reusable. Weller et al. (2005) suggest as a definition: '[a] digital piece of learning material that addresses a clearly identifiable topic or learning outcome and has the potential to be reused in different contexts'. Examples can vary in size, format and media. They include online articles, PowerPoint slides, digital images, animations, video clips and simulations.

Learning objects can be thought of as blocks of content that can be interlinked to produce a course (Duncan, 2003). This method of course building has been compared to building with Lego bricks: blocks of content can be recombined in different ways with other blocks and reused across a number of different courses. The Lego metaphor is helpful in also stressing that what is created from individual blocks is temporary and can be experimental. It can be easily changed and reformatted. However, there is a problem with this metaphor: this view of courses built of Lego 'bricks' is usually regarded as too simplistic. It can imply that every block must work with every other block. In reality, the blocks (objects) may be very diverse and – as with the more advanced 'Technic' Lego – may be special-purpose assemblages requiring a level of skill and experience (Pegler, 2004). Slapping one block (object) on to another will not usually make a worthwhile final product (for learning or Lego). You will get best results by understanding what the strengths and weaknesses of each type of object are and how they can reinforce each other. Other commentators prefer a different metaphor for courses made of learning objects, one of combining 'atoms' to form 'molecules'. This views educational *content* and *activities* as different types of 'atoms' that can be combined together. It is a metaphor that emphasizes that not every activity can join with each piece of content and that there are 'rules' as to how these might be combined (Wiley, 2004). Of course, the problem with this metaphor is that making molecules is not something that many of us would consider that we have the skill to do, and we would not usually pull apart and reuse those atoms again. Neither metaphor is perfect.

What both metaphors do make clear is that we have to think carefully about how we link content and activities if we want the final course to function effectively. As illustrated in Chapter 5, we can use LD_lite to help us think through a range of different possible combinations.

Tactic 5: Documenting courses within reusable templates

In Chapter 5 we saw how the design of learning activities can be based around the development and creation of electronic 'lesson plans' using a framework like LD_lite. These lesson plans not only are useful in terms of thinking through ways of blending activities, activity sequences, resources and tools, but also can be used to communicate a range of ideas on teaching practice within and across communities. We can think of the content of the LD_lite framework as a formal representation of the learning design.

- Within communities of practice, formal learning designs can be used to communicate ideas about professional practice. The lesson plans can be reused by tutors who wish to gain experience from colleagues or to transfer pedagogies across disciplines. The scenarios from Chapter 5 are available to communicate ideas in teaching practice to other tutors. These are likely to be of most benefit to tutors working within the same subject discipline as the examples. However, it is not difficult to see how ideas in practice might transfer across disciplinary boundaries.

- Within learning communities, formal records of learning designs can be used to communicate the complex interplay of interactions within and across the online and classroom environments. It is important that students understand the cross-linking of learning activities, teaching resources and assessment methods. Lesson plans like those in LD_lite are being used by the tutors from continuing professional development programmes to illustrate these associations to student teachers.

- Within formal and informal learning communities there may be benefits in LD_lite lesson plans or other formal learning designs being constructed collaboratively by tutors and students, allowing learners to reflect upon meta-cognitive processes and benefit from improved self-organization and informal learning. In the 'glossary construction' example in Chapter 5, students were given access to the lesson plan to allow them to understand why collaboratively constructing a glossary of terms might help them develop an improved vocabulary of terms. The students then had a good starting point to communicate to the tutor ways in which construction of the glossary might be most useful to them.

Examples of communities that are using shared lesson plans to disseminate ideas on practice include the international LAMS community (www. lamscommunity.org), based in Australia, and the UK Higher Education Academy (www.heacademy.ac.uk).

Tactic 6: Managing and moving materials

We have already seen that, although electronic learning resources are becoming increasingly widespread, it can be difficult to locate and select the most appropriate materials. Although you will be familiar with locating resources using search engines such as Google, you will also no doubt have been frustrated by the low level of information that these searches yield. A more effective way of managing learning resources may be to use digital repository software. A digital repository is essentially a 'storebox', or database that allows the storage, sourcing and retrieval of resources, or learning objects, in a variety of standard formats. These could be HTML files, images, audio or animations. The repository is often the file store within an electronic learning environment, allowing a single resource to be described once, and held in one location, but used many times across a number of student groups and courses.

The main difference between a digital repository and a digital library is that most repositories allow a range of users to upload resources, but libraries usually only allow 'download'. Institutions and organizations are implementing repositories at local (institutional), national and international level. Repositories are increasingly being used within specific classes (see, for example, Example 6.2, p. 154).

If you have access to a repository to deposit learning materials, you can use it in a number of ways to manage these. At a basic level, you (or your students or colleagues) can search for resources (or learning objects) by keying terms into a simple search tool. Search results will return information (metadata) about each resource. Figure 7.1 illustrates a screen shot from a search for resources on 'heart disease' from a collection of medical education resources within the IVIMEDS collection (www.ivimeds.org). The search yields a list of resources available for reuse. But how can you select the most appropriate resource? You can view the available 'metadata' information – or data about the resource – such as the author, format and description of the resource and how it could potentially be used. This information will help evaluate how useful each resource might be for any teaching situation. If the resource seems useful, it can be downloaded from the repository. Sometimes it is difficult to think of appropriate search terms, so some repositories will allow users to 'browse' through materials.

Institutions are implementing repositories like these at institutional, departmental, course or module level, allowing content to be stored in one location and reused many times. Some repository systems are independent of any particular electronic learning environment: they can be used across many environments located in different institutions, such as the IVIMEDS

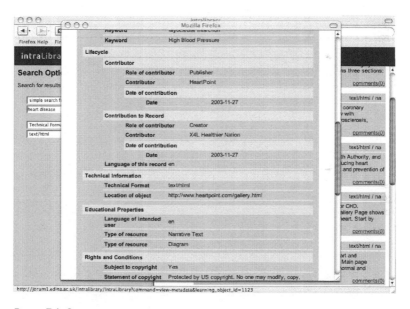

Figure 7.1 Sourcing resources within an international collection of resources (IVIMEDS)

international repository illustrated in Figure 7.1. However, other repository systems are built into electronic learning environments and are designed to store materials that can be reused across courses within a single environment system, such as the repository system illustrated in Figure 7.2. If the repository is part of an electronic learning environment, then a search may begin with a course title, for example 'supply and demand'. The search engine sources all relevant resources within the repository and displays the results, as illustrated in Figure 7.2. This helps the tutor to find objects, resources and activities that are of interest. This screenshot illustrates the kind of information about each learning object that may help evaluate the most suitable resource. As the materials are already stored in the electronic learning environment, they can then be linked to make them available to students within a specified group or course.

In general, repository systems are two-way. Many systems go beyond simple searching and download to allow users to upload their own resources (or learning objects) to the repository collection. Many of the

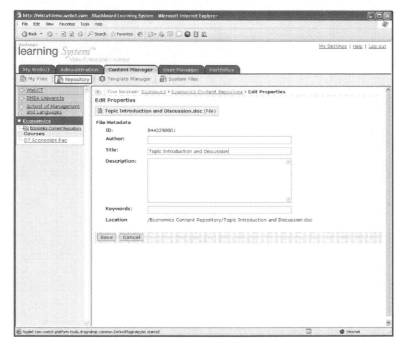

Figure 7.2 Metadata information about resources stored within a repository in an electronic learning environment

Source: Blackboard

electronic learning environments systems supported by institutions have integrated repositories that allow upload using simple browse tools, similar to those that you might use for saving and locating files on your personal computer.

During upload the system automatically records some metadata information – for example, the user's name (as resource author or contributor), the date and file format, and so on. This level of basic, automatically generated information helps to identify the learning object or resource. However, to make the repository really useful to educators there is usually an amount of description that the contributor is asked (or required) to fill in on an online form that asks for information about the resource – the sort of metadata information illustrated in Figure 7.1. At a minimum these metadata are likely to include a simple description of the resource and its intended use, to help others 'discover' appropriate resources and choose between them when searching on information about learning level or learning objectives and not just on topics. Metadata can potentially extend far beyond this and provide very helpful information to prospective users. It would, for example, be possible to provide sample lesson plans or other learning design information to help in using the resource. The metadata could also show what other resources are normally associated with this resource.

Figure 7.3 illustrates how to upload resource materials from a computer desktop to a repository within an electronic learning environment, in this case Blackboard. As illustrated in the screenshot, the system requires the user to add a file name and brief description of the resource. This information will help other users search for and source the resource as well as evaluate its potential for reuse.

But how can we ensure that this information is accurate and kept up to date? Larger, more formal repository systems have a process for metadata quality control, where a librarian makes sure the metadata information is correct and classifies learning materials to allow easy sourcing. While resource authors are best placed to describe the educational intent of their material (Currier *et al.*, 2004), they may not be the best people to describe resources consistently within an agreed framework. It is clear that effective reuse of collections of learning resources largely depends on tutors, students and library specialists working in partnership.

Resource collection repository facilities have only recently become widespread. Before that there was a tendency to duplication of materials within institutions, with multiple copies or versions of single resources being updated or amended individually. A recent survey exploring the way teachers store and reuse learning resources confirmed that many still have systems for managing resources which do not allow easy and

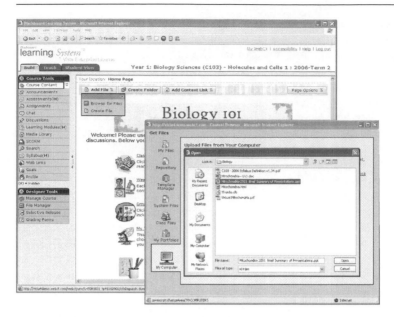

Figure 7.3 Uploading learning resources from a desktop into an electronic learning environment

Source: Blackboard

comprehensive searching or browsing by themselves or others (Margaryan, 2006).

While we have been talking about content within repositories as individual, unconnected items or objects, this is not how they will be used within a course. Some sort of judgement will need to be made in the learning design to determine what objects will be presented together and how, what order or sequence they will follow. Once those decisions have been made and we have a set of objects or resources and a learning design to hold them, we have what we might think of as a 'content package'.

The strength of a content package is that, if it has been produced in a consistent manner, following appropriate technical standards for content packaging, it can be 'played' in different systems. That is, a colleague could give you a content package from her or his electronic learning environment and you could import it into your own electronic learning environment and expect it to work. What you would be transferring between these systems is a compressed 'content package' – a very formal and systemized way of managing content so that it can be migrated across different systems, or within the same system.

Content packages are important for tutors who do not have the time to build a complete course from individual components and who prefer to work with a series of aggregated resources. Reload (www.reload. ac.uk; Figure 7.4) is one example of the type of software that you need to assemble content packages. It shows the sequence (left-hand frame) and a preview of the object (right-hand frame). You can navigate around the content package as you would around a learning environment to see how it works and change the selection of objects or their sequence until you have it right. Reload has been made freely available to the UK higher and further education communities, but the creation of content packages is still unusual in education. This application offers impressive potential benefits but is currently used by only a few early adopters.

Storing resources within a repository means that they can potentially be reused across several courses without copying and pasting the materials. This helps with versioning and, as the metadata contain information about authorship, rights and other users, they are automatically exchanged with (attached to) the object or resource. This sort of information must be shared across systems if we expect to extend the opportunities for reuse within blended and e-learning. For example, if we wanted to reuse a resource that you had created for one of your courses, we would need to know who

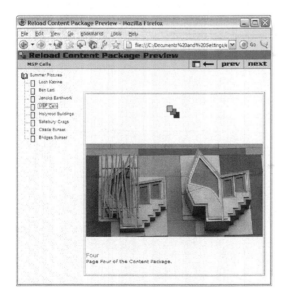

Figure 7.4 Packaging content using Reload
Source: Reload/JISC

had created it (so that we could provide appropriate attribution or acknowledgement). We would want to know who owned the rights and what restrictions on reuse there might be. We would also want to know what courses and what students it had been used with, so that we could avoid using a resource that students had already used elsewhere.

There are many advantages to having a single management system for resources such as a repository. It allows you to track down versions of the same object more easily and uniquely identify the version that you are using (which avoids confusion). You do not have to worry about adapting resources for use across a variety of different platforms, since you can 'point to' (hyperlink) a resource within a course, rather than uploading it to your section within an electronic learning environment. If you used content packaging you could go further: packaged chunks of learning resources and activities could be easily 'picked up' and 'dropped into' other courses. Finally, and perhaps most importantly, your department, school or faculty will have more flexibility in terms of choosing the electronic learning environment systems and tools to support teaching and learning. Your content is now more portable across different systems and accessible within them. This means that schools of social science may use content packages or learning objects within systems that emphasize the use of discussion boards, while engineering schools may use some of the same packages and objects within learning environments that focus on collaborative design tools, depending on their favoured teaching approach.

Moving and sharing across systems

Transporting and sharing of learning materials requires tools and electronic learning environments that can 'talk to' one another. New developments in standards for e-learning environments, portfolios and shared workspaces mean that future e-learning systems may not focus around one electronic learning environment managed by an institution, but may involve a range of different interconnected systems serving different purposes; some will be controlled by tutors and others by learners.

For e-learning systems to work together, they must have some standardized way of exchanging information. Currently, there are a range of international standards bodies working in this area (technologies, formats and methods). These include IMS, the ISO (International Organization for Standardization), CEN (Comité Européen de Normalisation), IEEE (the Institute of Electrical and Electronics Engineers), as well as national bodies such as BSI (the British Standards Institution). As IMS points out, 'The development of a framework that supports pedagogical diversity and innovation, while promoting the exchange and interoperability of e-learning materials, is one of the key challenges in the e-learning industry today' (IMS, 2002). Learning technology standards are now increasingly built into software systems, so that what you produce using these systems in the future will be 'standards compliant'. The development of these specifications will ideally be informed by clear identification of good practice in the use of existing electronic learning systems, but the very technical nature of the conversations around standards often precludes the involvement of any but the most technically competent teachers. The problem of making standards usable by users (and not just technical staff) is one that is now receiving more attention. Ideas from tutors who have experimented with electronic learning environments and have identified issues surrounding reusability of resources and transferability of information are essential to inform the development of future specifications and standards.

Partnerships and communities will be key to the success of sustainable blended learning – not only partnerships of those managing resources or devising the standards, but also communities of users sharing and reusing resources. For example, the 'LAMS Community' (www.lamscommunity.org) has been set up to allow users of the 'Learning Activity Management System' to share ideas about learning activity design with others around the globe. However, a word of caution: there needs to be clear communication between technologists and teachers if the technical developments that are now possible are going to support cost-effective blended learning and e-learning and be useful, attractive and inspirational as well.

Chapter 8

Support structures for blended e-learning

Support of students is perhaps the broadest activity that educators are involved in. It extends from the point at which the prospective student is deciding which course to choose, and perhaps choosing between modes of delivery (e-learning or not?) to the stage at which the student has completed the course (whether they passed or failed) and beyond into communicating with them as alumni or as students on a further course, in your institution or elsewhere. It covers both academic and non-academic support.

Most colleges and universities already have an established and comprehensive infrastructure for student support, since it is recognized that effective support plays an important role in retaining students and enabling them to complete their studies (e.g. Simpson, 2003). However, in many institutions the support systems will have been established with the assumption that contact between the student and support staff will be face to face. Before online learning, the rare exceptions to face-to-face support were where students were studying at a distance from the campus using supported open learning, perhaps never meeting staff face to face, or where large numbers of students studied part time and attended campus mainly in the evenings and at weekends, when key support staff might not be available. Even where distance and part-time courses existed, the onus may have been placed on the student to make time to visit the campus if they wished to use the support services.

Where courses are a blend of face-to-face learning and e-learning, the students may spend significant amounts of time on-campus and, depending on the timing of face-to-face teaching, may find it convenient to use established campus-based student support services. Where the support involves discussion of personal issues, or is a continuation of a previous service, the student may wish to retain contact with a single counsellor whom they know, rather than start afresh with online advice services. Even institutions using only distance learning generally offer students some choice as regards who to contact (i.e. some alternative to the default tutor or counsellor) and options about how to make and maintain that contact (e.g. face-to-face meetings, telephone contact, postal communication or email).

Individual student demands for support will also differ very widely, and this naturally makes planning such support problematic. There will be students who make extensive use of a variety of services, and who would not have completed their course without support. There will be others who rarely make use of any of the student services on an individual basis. Having a proportion of the student support service online, which makes sense within e-learning, and offers convenience in terms of access and smoothing peaks in demand, may not meet the needs of all students equally well.

For the purposes of this chapter we focus on the impact of e-learning and look in particular at the online support of students. In unpacking the services that make up student support, it is worth recognizing first the differences between academic and non-academic support services. These largely cover separate domains using different staff groups, even though the first point of call for many students seeking either academic or non-academic support for formal learning may, in practice, be the same person: their personal tutor or tutor-counsellor. Table 8.1 divides up student support into non-academic and academic activity but should not suggest that the two sets of activity work in isolation from each other. They share the same overarching aim of making the student experience as productive and pleasant as possible, and specifically addressing the need to retain students through to successful completion. Where the learning is more informal and flexible this presents new support challenges, since the student may not have a predictable pattern to their studies, and the 'course' may have open entry and negotiated outcomes. For maximum flexibility one can, and perhaps should, take the view that every staff member – from porter to principal – provides student support at some level. This would make it obvious that every member of staff needs to be aware of the kinds of services available and how to access these on behalf of students. However, where the students are studying some or all of their course using e-learning, perhaps as part of a learning community or within a blended learning work-based context, the institution will need to be flexible and innovatory not only in how it provides learning, but also in how it supports learning.

Many established non-academic support services are directed at providing pastoral care to relatively young students who not only study, but

Table 8.1 Examples of academic and non-academic support for students

Academic support includes:	Non-academic support includes:
Individual tutorial support (e.g. advice on course content and feedback on individual student performance)	*Financial advice* (e.g. advice on how to apply for bursaries and grants, debt counselling and advice on student loans)
Study preparation (e.g. courses in English for Academic Purposes, course induction)	*Course and careers advice* (e.g. information on which courses, or further degrees to choose; support in applying for jobs prior to and after graduation)
Courses office (e.g. contact point for academic advice, distribution of handouts, preparation of timetables)	
Library services (e.g. information literacy and research training, loaning books, locating resources, photocopying services)	*Accommodation and welfare* (e.g. finding somewhere to live, providing on-campus healthcare and security services, offering personal counselling)
Technical support (e.g. supporting technical lab work, field trips or computing)	*Social, cultural and religious support* (e.g. student societies, chaplaincy, sports facilities, alumni activities)
Academic services (e.g. administration of examinations and assessment, preparation of transcripts, award of degrees)	

also live on or near to the campus. For example, the focus of accommodation and healthcare services is often on helping students who are living away from their normal home environment for the first time. These are unlikely to be important services to students who are studying remotely using e-learning within their own home. We also know that e-learners who study at a distance, and thus may need most of their support online, will be more mature and are likely to be in employment or have families. They may need work-related advice (e.g. on how to balance work and study commitments), which could be irrelevant for full-time on-campus students.

A different set of non-academic services may be critical for the e-learner yet little used by the student being taught face to face. The technical helpdesk is an important e-learning support facility and is dealt with in more detail below. If a student has unresolved technical problems at the start of an e-learning course, they may fail to start the course at all.

Effective student support for e-learning needs to be both proactive and reactive. It should anticipate what difficulties students may have, and make decisions about how to provide support for these before those problems occur. It also needs to address the unanticipated support needs that students may present. While it is possible to take a wholly reactive approach to support, dealing with problems as they become obvious, or when the student explicitly asks for help, this approach carries risks, as it generally relies upon knowing the student well and being proximate to them. For a purely reactive approach to work well in an online environment the student must be confident enough and competent enough to ask for and receive help online. This may not be the case for many learners.

If alerting students about the student support services available is the first hurdle, then making sure that they use them when required is the next difficulty. There are many reasons why a student might fail to take advantage of support even if they know that it is on offer. Students may be concerned with how they will appear (to their tutors or peers) if they ask for more support than their fellow students. They may also be concerned about matters of confidentiality. Where communication with others is expected to be wholly online, students need reassurance that their requests for support will not be visible to others. They could feel daunted by the prospect of revealing problems to someone whom they may have not met face to face, and using a medium (email or conferencing) they may be unfamiliar with to ask for help. The problems that they need to discuss may be about the use of technology, or their discomfort with the lack of face-to-face contact. For this reason, even with fully online courses it is advisable to offer an alternative means of making contact (e.g. a telephone contact number for the technical helpline).

If the student is studying and living on-campus, help can be requested and proffered quickly. But where support is not visible and accessible (e.g. where the student is studying at a distance), a major risk is that students will not be aware of the help that is available, or will not be able to use it. They may leave the course because of their problems without having realized how student support could help them. This is particularly the case with issues addressed by non-academic student support, which may require disclosure of personal difficulties and which includes services that the student may have no prior experience of using.

Supporting blended e-learning: the impact of distance and experience

If we return to the matrix introduced at the start of this book, we also see that students who may be experienced in terms of face-to-face learning may at the same time be inexperienced e-learners. In fully e-learning mode they will typically be studying away from the campus for much of the time and so have less opportunity to access on-campus student support. During the online elements of blended e-learning they may also be away from campus, for example on work placement. This has an impact on the type of student support that they will need and also on where they should go to access this.

The student who is experienced in studying face to face may have little experience in studying online, where different study skills are required and the academic support services are often offered in unfamiliar ways. For example, locating a resource online is not the same as locating one in a physical library, and the resource may be presented in a format unlike that which the student is used to.

This means that the academic support services that students require when they start to e-learn are not the same as those required to study on-campus. A student who is well prepared to study on campus (a relatively expert student in a face-to-face context) may be unprepared to be an e-learner (i.e. an e-learning novice). Students' access to support is also, in part, determined by their physical location in relation to the campus, and the blend of e-learning with other coursework. Just because one of the courses or modules taken by a student is online does not mean that the student is studying entirely off-campus.

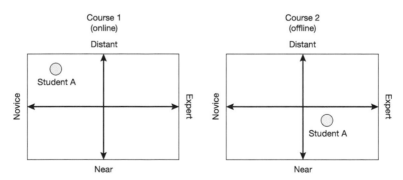

Figure 8.1 Location/experience in relation to e-learning and on-campus courses (single student, different courses)

The same student is represented by both matrices within Figure 8.1. Depending on the course that they are studying, or – with blended learning – the element in that course, their location and experience position relative to support changes. The same student could be a novice when studying online (Course 1) and yet relatively experienced, requiring low levels of study support, when studying in a familiar on-campus environment (Course 2). This will have implications for how much support the student requires when they start e-learning activities. It affects where that support should be located and when it should be offered.

The position on the Near–Distant axis shows the student's proximity to campus and indicates where support may need to be accessed (i.e. on-campus or off). In Figure 8.2 at least some support will need to be provided off-campus for Course 1 as the student is relatively distant. By contrast, the same student is on campus at least some of the time for Course 2, so providing on-campus support is an option. The student also has experience as a face-to-face student, so is unlikely to need basic (getting started) study support for Course 2.

Both the relative expertise of the student in studying within a particular course environment, and their proximity to the campus, will determine what academic support services they need and how these should be provided. In Figure 8.2 the four students need different levels of support and need support at different locations. While Student C is very distant from the campus, as far away as it is possible to be, she has a high level of experience in studying in the way that this course demands. Student B is

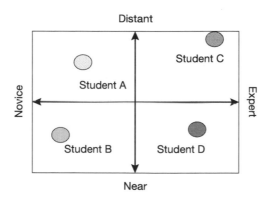

Student A: low experience, long distance; Student B: low experience, long distance; Student C: high experience, short distance; Student D: high experience, short distance.

Figure 8.2 Location/experience in relation to an e-learning course (different students, same course).

of low experience but also near to the campus, so he could possibly choose on-campus support to supplement any online support. Student D is in the strongest position, able to choose on-campus support but also having relatively high expertise in studying (and being supported) online. Perhaps he has good online skills because of work-related use of computers, or has studied via online courses before?

Some support needs can be predicted (e.g. careers advice as students prepare to graduate). But at least some non-academic support, and the more urgent demands on support, will address life events that could not have been, or at least were not, predicted (e.g. dealing with serious health problems). Where the student is studying primarily online there should ideally be online access to non-academic as well as academic support, although this may also be offered in a variety of other modes (post, email, telephone, audio or video one-to-one conference, self-help discussions and face-to-face meetings).

Web-based student support

As the numbers of students entering further and higher education has risen, so has the demand on colleges and universities to support larger numbers of students from increasingly diverse backgrounds. One of the ways in which initial student support is now provided is through an institutional, departmental and course web site. Aimed at students trying to shortlist universities, or overseas students who have no opportunity to visit campuses before the course starts, the web sites of twenty-first-century colleges and universities are often information rich, complex and technically refined.

This early introduction to e-administration may be supplemented by further student support material online, particularly material that needs to be consulted before the official course start. Even for students on more conventionally taught courses, the university web site, and later the university intranet or electronic learning environment, are often chosen to address initial study skills support requirements. This has the advantage that each student can choose the level of support that they need and can spend as much or as little time on the activities as they wish. This type of support is often generic, common to several related disciplines and students in different institutions. In some cases, as in Example 8.1, online study support resources may be developed at one site and then reused on others.

Where the student is expected be off-campus for the whole of their studies, the student intranet or electronic learning environment may act as a portal to all academic and support services. In this case, organizing

Example 8.1:

eLanguages support for new students

The eLanguages project at Southampton University offers a number of online activity-based modules on preparing to study in the English language at UK institutions. The material was written as reusable learning objects and is now used by many UK universities as well as being offered through the British Council India as support for Indian students wishing to study in the United Kingdom. This material is focused on the skills needed for effective communication, using audio-, video- and text-based conversation practice online.

Although some students studying the English for Academic Purposes module are clearly located at a distance from their university or college, Southampton also blends these online resources with face-to-face support for its own on-campus students.

(*Source:* www.elanguages.ac.uk/students/index.html)

and presentation of support services becomes a challenge. The student needs to know that these are there when needed, and to be able to find them.

To the student entering the campus of their college or university for the first time it is initially surprising to them just how huge it is and how much physical space it occupies. The library, the registry, the student union, the lecture theatres, etc. will each have a different location, often in separate buildings. These differences, although initially confusing, eventually help the students to find their way around. Students also become aware that their own behaviour in each space may need to be modified. They need to adapt to being quieter in the library, social in the student union, orderly in lectures and more interactive in tutorial and break-out rooms. They know that if they have a security problem then they tell the porters; if they have a personal finance problem they talk to a student counsellor. If they are not yet sure who to ask, then they can consult notice boards, friends, tutors, or courses office staff.

Online, there is not the same physical differentiation between spaces or the same cues about behaviour. There is no immediate indication of scale, so it is not as immediately evident to the student that there may be an extensive support system associated with their 'virtual institution'. To even

Example 8.2:

Supporting 220,000 students

The Open University (OU) is well known for its supported open learning model of distance education, with emphasis on 'support'. Distance learning was an unfamiliar approach to study for many students when the OU was established, just as e-learning is today. The extensive information that the OU has always provided to prospective students is now made available online. It is very comprehensive: the screenshot shown in Figure 8.3 shows some of the resources that are available on part of the pre-registration (public) web site. Each link is described so that visitors will know what to expect before navigating beyond the link. Registered students will be able to access more specific and detailed resources when they log in.

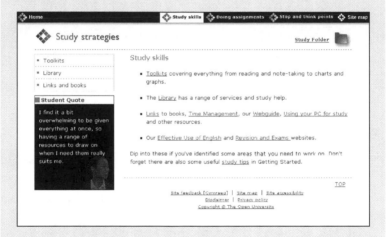

Figure 8.3 **Screenshot showing some of the resources available on the Open University's pre-registration web site**

(*Source:* www.open.ac.uk/learning/index.cfm)

an experienced e-learner, what is beneath the surface of the home page, or their student portal, will not be obvious unless they explore, or someone else tells them what is there. Think about the front page of Google (www.google.com). This is the gateway to billions of resources, yet there are no clues as to what can be accessed from this single, very simple page.

It is precisely because there is such a lot of information now available online, on college virtual learning environments and in university intranets, that some level of personalized or individualized access to that information is now so necessary. To offer every possible support option to every student from a single entry point would create a crowded and confusing online learning environment. In order for a simplified and more tailored view to be offered, the student is usually supplied with a student ID and password that allow them to view a personalized version of all that is there. Their ID acts as a filter so that they can see or access only that information that is relevant to their needs. It can also be used to remember personalized settings, for example to increase font size by a set amount for a student with particular sight problems. The most user-friendly systems will also offer students the options of searching or browsing, and may incorporate personalized alerts, prompts and hints to bring features to the attention of students at appropriate times using RSS feeds and SMS messaging (mobile phone texting). These may remind students that assignment deadlines are approaching, that books that they reserved are now available, or alert them about server downtime during which they will not be able to access the online course resources.

The technical helpdesk

One additional student support overhead that any substantial implementation of e-learning introduces is the technical helpdesk. At the least, this may be the services of the tutor or course creator helping students and other tutors as and when they are able. At the other extreme it may be outsourced to a 24/7 service meeting the needs of hundreds of students studying dozens of courses globally. On many e-learning courses it will quickly become obvious that students are studying outside the normal institutional working hours. It is not unusual for parents of young children, or night-workers, to opt for e-learning precisely because they can study in the middle of the night when others are asleep. In some countries and regions (e.g. the Netherlands) there may be initiatives that expand access to broadband or subsidize mobile phone costs. If students use helpdesk services at non-standard times, who will be answering their queries? Although many technical queries can be anticipated and dealt with through help systems, guides and FAQs, many students and tutors will still often need someone to talk them through their problems. For this reason it is common practice to make the technical helpline available by telephone, as well as email.

Even given the best e-learning design and implementation there will be students on technically complex courses who need help in installing specialist applications. Others, on courses with only moderate computing use, will have little prior experience and may need more basic assistance. Where the students are required to submit assessment items online, and where staff need to download, upload and mark work electronically, there will be a particular requirement for reliable and patient technical advice. Advising a student who is panicking because they have just 'lost' their assignment, or forgotten their password, moments before the submission deadline requires tact as well as technical expertise.

In order to reduce the complexity of the queries dealt with, and thus the costs of technical support, most institutions require a minimum specification of computer and browser for students taking their courses. This at least avoids having to ensure that the newest online courses will work with legacy or unusual systems. However, such a requirement may give rise to queries about social inclusion and accessibility, as it can be argued to be one way in which the costs of education are being driven upwards. Some institutions have laptop loan schemes to try to address both problems. This uses a standard item that can be exchanged for another if it fails (rather like current staff equipment loans). This solves the problem of providing computers to those who cannot afford to buy them. As students increasingly use their computers for a variety of purposes, not all connected with study, any requirement to use *only* university-approved equipment and applications becomes less workable. Students may prefer the devices that they have experience in using.

Librarians on call

Library staff are perhaps foremost among the support staff who find their role broadening with the move to blended learning and e-learning. They are likely to be called on to support both staff and students in locating online resources, and they have often taken the lead in teaching new study skills such as 'information literacy' and 'searching online'. We have already seen how new buildings such as the Saltire Centre at Glasgow Caledonian University (www.gcal.ac.uk/thesaltirecentre/) offer exciting and flexible spaces built with the use of new learning technologies in mind. These integrate all the student services and are increasingly seen as social centres and meeting places as well as learning and library spaces – effectively as a 'one-stop shop' for students. They can be used for lively discussion as well as providing an attractive portal to vast stores of academic content.

The 'stock' of the college and university library has also fundamentally changed with the addition of electronic resources and searchable databases that students and staff can access even when the library is otherwise closed. This has improved reliability and speed in locating named resources within a reading list (which in their physical form could be on loan, defaced or missing). It also improves the ease with which students can locate (search and browse) resources that take the student beyond the standard reading list. Easier access to searchable databases and specialist online collections has opened up the potential for student research – even for part-time students with limited physical access to the campus library.

Example 8.3:

Accessing law reports online

Digital curation (the preservation of materials in digital form) has also opened up access to resources that were previously very restricted, even for on-campus students. For example, the British and Irish Legal Information Institute (BAILII) project at Oxford gives online access to a searchable database containing the full text of legal judgments made in England, Wales and Ireland. These include historically significant documents which are only available in handwritten and microfiche format, neither of which is a particularly accessible form for students to search, and both of which may be restricted access. As BAILII is an open access resource, members of the general public, non-academic researchers and students studying UK law in overseas locations also have access.

Because of intellectual property rights issues the BAILII database does not contain the most authoritative law reports, but the judgments it does contain are used by law students as a means of accessing a wider set of information and for comparing different records of judgments. Students learn to skim-read the online judgments to choose which they wish to track down in hard copy or through the formal, more restricted access, legal databases.

(*Source:* www.bailii.org/)

Supporting staff to support students in blended e-learning

Many college and university staff will be unfamiliar with blended e-learning either as a means of supporting study or as an approach to study that requires supporting. They will need help in adjusting not only to the use of unfamiliar technologies, but also to the practice of working with students whom they may not see or speak to, and at one extreme may never meet in person. The lack of body language and reliance on text-based communication common in online learning introduces both challenges and opportunities for those supporting students.

The principles underpinning good teaching and support of learning are, unsurprisingly, fundamentally the same whatever the tools. Experience teaches us that good teachers offline are likely to be good teachers online. The introduction of e-learning simply brought in new tools, tools that can be used well or poorly (Mason, 2001). These new tools do, however, introduce variety into the way in which staff can communicate with students, taking advantages of ICT features. Some examples of how to use these tools to support learners are shown in Table 8.2.

Table 8.2 Examples of using ICT tools and techniques to support students

ICT tools and techniques	Uses for supporting students
Broadcasting online messages to all students, or to a specific set of students	Most electronic learning environments allow you to send a message once which is read by many – either the whole class, or specified sub-sets of it. This can be an effective way of answering a question so that many can share in the answer. Some systems offer a 'message history' that allows you to check that all students have spotted the message. This can work better than messages in pigeon-holes or on noticeboards, which may be lost or overlooked.
Keeping a record of electronic correspondence with students	Most systems will automatically save email and other correspondence, allowing you to review and build on advice that you may have offered the student in earlier correspondence. With the student's permission you can also forward specific queries to other staff who are equipped to provide specific help. The quality of support of students via email will of course depend upon the skills of the students and staff involved.

Table 8.2 continued

ICT tools and techniques	Uses for supporting students
Cutting, pasting and customizing support messages and feedback	It is easier to use ICT to update not only handouts and other documents (as you may already do for your teaching material) but also to update and repurpose messages. Tutors can share and then personalize a pool of introductory messages, or activities, adjusting these to individual taste or to make the message topical for each course presentation. One Australian system (Bell, 2005) helped staff to develop a database of feedback comments to students which can be adapted and reused. The research shows that students appreciate more detailed comments delivered through use of this system.
Using alerts and other timed-message features	These can be used, via the electronic learning environment, or through mobile phones or shared course calendars, to remind students of important events (e.g. examination times), or to advise them of changes (e.g. to tutor availability).
Incorporating hyperlinks to online resources	This offers the student instant access to the resource, which could be an external web site, movie or podcast. It can be especially useful if the resource is hard to locate, or it is beyond the material originally cited within the course. Many online libraries can now supply URLs (web addresses) that will take the student directly to the journal paper or other resource. Inserting links into messages to students, or into course web sites, can be a good way of bringing in topical new material, or encouraging a broader view of the topic.
Attachments to messages	It is possible to attach images, screen dumps (replicas of what is showing on the computer screen) or even audio and video clips to messages sent to students. Students can do the same in messages to tutors or peers. This can support social interaction (e.g. exchanging holiday pictures), and allows each party to be crystal clear about what they mean. Use of audio and images (photos, smiley icons or avatars) can overcome some of the impersonality of email and other purely text-based systems. They can also provide valuable cues for students whose preference is for a visual or aural learning style.

continued

Table 8.2 continued

ICT tools and techniques	Uses for supporting students
Using polling devices	These can be online polls or surveys to check what the class as a whole may think on a certain issue or to collect feedback part-way through the course. Or this could be use of hand-held devices during a lecture to engage students in decision making and collect feedback quickly.
Reviewing student tracking data	Knowing how each student is using the online course material can help determine how well students are progressing individually, or as a class, while the course is still in progress. This allows you to review material that students appear to find difficult or target particular students with offers of help, fulfilling the adaptive stage of Laurillard's conversational framework.
Easy access to e-administration	Being able to call up the student record as soon as you need it, and being able easily to locate suitable support online (names of human advisers as well as web sites and guides) can improve the quality and timeliness of the information that you provide to students, without requiring them to repeat the same information to you that they have already supplied elsewhere.
Reflecting on your advice before responding to a student	Students presenting with a problem which requires support often need a considered answer. This may not be as easy in a time-pressured face-to-face meeting as it could be when using an asynchronous communications system.
Using conferences, blogs, wikis and instant messaging to encourage peer support	Some of the newer technologies, particularly instant messaging, blogs and wikis, are being used to help build and maintain communities with shared approaches to problem solving. This is a 'traditional' role of the tutor group conference, where support from other students often arrives before the support from the tutor. However, while that resource is often controlled by staff, blogs, wikis and instant messaging may be set up outside the formal college or university systems and controlled by students.

Just as with any other change in delivery format, there are some problems that arise within blended e-learning which might not have been so obvious if the student were being taught differently. For example, while some disabilities can be accommodated and ameliorated through use of assistive technologies, others may be exaggerated by reliance on certain technologies (e.g. text-based discussion). Using writing rather than spoken communication to exchange information with students can highlight problems that some students, such as dyslexic students, may have with text-based communication. Using moving images can create problems for students with visual impairment. Even if best practice is followed in creating and displaying institutional materials accessibly, controlling the accessibility of external resources (e.g. web sites) is still a problem.

The impact of e-learning on student participation is still a new and contested area. However, it has been recognized for some time that certain students who may have anxieties about speaking in class can make more extensive and reflective contributions when they are allowed to take their time and check their responses before sending them. This may be one particular advantage of asynchronous communication where students are not native speakers of the language used for instruction (Skinner and Austin, 1998).

Online peer support

Use of blended learning and e-learning may not necessarily mean that the course is taught off-campus, but where it is, there is often a perception that reliance on web-based communications must be a very impersonal and isolating experience. The idea of building an online relationship with someone whom you do not know and may never meet is certainly a strange one until you try it (Joinson, 2003). However, experience shows that many students can and will establish effective working relationships with other students online. As students become more used to using online communications for social networking outside their studies, their skills increase and the barriers to building strong online study relationships are reduced. The importance of peer group support should not be underestimated; it has been rated by some distance learning students as highly as tutor support (Simpson, 2002). The motivation to carry on with a course when things become difficult often comes as much from the encouragement of fellow students as from the support of institutional staff.

Students supporting other students is not a new idea. Support may be course cohort specific (all participants are studying the same course at the same time), it can be course specific but not cohort specific (they have studied the same course in the past), or it can be unrelated to course or cohort (generic support). The support may be in the form of social support or encouragement, rather than directed at study tasks. It is one of the features of e-learning that students studying on different courses and in different cohorts can establish and maintain contact as long as the online systems are set up to allow this. Indeed, it is one of the advantages of online communications that students can converse with peers in relative safety. To communicate using personal email, telephone, post or meetings raises more safety concerns than the sharing of course-related email addresses, as long as an appropriate computing code of conduct is followed.

While it is usual for students to be able to read and respond to messages only from students within their own course or tutor group, the idea of extending the scope of the students' discussions into other groups within the same cohort is one that may be considered useful. For example, in the Open University's MA in online and distance education students are able to see and respond to messages within other tutor groups so that they can, if they wish, compare the approaches and discussions in their own group with those of other groups. This developed into what one student (later an OU tutor) called 'super-lurking'. Students from one group would enter and lurk in the conferences of another group, capturing the content of some of the messages and presenting a summary of this to their own group. This developed into an exchange of views across the groups and has been successfully reapplied in subsequent cohorts.

This movement across boundaries within an online course where tutor groups are relatively small (typically twelve to eighteen students per tutor) is perhaps unsurprising. Where a course is organized into much larger tutor groups this cross-group boundary hopping may be less attractive and less feasible. However, it is common on online courses for the online social space of the course – the café or online common room – to be shared across the cohort. Interaction here can be more relaxed. It may be a tutor-free zone where study-based discussion only rarely makes an appearance. It is often a place for exchanging recipes, advice on holiday destinations and photos of newborn babies, suggesting the unexpected level of intimacy in online relationships that Joinson (2003)has commented on in other internet environments.

While positive experiences outnumber negative ones, it must be remembered that online communications can support antisocial as well as social behaviour. Although it rarely happens, online conferences can allow 'publication' of racist or sexist views, or bullying, harassment and ridicule of others. Such behaviours exist on campuses too, but in online environments are very visible and if not dealt with can escalate to a form of online aggression known as 'flaming'. In this, students argue online and post hostile views about each other within student forums, turning their peers into reluctant and uncomfortable spectators. If nothing is done to intervene, the messages can build to a point at which other students feel uncomfortable within this study group and may stay away from the forums altogether. Computing codes of conduct that are well understood by all students will help prevent such situations occurring and make them easier to address, for example by deleting offensive messages and withdrawing the ability to post messages for a while. The issue of 'netiquette' (appropriate online behaviour) is one that we return to in Chapter 9.

Where is student support heading?

It is always a challenge to offer predictions about what will happen next, particularly when you are talking about e-learning. It may, however, be useful to highlight some of the current initiatives that we could expect to see impact on student support in the future. The three that we have chosen all offer some aspect of personalization.

Personal development portfolios (PDPs) are envisaged as records of achievement and development that students will continue to use throughout their educational careers. Using e-portfolio technologies, they allow students to have a single integrated record, which will include a record of appropriate student support activity. Over time this will allow students to take a much clearer view of how they have been supported in the past and anticipate what support they may need in current and future studies. It will be an effective long-term planning tool for future students as well as a reflective log of progress made.

Current discussion about *personal learning environments* (PLEs) (Downes, 2006) recognizes that many students enter further and higher education with advanced skills in using communication technologies. They may already own devices and use applications which, in user-friendliness and functionality, offer improvements on the standard communications technologies used by the institution. However, the students' devices may all differ from each other, and the institutional networks will often not allow their use. We can expect to see institutions starting to make more use of students' own devices to communicate with them and support their studies. The student who is struggling may be more likely to see a message on their mobile phone than one posted to the email account on the college learning environment. The student will also know how to use this technology to respond and ask for help. We can expect there to be more use of students' own communication channels as well as, or instead of, those that the institution provides.

These are both, arguably, part of a wider trend to personalized education, or *personalization* in education. We have touched on this in earlier chapters in the book in talking about how content can be personalized so that it better fits the student. We can also expect to see better – more seamless and integrated – personalization of student support. The technology will increasingly support the student in offering them access to support services as they need them and flagging their availability in response to particular signals. For example, a missed deadline or failed test may lead to offers of assistance. Alternatively, a new journal article in their research area may be flagged as soon as it becomes available online.

Support staff will also become more adept at using the data from electronic learning environments to recognize students who are at risk. Through blended learning and e-learning, and particularly through personalized learning, they will have more choices about how to address those risks.

Chapter 9

Ethical issues in blended e-learning

When talking about e-learning, we often use terms which suggest that elements within this are equivalent or analogous to the face-to-face teaching and learning elements that we are already familiar with. We use terms like 'conference' or 'forum' to describe environments where there are many people conversing in the same place; we talk about 'bulletin boards' or 'notice boards' when we want to talk about places where items can be 'posted'. We talk about 'virtual' or 'online' or 'electronic' learning environments, lectures or classrooms. At the less formal end of the spectrum we talk about 'chat' to describe more spontaneous, ephemeral conversations with a single person or small group. We understand that our 'mailbox' is where our personal messages reside.

It is useful to have this idea of broad equivalents, or to use metaphors to make sense of an unfamiliar working environment, but there are aspects of online interactivity that deviate from what we are accustomed to. By using e-learning, as this book shows, we can support activities that would not be possible if we were teaching and learning offline. The experience of learning and teaching using computers and the internet *is* different, and individuals and institutions that use e-learning need to recognize what these differences are and how to work with them. At some stage they will also need to consider the ethical and policy issues that these differences present.

In a sense, all e-learning is a form of publication, whether this is publishing a set of handouts to a class, or privately 'publishing' a message to a classmate or teaching colleague. Online communication – unlike the student–lecturer or student–student communication in lectures, seminars or 'chat' – is very often text based, and will usually result in the creation and storage of digital files. Online communications can often be saved, distributed, edited, searched and tracked. What started out as private one-to-one communications can be made visible to others at a later date unless there is clear understanding and agreement that this should not happen. It may occur even when there *is* such an understanding. Ensuring an appropriate level of confidentiality and security for online resources and communications is an important aspect of developing e-learning courses and resources. The course developer, or the institution, needs to understand why certain online communications and resources are used and what the ethical and policy implications may be. They need to be prepared to explain why certain people will have access to certain resources and others will not, why some people will have online permissions and privileges and what the limits on these are. This is just one of the ethical concerns arising from the use of e-learning, and is considered in more detail below.

Sometimes the institution or lecturer will be forced into developing a policy, or at least producing guidelines, in order to fulfil its legal obligations to staff, students or others. These may be clear obligations to meet legal requirements relating to the security and type of personal data held (e.g. the Data Protection Act 1998), or it could relate to government policy on public accountability (e.g. the Freedom of Information Act 2000). There will be established policies for other types of courses which will apply to e-learning or blended learning provision. However, the institution will also be faced with the task of generating policies on a more discretionary basis where there is no established practice and no governmental guidance.

The ease with which students and staff can publish files online, perhaps incorporating parts of files drawn from other sources within their own material, can raise concerns about copyright. When the only materials produced within a course are printed handouts there is a relatively low risk of copyright infringement if the institution has an appropriate copyright licence. However, where students are incorporating images and text from multiple sources into documents that they share online with others, the resulting publication is unlikely to be covered by existing licences and may attract prosecution of the individual and institution. In the world of copyright, ignorance is *not* a viable defence, so the institution will need either to restrict the potential for students to publish, or to adopt a policy that reduces the risk of infringement occurring. There is a great deal of confusion and worry around the area of copyright and online courses, making this a 'hot topic' for most universities and colleges. Some of the issues here are examined in more detail below.

Finally, although we may use the term 'environment' to talk about the online world in which e-learning occurs, we often do not consider what practical consequences there may be in shifting learning and teaching into an e-learning environment. There may be consequences for students and staff when adapting to the use of new types of tools for their work and study. For example, the institution will have had to take account of staff and student training and support (including accessibility concerns) so that there are no undesirable and avoidable consequences from introducing these changes. There needs to be a shared understanding of what is appropriate and what is proscribed behaviour in the new environment. On a very practical level there are health and safety implications of using computers, and these need to be addressed.

Unlike the previous chapters, this one is looking at issues and policies over which you may have little personal influence. Many of them extend beyond a single course or programme, and some of these decisions may already have been made within your own institution (although with changes in technology they may need be revisited as new challenges and queries occur). Although it is unusual for any one person to have been the only influence in deciding on institutional policies and practices, everyone in the institution should be aware of what these are and, ideally, why they are considered to be important. The focus in this chapter is on those issues over which the institution or individual is likely to have some discretion, those concerns where there is more than one possible response. We will particularly focus on the underlying reasons why policies may have evolved in the form that they have, and how they can impact on the design of e-learning resources and courses.

Computing codes and controls

It is one of the apparent contradictions of the internet that it can afford exceptional levels of both anonymity and intimacy. A Peter Steiner cartoon published in the *New Yorker* in 1993 showed a dog typing at a computer while observing to another dog, 'On the internet nobody knows you're a dog'. Online, correspondents are often not visible to each other. It is not immediately obvious to a reader of a bulletin board posting whether the author is male/female, young/old, stranger/acquaintance, disabled/able-bodied, local/distant, expert/novice, etc. unless some clues are provided in the message, in the name used, or within a biographical résumé. It is possible that even with this additional information there may be some level of deceit being practised. This could be simply a prank, or could signal more sinister intent. It could be a 'joke' that escalates beyond the control and intentions of the initiator, as for example in the case with the Anandtech forums, where a member created a fictitious female contributor, responding to messages in role and even flirting with 'her' online using his own established ID. (Anandtech forums are asynchronous bulletin boards used by information technology professionals.) You could be suggesting that students, particularly vocational students, use such specialist fora as a learning resource. It is interesting that in this case the users were IT professionals and not new or naïve users of the internet. When it became too difficult to maintain this deception, he reported her tragic 'real-world' death. The reaction to this fraud was initially grief and shock at the loss of a 'friend'. That then degenerated into a torrent of increasingly angry emails when the deceit was discovered. There were over 450 messages posted on this topic within twenty-four hours of his confession/apology and he was banned and stigmatized, perhaps being treated more harshly because he was a member of the community than he would have been if he had been an 'outsider' – what Joinson and Dietz-Uhler (2002) call 'the Black Sheep effect'.

While within an institutional e-learning environment some verifiable information will usually be known about participants – at least by the tutors – the above example shows how abuse of trust can escalate in online environments and how even experienced internet users can be deceived. The more informal the learning context, the more possible it is for a learner or tutor to abuse it. The more formal the context, the more likely it is that the student will rely upon e-learning to complete their studies, and hence the more vital it is to retain their confidence in the learning environment. The external sources that students locate themselves carry a greater likelihood of exposing students to unsolicited sales pitches (spam) and possibly fraud: false information (e.g. emotional but fictitious chain letters), or viruses. These experiences will waste students' time and, perhaps more seriously, erode their confidence in using the internet for their studies. This is one of the arguments for ensuring that all students new to e-learning understand some of the basic principles of information literacy and security.

Within blended and e-learning it has been suggested that students find it easier to engage in online learning with others when there is an opportunity to meet at least some of the cohort face to face (Nicol *et al.*, 2003). We could speculate that one of the reasons for this is a natural caution about talking to someone online whom you have never seen and who is effectively a stranger. It may be difficult for students, particularly for computer novices, to trust the technology, or the other unseen participants. If the course uses a blend of face-to-face and online conversation, then this is less likely to be a problem. If the course population is dispersed, for example in the case of an international course, then it may be more difficult, particularly when we factor in the difficulties of managing effective communication across different cultures.

One way in which the problem of trust may be addressed is through developing a clear code of conduct that is understood by all participants.

Courses that use computers will normally have a stated policy which prohibits students from using the institution's computing network for purposes that are inappropriate (e.g. making racist comments about other students) or are not connected with valid education or research use (e.g. publishing pornography). These are clear-cut cases of abuse that would normally result in the student being reduced to 'read-only' access, or denied access entirely. There are, however, many 'grey' areas in computer use and communications that may also require some policy or guidance, simply because these are still new technologies for many students and they may not recognize what is appropriate behaviour in an e-learning context. A thoughtless remark or off-colour joke that would be easy to rectify or ignore in a face-to-face setting may have a much greater impact within an online educational environment because:

- It is 'published' and therefore can be more widely disseminated (e.g. by forwarding to other forums reaching audiences for whom it was never intended).
- It is 'persistent' (unless deleted by the author or tutor), so that it may still be read and referred to long after the event to which it relates. This makes it more difficult to forget that the remark was made.
- The written form may prompt a written response which is itself published and persistent and, if sent in the heat of the moment, may lead to an escalation in hostility (sometimes called 'flaming') in the public gaze.
- It is visible to the tutor, which may imply to some students that the tutor should do something about the message. Not doing so may lead to the assumption that the tutor is endorsing what has been said (although in fact they may simply not have seen it).

Some courses offer students an induction into appropriate 'netiquette' (internet etiquette) to try to reduce the likelihood of problems occurring. Some researchers have gone further, to suggest that students adopt a protocol or template for posing and responding to online messages in order to reduce conflict and foster empathy (Zimmer, 1995). However, it should be borne in mind that argument and dissent can be very positive signs that students are actively engaging with the content of the course, and the role of the online tutor is to ensure that the energy generated is used to positive rather than negative effect. The online tutor's role here is very much like that of the lecturer in a tutorial who helps students to resolve an argument, sometimes through consensus but often by respecting each other's opinions. Tutors can use the online tools to good effect in doing this, incorporating abstracts from previous messages to weave a summary of the argument. This has the additional advantage of opening up the discussion to course participants who would otherwise have missed it – a positive aspect of the published and persistent nature of online communication.

A brief guide to netiquette

The 'rules' set out in a netiquette guide will differ with context and with the system. They tend to cover three distinct areas:

1   *Message formatting guidelines.* These concentrate upon making the conference or forum as usable as possible for everyone. For example, they may include advice on:

   • *Making the subject header meaningful.* Ideally, the message title should be descriptive of the content, to help participants decide in advance whether they need to read the message.
   • *Placing messages sensibly* – for example, within the appropriate sub-conference or within a message thread to which the message refers.
   • *Using separate messages for each topic.* This makes each message easier to locate, read and respond to in context.
   • *Keeping messages short* – for example, by quoting only parts and not the whole of messages that you are responding to in order to save the downloading and reading time of others.

2   *Expressing and managing emotion.* This offers guidance on making the conference messages more 'human' and taking account of the diverse humans using the system:

   • *Cautioning against unexpected use of humour.* Where forum messages are text based there is no body language to signal whether someone is joking. Jokes may fall flat or be misinterpreted, and novices are advised to signal whether they are joking or not when writing in forums with which they are not familiar.

- *Use of emoticons.* Some will use smileys or abbreviations to show mood or signal intent. This works well when the readers are familiar with the notation. Figure 9.1 shows some common examples.

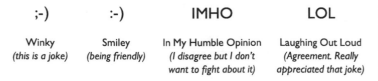

;-)	:-)	IMHO	LOL
Winky	Smiley	In My Humble Opinion	Laughing Out Loud
(this is a joke)	*(being friendly)*	*(I disagree but I don't want to fight about it)*	*(Agreement. Really appreciated that joke)*

Figure 9.1 **Some emoticons and what they mean**

- *Elimination of 'flaming'.* Flaming is the term used for highly charged and sometimes abusive online exchanges. Guidance given about this can encourage patterns of inquiry and agreement to try to ensure that flaming does not occur, or at least inform participants in advance that messages or threads may be 'locked' or deleted by a moderator.

3   *Advice on conference/forum-specific behaviour.* This will include advice on the use of specific conferences or fora. For example:

- *Advice on confidentiality and privacy.* With a private forum this advice is likely to stress that postings there cannot be referred to or circulated externally. The forum may have been set up so that it is not possible to determine individual and e-mail addresses.
- *Restrictions on what can be posted.* It is common to prohibit the use of conferences for spam messages (i.e. messages that are attempting to sell things rather than inform or help the users of the conference/forum), or for forwarding of chain e-mails.
- *Moderation arrangements.* Some online forums and conferences will use moderators (who could be students or staff) to approve messages before they are published, or to keep conferences tidy – moving and archiving messages and threads. The rules of moderation (if any) will vary.

It can be very tempting to try to avoid 'trouble' by trying to reduce the opportunity that students have to make problems for themselves and others. For example, the institution may decide to use a 'profanity filter' to ensure that messages cannot include swear words, or use other controls to restrict which sites students can access, for example to avoid access being gained to 'adult' sites either by accident or by intent. Such controls need careful consideration and are not in themselves sufficient to avoid offensive messages or access to unsuitable materials. It is, after all, very possible to send offensive messages without the use of profanity, and if this is the only form of moderation, some students may see that as a challenge. Such devices can also have unintended and undesirable side effects, for example blocking content from sites that merely *sound* as though they may be offensive, or preventing students from accurately recording verbatim interview dialogue.

Privacy and confidentiality online

In 2001, Scott McNealty (the chairman and CEO of Sun Microsystems) made a provocative and much-reported statement about online privacy: 'You have no privacy – get over it'. Taken in the context of online commercial transactions this is probably close to the truth. If you do business online, individually or corporately, then an astonishing amount of information will be held about your online behaviour (sites visited, items purchased, even your address book).

To some extent this is also true with e-learning – if we choose to take this path. Most virtual learning environments can provide student tracking information in a detail and depth that extends far beyond the routine progress reporting that we are used to receiving. It is possible not only to collect data on student test scores (online formative tests as well as the more usual records of achievement in summative assessment), but also to note which pages students have visited, downloaded and bookmarked, which messages they have read, responded to or forwarded, how much time they have spent online during different activities and when they last were online.

Some of this information may be of use to tutors in spotting students who are experiencing difficulty in the course – for example, students who have not yet logged in when the course has been up and running for a week or so. However, much of the information is unlikely ever to be used. It will often require additional effort to generate it in a form that *could* be useful. You have to be realistic about the gains and costs. It is possible to become carried away with ideas about complex data mining, for example identifying every student who scored less than 30 per cent on a certain test *and* who last logged on more than a week ago *and* downloaded only two articles from an extensive reading list. We could argue that this kind of check can help us to identify and offer assistance to 'weaker' students. However, such information will require careful analysis and sensitive intervention. Students might reasonably be expected to become nervous about their online activity if they believe that their every keystroke is captured, analysed and acted upon. This could be seen as unwarranted surveillance and an invasion of privacy. After all, we do not know how much time each student spends studying a single page in a textbook and whether they attempt any of the optional questions or follow up references. Even if we did, it is unlikely that we would have the resources to offer assistance at this personalized level, and it might even be counter-productive to do so. We need to ask ourselves whether there is any need to have highly detailed knowledge about the online student simply because we can. We need to establish what information is appropriate and usable and useful.

In praise of 'message history'?

Some online forums and conferencing systems offer a facility usually described as 'message history'. This allows students and staff users of those forums or conferences not only to view a message but also to view a list of who else has read, forwarded, downloaded or responded to the message (Figure 9.2). This can be very useful if you are the sender of the message and want to check which students have noted its content – something that you would probably not otherwise know with any degree of certainty. The student can also check that their tutor has read their own messages without the tutor having to leave a message to that effect. Students have commented that this helps them to feel that the tutor is keeping an active eye on the online discussion even when not posting messages there. For the tutor it helps to identify lurkers and note their activity, rather than simply assuming that anyone who does not post messages is being inactive.

It can, however, lead to anxiety for message posters, either because they can see that many have read their message and *not* responded (leading to doubts along the lines of 'Why doesn't anyone answer me?'), or it can result in pressure to respond because the message sender will 'know' that you have read their message.

☞ **History: Revitalising the course**		_ □ ×
File Edit Format Message Conferencing Connection View		
Help		

What	When	Who
✍ Created	22/05/2006 15:08	Chris Pegler
✉ Sent	22/05/2006 15:08	Chris Pegler
✷ Read	22/05/2006 15:41	James McLannahan
✍ Modified by	22/05/2006 17:40	James McLannahan
✷ Read	22/05/2006 18:33	Arnold Muhren 2
✷ Read	23/05/2006 09:25	Sarah Cornelius
◄✉ Reply	23/05/2006 09:26	Sarah Cornelius
✷ Read	23/05/2006 10:08	Martin Weller
◄✉ Reply	23/05/2006 13:19	Sarah Cornelius
✷ Read	23/05/2006 16:46	Chris Pegler

Figure 9.2 Message history from online Firstlcass forum

Another aspect of lack of privacy can be seen in the use of some instant messaging (chat) systems that indicate whether a particular person is online and show whether they are currently active or inactive. Ideally, such systems will also allow users to flag that they are unavailable for conversation. If not, there is a danger that they could be distracted by intrusive chat invitations eating into online time scheduled for other, possibly more urgent, purposes.

Associated with the idea of online privacy are concerns about online confidentiality. In some discipline areas, for example social work, students will be aware of the need to anonymize case histories and other material that they wish to discuss with course colleagues. Business students may decide to change financial information that they submit to an online forum so that it is of no value to competitors. While these same issues of confidentiality may be familiar in class discussions, wherever the information is submitted to a group of fellow students in writing there is a greater risk that it may be abused (e.g. by wider circulation), perhaps after the course has finished. Whatever the discipline area, the content of email (one-to-one messages) should generally be treated as confidential correspondence to which no reference should be made without the consent of the author(s). Many courses will also choose to adopt the same principle for forum messages: that they should not be referred to or quoted without the prior consent of their creator, and/or be rendered anonymous. It is easy to forget that in submitting quotations from online messages within a course assignment, or within a research article about the course, the wish of the author to retain control of their work is being infringed. Their views may be receiving a much more public airing than would have happened with conventional classroom interaction, so additional precautions are necessary.

Digital rights

The issue of intellectual property rights in educational materials has a significant impact on e-learning. It can sometimes be put forward as a barrier to engaging in e-learning at all. The issues generally manifest themselves as:

* concerns by academics and publishers that the materials that they have invested time and resources developing will now be freely available and their rights regarding that material will be eroded or infringed;
* worries by individual academics and their institutions that they will need to engage more actively in understanding and managing this area, as material that they create may now be visible beyond the class-room, making more obvious any existing infringement of copyright.

It is possible to see these as two sides of the same coin. Teachers may have used material in their teaching without being overly concerned about the rights issues. They may have taken or adapted resources from sources that gave no information about the rights, or they may have assumed that as they were involved in teaching and learning, or academic research, they were protected under some sort of 'fair dealing' provision. Before e-learning, they might have been comfortable about this line of thinking because the likelihood of infringing copyright was quite low and the impact of any single infringement (if infringement it was) was probably quite minor. The materials would have been shared in hard copy form within a single class and this use was usually covered by a licensing arrangement that gave 'blanket rights' to produce reprographic copies from many different print sources. Even if the licence did not cover this specific use (context or content), the likelihood of being 'found out' was quite small. The materials distributed in the classroom were not likely to be seen by those outside it.

There were concerns about infringing intellectual property rights before e-learning, but in many cases it was regarded as almost an occupational hazard – sometimes difficult to avoid doing in practice and with little likelihood of unpleasant consequences (a little like exceeding the speed limit when no one is looking). Like so many of the problems identified with moving into online learning, this is not an entirely new concern, but has become one that it is now impossible to ignore. The move to storing and distributing material in digital form, whether on individual machines or in repositories, has had an impact on the scope of any single infringement and increased the chances of its detection. The situation is further complicated by the fact that the laws which govern copyright were written before digital rights became an issue, and the licensing agreements with publishers (e.g. the Copyright Licensing Agency agreement in the United Kingdom) in the past specifically excluded any right to make or share electronic copies.

Lecturers, particularly those who are working on fixed-term contracts, have always been concerned to protect their materials and ensure that, where these are reused by others, there should be some acknowledgement. The right to be identified as the creator of the material is the author's 'moral right'. There may also be an issue of receiving a fee for using the material – the 'economic right'. Plagiarism, the reuse of material from one source in another without acknowledging provenance, is regarded as one of the cardinal sins within academia, so the need to respect moral rights is already appreciated. The problem is often with adaptations of the original. Whenever a resource is made available in electronic form it becomes easier to adapt it, and unattributed copies may be further distributed and adapted using electronic means, increasing the impact of infringement as well as making it more difficult to spot when it has happened. This applies whether the copying is done by a student completing their assessed work, or by a teacher using third-party material – knowingly or otherwise – without the correct permission or attribution.

Although it is often assumed that authors and publishers are most concerned with protecting their income – and indeed this may be true of best-selling authors – academic authors are accustomed to not receiving income for most of their research publications. They generally publish in academic journals for no fee, to raise the profile of their research and disseminate their findings but not in expectation of monetary reward. This has led in the past decade to moves towards electronic publishing of academic research under arrangements that maximize the potential for dissemination and reduce the costs. One example is the eprints www. eprints.org) service, which helps academics and institutions to provide free-of-charge access to their research outputs. As this type of licensing arrangement (emphasizing rights to attribution while minimizing economic rights) has increased, so has interest in equivalent arrangements for sharing teaching material within structured but free-of-charge licensing arrangements.

There is an important difference between the cost-free dissemination of research output and the equivalent arrangements for sharing teaching resources, although you may use both types of material within your own teaching. Whereas the first is generally taken as a finished resource to which the end user refers without changing it, the latter may need to be repurposed for each new context and could become, in this reuse, significantly different from the original. Teaching materials are essentially evolving resources, with many versions, and they need a different sort of licensing arrangement to reflect this. Licensing under Creative Commons (www.creativecommons.org) options takes account of versioning issues (where the original resource is adapted) to allow an 'open content' approach to reuse. 'Open content' licensing arrangements put the onus on the community who take and use the material to keep this up to date and relevant. This mirrors the 'open source' software movement in seeing the usefulness of the resource as being increased through updating and revision by users. The new versions are then deposited back to the original repository for sharing, extending the variety of resources available. One of the important contributions that electronic learning environments and repositories can make is in keeping track of intellectual property rights.

The ethics of access

In Chapter 8 we considered the issues of accessibility and the digital divide, and from those discussions it is easy to see that access to education can be affected positively or negatively by use of e-learning. For some severely disabled students it may be their only option if they are to study at home, or undertake studies independently. For other students, both able-bodied and disabled, the change to a new style of learning and teaching may be a barrier, actual or perceived. Simple geography can make some e-learning courses and course elements more convenient for some students than others, reflecting the unevenness of telecommunications provision both nationally and globally. Sometimes these issues can be addressed by innovative solutions. One initiative in South Africa (the Freedom Toaster www.freedomtoaster.org/) offers kiosks that will burn on to CD-ROMs free open source software so that those without fast internet connections can benefit from resources that normally require large downloads. It would be possible to offer similar services to disseminate open content.

Without initiatives to overcome the digital divide, the concern is that the potential of computers to help widen participation will be lost or dissipated. While in some areas the access to personal computers may already be good (in the United Kingdom is estimated that over 50 per cent of households are connected to the internet and thus significantly over half the population), in other areas of the world it may be necessary to arrange for some sort of laptop loan scheme for students, or even to create learning resource centres to which students travel for their e-learning sessions. Part of the interest in mobile learning is that the use of satellite technologies in telecommunications now means that isolated students in countries without good conventional telecommunications can access the internet using mobile phones. The compact, and increasingly powerful, nature of PDAs and notebook computers also means that tutors who travel between classes can take student equipment with them. Although the ideal may be the use of personal computing devices that are owned by students, and therefore familiar to them, these initiatives help to build familiarity and improve access for what would otherwise be technologically disadvantaged groups.

The implications of teleworking and the 24/7 network

This book has largely focused on e-learning and e-teaching from the point of view of the student. However, it is likely that the impact on lecturers and tutors will be even more significant as they may well be using computers more intensively than their students. The tutor may be reading, marking and commenting on thirty assignments online while the equivalent student activity requires composition of a single piece of assessment.

This means that the teacher's range of technical skill not only will need to be as good as that of most students, and needs to encompass activities and systems that students are not expected to engage with. That can translate into additional training and a sharp increase in on-screen work, which can in turn raise questions about health and safety. Many institutions will already have in place procedures for advising on, and even auditing, the workspaces of staff so that they are not running undue risks from eye strain or repetitive strain injuries. Just as employees operating a new and potentially dangerous piece of heavy machinery may need advice on safety, so too do staff and students using computers for any sustained period. The problem with ensuring that this advice is observed is made more difficult by the tendency towards mobile computing. While the office set-up may be appropriate, the lighting and seating arrangements in the tutor's 'home office' (perhaps the end of their dining room table) may be less desirable. As students are often studying on e-learning courses out of normal office hours, so staff are often teaching and supporting students outside their normal offices.

Apart from the concerns about the health and safety aspects, there are also issues about the transfer of costs of the course from the institution to the individual (tutor or student). If students are expected to make extensive use of computers, they probably need to own one, or at least own one jointly with other household members. They will also need an internet connection and may need to upgrade this to a faster connection. This introduces an expense into their course that would otherwise not have been there.

The tutor who is supporting students may also need to arrange for access to a computer at home and could find that there are significant 'hidden costs' in terms of computer consumables (paper and printer cartridges). They can reasonably expect the institution to provide allowances for these work-related expenses – although where there is a choice of workplace, the institution may expect those staff who choose to work from home to offset some of these expenses against savings on travel costs. The less generous the allowances for online working, the more resistance staff may have to shifting to e-learning.

Observations about teleworking in other employment sectors suggest that staff have very mixed experiences. There may be an erosion of the concept of a set pattern of working hours so that evenings and weekends become times spent online. Some tutors are careful to set out what their online 'office hours' are so that students do not expect immediate responses to queries sent in the middle of the night. Other tutors really appreciate the flexibility of being able to work at unsocial hours – particularly those for whom tutoring is a part-time additional job, or who have childcare responsibilities. As with so many other aspects of e-learning, there are benefits as well as disadvantages, and the disadvantages are often avoidable.

Good e-learning does not just happen by accident, any more than effective teaching and learning 'just happens' within a more traditional educational context. It is for us all to share and use and extend the knowledge that we have about what works and what does not, being honest and curious about failures as well as open and enthusiastic about success. For most educators today, e-learning will become, or already is, part of their professional lives. It offers enormous potential, but, as with any area with huge potential, this needs active and informed engagement by professionals working in that area if the full potential is to be realized.

Glossary

Accessibility A characteristic of a tool or system that enables people with disabilities to use it. An accessible web site could be navigated by users with visual, hearing, motor or cognitive impairments. Accessible design can also benefit people with older or slower software and hardware.

Affordance A property of an object, environment or tool that indicates how to interface with it. (An empty space within an open doorway affords movement across that space.)

Assistive technologies Technologies used by individuals with disabilities in order to perform functions that might otherwise be difficult or impossible.

Asynchronous communication Communication that occurs intermittently rather than in 'real time'. An example used in this series is **online** forums, where students can read and respond to a message some time after it was posted. Another very familiar example is email.

Audioconferencing Communication between two or more sites using standard telephone lines to allow participants to hear and speak to each other.

Blended learning Learning that combines different technologies, in particular a combination of traditional (e.g. face-to-face instruction) and online teaching approaches and media.

Blog (weblog) An easy-to-publish web site consisting of entries posted in date order. Blogs can contain links, images, sound and video (sometimes called *vlogs*). Blogs are usually personal but may invite comments from a wide audience.

Bookmark A way of noting a link using browser software. Bookmarking allows users to return to web pages quickly without remembering or searching for the **URLs**, for quick and easy retrieval. See also **Social bookmarking**.

Broadband A means of allowing high-speed transmission of data and therefore a quicker connection to the internet than **dial-up** modems permit. This makes learning and teaching at a distance possible using audio and video without lengthy waits for files to **download**.

Browser An application such as Firefox or Internet Explorer that displays web pages in a user-friendly graphical format. Browser software may also be used to **navigate** and display the contents of a personal computer.

Chat Real-time text-based communication, usually on a one-to-one or small-group basis. Chat can be used in **e-learning** for students to ask questions of peers or the instructor as they work through problems. It is often used to describe **instant messaging (IM)**.

Chat room A virtual meeting space used for real-time text (**chat**) discussions among several users.

Collaborative knowledge construction Collaborative development of an awareness and understanding of facts, truths or information gained in the form of experience or learning (see **Knowledge construction**).

Computer conferencing Refers to forums on the internet or an intranet where users can post messages for others to read (other terms include *discussion boards* or *bulletin boards*).

Constructivism A philosophy of learning founded on the premise that, by reflecting on our experiences, we construct our own understanding of the world.

Continuing education Courses designed for part-time adult learners.

Continuing professional development (CPD) Work-related training or updating that is required to maintain professional standing. This may take the form of formal courses provided by, or accredited by, colleges and universities.

Convergence A way of describing the combination of separate digital information formats, such as text, audio and video, into new, integrated forms. **Podcasting** is an example of convergence between audio broadcasting and personal **MP3** players.

Courseware Instruction or education delivered in the form of courses using a software program. Can be delivered online or using disks, CD-ROMs or DVDs.

Data mining Analysing data relating to online activity to identify patterns and establish relationships.

Delivery Any method of transferring content to learners. This can be via face-to-face (traditional) delivery or done at a distance. In either case it may include use of the internet, DVDs, CD-ROM, books and other media.

Dial-up A way of accessing the internet using a device called a modem. This allows a computer to connect using a phone line. The connection speed is much slower than for **broadband**.

Digital divide A term used to describe the gap that exists between those who can afford technology (or can afford the best or fastest technology) and those who cannot.

Distance education or **Distance learning** Teaching where the student is separated by time or location from the teacher and, usually, other students. Courses are delivered using a variety of synchronous or asynchronous technologies. The Open University is an example of a distance teaching university, but many traditional colleges and universities offer some of their courses 'at a distance'.

Download Transfer of a file to a user's computer from another, connected computer or service, usually using the internet. Download time refers to the amount of time taken to complete a file download. For large (e.g. media) files this could be significant, hence the use of streaming media.

e-Administration Electronic administration. This term covers a wide set of course management applications that take place **online**, e.g. registration of students, or reservation of library books.

e-Content Refers to the electronic content of a course. Covers a wide range of resources for learning, from specifically created **learning objects** to the content of third-party materials such as external web sites.

e-Learning Broad term used to describe electronic teaching and learning using computers, usually through access to **online** materials or the internet.

Electronic learning environment An integrated set of electronic teaching and learning tools which combine to form a learning environment (similar to *content management system* (CMS), *virtual learning environment* (VLE), *managed learning environment* (MLE) and *learning management system* (LMS)).

e-Portfolio A collection of electronic files used to support development, dissemination, reflection and/or assessment. Often uses a specialized system for managing and displaying the files and can be accessed once the course is over, or away from campus.

e-Tool Term used to describe electronic software or hardware tools. Examples of software e-tools range from Microsoft Word or **Skype** to **Google**. Hardware e-tools include phones, DVD players, **iPods**, etc.

Experiential learning Learning through experience, either in a real situation, such as a workplace, or in a simulation or role-play.

f2f (face-to-face) Used to describe synchronous interaction between students or students and teachers within the same space. An example is the traditional classroom setting.

FAQs Abbreviation of 'frequently asked questions' – a format for presenting information as a list of questions with answers. FAQs often appear on web sites and may be used as a way of answering anticipated student queries such as 'How do I get a password for the network?'

Formative assessment Assessment intended to give students feedback on their learning progress and to give the teacher an indication of students' areas of difficulty. **Multiple-choice questions** are a popular way of providing formative assessment within **e-learning**.

Further education (FE) Post-compulsory education offered by colleges in the United Kingdom. The 'FE sector' includes tertiary colleges, agricultural colleges and sixth-form colleges.

GB (gigabyte) Just over 1 billion bytes; 1,000 megabytes (MB).

Google A very well-known example of a **search engine**. The term 'googling' refers to searching the web using any search engine.

Granularity The size of a learning resource. The smaller the resource, the higher the level of granularity.

Higher education (HE) University-level education, usually leading to the award of a degree.

Higher Education Academy (HEA) The professional organization of higher education teachers in the United Kingdom. The HEA aims to help institutions, discipline groups and all staff provide the best possible learning experience for their students.

HTML (Hypertext Markup Language) The programming language used to create documents for display on the World Wide Web.

ICT (information and communication technology) A catch-all phrase used to describe a range of technologies for gathering, storing, retrieving, processing, analysing and transmitting information. The emphasis is on communication, differentiating it from **IT (information technology)**.

Informal learning Informal learning activities that take place without a teacher and may also take place outside the classroom.

Instant messaging (IM) An application that can be installed to let users '**chat**' to others, sending short text messages to selected 'buddies' (e.g. friends, colleagues or fellow students) who are online. MSN (Microsoft Network) is a popular instant messaging system.

Interoperability When hardware or software is 'interoperable', it has been designed to work effectively with other systems. Interoperability improves the opportunities for reuse and also underpins mobile learning.

iPod The brand name of Apple's **MP3** player. Often used as a generic term to describe all MP3 players. Gave rise to the term **podcasting**.

IT (information technology) In education this term is usually used to describe the use of computers and often refers to the technical skills (IT skills) needed to use them.

JISC (Joint Information Systems Committee) A strategic advisory committee working on behalf of UK **higher** and **further education** that aims to promote innovative applications of information technologies and systems.

Just-in-time Characteristic of **e-learning** which means that learners are able to access the information they need exactly when they need it. This approach is particularly popular in **work-based learning** and training.

Knowledge construction Building an awareness and understanding of facts, truths or information gained in the form of experience or learning (see **Collaborative knowledge construction**).

LD_lite A framework for documenting teaching and learning practice.

Learning Design IMS Learning Design specification, which supports the use of a wide range of pedagogies in online learning (www. imsglobal.org).

Learning environment The physical or virtual setting in which learning takes place.

Learning object (LO) Sometimes referred to as a *reusable learning object* (RLO). A learning object is a digital piece of learning material that addresses a clearly identifiable topic or learning outcome and has the potential to be reused in different contexts.

Learning object economy Activities related to the production, sharing, distribution and reuse of learning resources.

Learning objective A statement that sets out a measurable outcome of the learning. May be used within a course description. See also **Learning outcome**.

Learning outcome Statement of what a learner is expected to know, understand or be able to do at the end of a period of learning.

Link An icon, text or image within a web page which, if clicked, will display another web page, or resource. Used in the design of hypertext. A set of linked web pages is a web site.

Metadata Information (data) about a resource which is used to classify and describe it (e.g. name of author, when created). Standards exist for writing metadata which aim to make its use consistent and helpful for retrieval and reuse. A **repository** will include resources with metadata attached. The metadata will help to locate usable and relevant resources.

M-learning or **Mobile learning** Teaching and learning using technologies such as mobile phones, **PDAs**, wireless notebooks or **MP3** players.

MP3 A format for audio file compression that allows users to **download** or **upload** recordings over the internet. These files can be organized, stored and played back (or recorded) using an MP3 player or a conventional laptop or desktop computer.

Multimedia Refers to the use of more than one medium (print, online, audio or video) within a single resource. May be delivered online or using CD-ROM or DVD format.

Multiple-choice questions (MCQs) Questions where the learner selects from a number of choices as answers in reply to a text or formula question. Some MCQ software will allow construction of mazes or crosswords.

Navigation Refers to the process of moving through a series of pages, either those that are connected to the same site, or pages from separate sites that are linked together.

Netiquette Etiquette for 'net' users. Suggested or required rules of conduct for online or internet users.

Online The state of a computer when it is connected to another computer via a network. Also used in **e-learning** to describe being connected to the internet, as in 'Now go online and . . .'

Online learning Refers to learning delivered using internet-based technologies. Also sometimes described as *web-based* or *internet-based learning*.

Open courseware Courseware or learning resources that are made available free of charge, often with some educational licensing restrictions.

Open source software Software for which the original code is made available free of charge so that users can access, modify and republish it. The Linux operating system is an example of open source software.

PDA (personal digital assistant) An ultra-portable hand-held computer commonly used to organize personal information such as contacts, schedules, etc. Can also be used to display electronic texts, complete **multiple-choice question** activity and to take notes.

PDF or .pdf (portable document format) Adobe document file format that allows documents to be displayed with fonts, images, links and layouts as they were originally designed.

Personalization or **Personalized learning** Tailoring content within a course, and/or student support, so that it reflects the requirements or preferences of the individual user. Can be informed by **student tracking**.

Podcasting A method of uploading and publishing audio files to the internet. Many podcast services allow users to subscribe to a feed and receive new files automatically by subscription. Outside of education this may be a free service provided by broadcasters, e.g. the BBC.

Real-time communication Communication in which there is no obvious delay between the time when the information is sent and when it is received. Characteristic of **synchronous learning**, this describes communication that can be close to conventional face-to-face conversation.

Repository An electronic database of materials together with detailed information (**metadata**) about them which helps users classify and identify the contents. Contents can be learning resources deposited for reuse, or research or other documents deposited for dissemination.

Repurpose To change content by revising or restructuring it so that it can be used for a different purpose or in a different way. Updating is a very light level of repurposing.

Reusable e-Learning content that has been developed to be usable in more than one context, or for more than one cohort. This may include a special format (see **Learning object**) that allows import into different systems or delivery mechanisms, usually without the need to make changes to the resource.

RSS feeds A form of 'news feed' used for supplying (serving) users with frequently updated content and increasingly used as a means of automatically updating **blogs** and other frequently revised sites.

Scalability The degree to which something (cohort size, computer application, etc.) can be expanded in volume and continue to work effectively.

Screen reader Computer software that can be used to read aloud content displayed as text on the screen. This may be used as **assistive technology** by some disabled students.

Scroll To navigate around the screen by moving through text and images on a computer screen in a constant direction, e.g. down, up, right or left.

Search engine Software that helps users to locate web pages based on a search of keywords. The search engines maintain databases of web sites and use programs (often referred to as 'spiders' or 'robots') to collect information, which is then indexed by the search engine. The most commonly used search engine is **Google** (www. google.com).

Skype A form of VoIP (voice-over internet protocol) whereby voice is transmitted digitally. Can be used to avoid fees charged by telephone companies.

Social bookmarking A form of **social software** which allows users to build sets of annotated bookmarks and share information about these with others. Systems such as deli.cio.us (www.deli.cio.us) can identify common 'tags' (descriptions) used to describe bookmarks and can flag up popular or linked themes.

Social software Software that allows users to connect or collaborate by use of a computer network and encourages sharing and commenting on content. Commonly used examples are MySpace (www.myspace. com) and YouTube (www.youtube.com).

Spam Unsolicited junk e-mail, usually offering products or services.

Standard A specification established as a model for some element of e-learning by an authority (e.g. the International Organization for Standardization (ISO)). **e-Learning** standards are usually aimed at ensuring quality, consistency and interoperability.

Student tracking The use of software to monitor the progress of a learner through **courseware**. These data can be used to analyse the effectiveness of a course or environment.

Summative assessment The process of evaluating (and grading) the learning of students at a point in time.

Synchronous learning A real-time learning event. If online rather than **face to face**, it requires all participants to be logged on at the same time so that they can communicate with each other. Interaction may occur via text-, audio- or **videoconferencing**, internet telephony or two-way live broadcasts.

Thread A related set of messages on a particular topic posted within a computer conference or forum.

Upload To send a file from your computer to another (e.g. as an email attachment), or to publish a file on a web page.

URL (uniform resource locator) The unique address of an individual web page or the address of a web site, for example www.open. ac.uk (the Open University).

Usability The measure of how effectively, efficiently and easily a person can **navigate** an interface, find information on it and achieve their goals.

Videoconferencing Using video and audio to allow synchronous communication between participants at different locations. This can be based on a personal computer (desktop videoconferencing), for use as needed, or it can be located at a particular site as a fixture.

Virtual Not physical. Usually used to refer to something that is happening online, for example a virtual lecture.

Webcast A way of transmitting video via the web that allows the content to be viewed as it 'streams' so that users do not need to download large files. To receive lengthy streamed webcast it is usually necessary to have a fast computer connection (see **broadband**).

Web conference A virtual meeting of participants from different locations. Communication can occur using text, audio, video or a combination of these. Used in contrast to **computer conferencing** (which refers to text-based online forums).

Wiki A web site or similar online resource that allows users to add and to edit content collectively. A well-known example is Wikipedia (www.wikipedia.org).

Wireless or **Wi-fi (wireless fidelity)** A means of connecting to the internet that relies upon radio-based systems. A 'wired' classroom or building will allow students and teachers within that space to connect to the internet using wi-fi devices without the need to make a physical (cable) connection.

Work-based learning (WBL) Courses that may or may not include classroom components but will integrate a range of learning activities that focus on work-based problems, learning resources sourced from the workplace, times and places for learning (with an emphasis on activities being carried out in the workplace), and different ways in which learners work and network together.

WYSIWYG (what you see is what you get) Pronounced 'wizzywig', a WYSIWYG program allows users to see text and graphics on screen exactly as they will appear when printed out or published **online**. It allows users to format text without using programming code.

References

Alexander, S. (2002) 'Designing learning activities for an international online student body: what have we learned?', *Journal of Studies in International Education* 6(2): 188–200.

Ally, M. (2006) 'Distance learning, online learning and mobile learning at Canada's Open University', Paper presented at the Telelearning Research Group Seminar, 8 March, The Open University, Milton Keynes, UK.

Attwell, G. (2006) 'Personalised learning environments', Position paper for CETIS PLE Workshop, Manchester, 6–7 June, www.project.bazaar.org/2006/06/01/personal-learning-environments/.

Bacsich, P. (2005) The UKEU Reports, Publications from the Archives of UK eUniversities Worldwide Limited. Report 01 Overview, July 2005, HE Academy, York, www.heacademy.ac.uk/documents/r01-ukeu.doc.

Bacsich, P., Ash, C., Boniwell, K. and Kaplan, L. (1999) *The Costs of Networked Learning: Report 1*, Joint Information Systems Committee (JISC) Project Report.

Bacsich, P., Ash, C., Boniwell, K. and Kaplan, L. (2001) *The Costs of Networked Learning: Report 2*, Joint Information Systems Committee (JISC) Project Report.

Becta (2003) *ILT in Further Education: Laying the Foundations of e-Learning*, A report to the National Learning Network Transformation Board, Coventry: Becta.

Becta (2005) *ICT and e-Learning in Further Education: The Challenge of Change*, A report to the Post-16 e-Learning Policy and Project Board, Coventry: Becta.

Beetham, H. (2001) 'How do representations of practice enable practice to change?', *Educational Developments* 2(4): 19–22.

Beetham, H. (2004) *Review: Developing e-Learning Models for the JISC practitioner Communities: A Report for the JISC e-Pedagogy Programme*, JISC.

Bell, J. (2005) 'Evaluation of a learning repository in schools and faculties of information technology and computer science in three large universities', Paper presented at ALT-C 2005: Exploring the Frontiers of e-Learning: Borders, Outposts and Migration, 6–8 September, Manchester.

Britain, S. (2004) *A Review of Learning Design: Concept, Specifications and Tools: A Report for the JISC E-learning Pedagogy Programme*, JISC report, www.jisc.ac.uk/uploaded_documents/ACF1ABB.doc (retrieved 14 September 2006).

Britain, S. and Liber, O. (2004) *A Framework for Pedagogical Evaluation of e-Learning Environments*, JISC e-learning pedagogies programme report, www.jisc.ac.uk/elp_outcomes.html (retrieved 19 March 2007).

Clark, D. (2001) *e-Learning: Return on Investment*, Brighton: Epic Group plc.

Collis, B. and Margaryan, A. (2005) 'Multiple perspectives on blended learning design', *Journal of Learning Design* 1(1): 12–21.

Collis, B. and Moonen, J. (2001) *Flexible Learning in a Digital World: Experiences and Expectations*, London: Kogan Page.

Collis, B., Bianco, M., Margaryan, A. and Waring, B. (2005) 'Putting blended learning to work: a case study from Shell Exploration and Production', *Education, Communication and Information* 5(3): 233–250, www.academy.gcal.ac.uk/anoush/fulltexts/RECI2005-eprint-collis-bianco-margaryan-waring.pdf (retrieved 19 March 2007).

Conole, G. and Fill, K. (2005) 'A learning design toolkit to create pedagogically effective learning activities', *Journal of Interactive Multimedia*, 8, www-jime.open.ac.uk/2005/08/conole-2005-08.pdf (retrieved 14 September 2006).

Conole, G., Dyke, M., Oliver, M. and Seale, J. (2004) 'Mapping pedagogy and tools for effective learning design', *Computers and Education* 43(1–2): 17–33.

Conole, G., Littlejohn, A., Falconer, I. and Jeffery, A (2005) *Pedagogical Review of Learning Activities and Use Cases*, LADIE project deliverable to JISC, August, www.elframework.org/refmodels/ladie/ouputs/LADIE%20lit%20review%20v15.doc (retrieved 14 September 2006).

Cowan, J. (1998) *On Becoming an Innovative University Teacher: Reflection in Action*, London: SRHE and Open University Press.

Currier, S., Barton, J., O'Beirne, R. and Ryan, B. (2004) 'Quality assurance for digital learning object repositories: issues for the metadata creation process', *ALT-J: Research in Learning Technology* 12(1): 5–20.

Dalziel, J. (2003) 'Implementing learning design: the Learning Activity Management System' (LAMS), *Proceedings of ASCILITE*, www.ascilite.org.au/conferences/adelaide03/docs/pdf/593.pdf (retrieved 19 March 2007).

Daniel, J. (1996) *The Mega-universities and Knowledge Media*, London: Routledge Falmer.

Department for International Development (DFID) (2003) 'E is is for education', *Developments*, Issue 22, www.developments.org.uk/data/Issue22/e-for-education.htm (retrieved 25 January 2007).

Downes, S. (2000) *Learning Objects*, Edmonton, Alberta: Academic Technologies for Learning. www.downes.ca (retrieved 25 January 2007).

Downes, S. (2006) 'The student's own education', webcast seminar at Knowledge Media Institute, The Open University, Milton Keynes, UK, 5 June.

Duncan, C. (2003) 'Granularity', in A. Littlejohn (ed.) *Reusing Online Resources: A Sustainable Approach to e-Learning*, London: Routledge.

Falconer, I. and Littlejohn, A. (2007) 'Designing for blended learning, sharing and reuse', *Journal of Further and Higher Education* 31(1): 41–52.

Fielden, J. (2002) *Costing e-Learning: Is It Worth Trying or Should We Ignore the Figures?*, The Observatory on Borderless Higher Education, Report, August.

Garrison, D. R. and Kanuka, H. (2004) 'Blended Learning: uncovering its transformative potential in higher education', *The Internet and Higher Education* 7(2): 95–105.

Gibson, J. J. (1979) *Ecological Approach to Visual Perception*, Boston: Houghton Mifflin.

Golden, S., McCrone, T., Walker, M. and Rudd, P. (2006) *Impact of e-Learning in Further Education: Survey of Scale and Breadth*, Department for Education and Skills (DfES) Research Publication, Brief no. RB745, www.dfes.gov.uk/research/data/uploadfiles/RB745.pdf (retrieved 29 January 2007).

Guardian (2006) 'Exam authority finds rise in mobile phone cheats', 27 March, education.guardian.co.uk/schools/story/0,,1740396,00.html (retrieved 19 March 2007).

Ha, D. and Dobson, M. (2005) 'Designing an interactive simulation to support expansive learning', Paper presented at ALT-C 2005: Exploring the Frontiers of e-Learning: Borders, Outposts and Migration, 6–8 September, Manchester.

IMS (2002) *IMS Meta-data Best Practice Guide for IEEE 1484.12.1-2002 Standard for Learning Object Metadata* (retrieved 29 December 2006 from www.imsglobal.org/metadata/mdv1p3/imsmd_transformv1p0.html).

JISC (2001) 'Disability, technology and education: new pressures and opportunities for further and higher education institutions and staff', Senior Management Briefing Paper 15, www.jisc.ac.uk/uploaded_documents/smbp15.pdf (retrieved 29 January 2007).

JISC (2005) *Effective Practice with e-Learning*, www.jisc.ac.uk/elp_practice.html (retrieved 29 January 2007).

JISC (2006) *Designing Spaces for Effective Learning: A Guide to 21st Century Learning Space Design*, Bristol: JISC, www.jisc.ac.uk/uploaded_documents/JISClearningspaces.pdf (retrieved 29 January 2007).

Joinson, A. N. (2003) *Understanding the Psychology of Internet Behaviour: Virtual Worlds, Real Lives*, Basingstoke, UK: Palgrave Macmillan.

Joinson, A. N. and Dietz-Uhler, B. (2002) 'Explanations of the perpetration of and reactions to deception in a virtual community', *Social Science Computer Review*, Special Issue on Psychology and the Internet, 20(3): 275–289.

Kirkwood, A. and Price, L. (2005) 'Learners and learning in the 21st century: what do we know about students' attitudes and experiences of ICT that will help us design courses?', *Studies in Higher Education* 30(3): 257–274.

Koper, R. (2003) 'Combining reusable learning resources and services to pedagogical purposeful units of learning', in A. Littlejohn (ed.) *Reusing Online Resources: A Sustainable Approach to e-Learning*, London: Routledge.

Koper, R. (2004) Editorial: 'Technology and lifelong learning', *British Journal of Educational Technology* 35(6): 675–678.

Koper, R. and Olivier, B. (2004) 'Representing the learning design of units of learning', *Education, Technology and Society* 7(3): 97–111.

Kukulska-Hulme, A. and Traxler, J. (eds) (2005) *Mobile Learning: A Handbook for Educators and Trainers*, London: RoutledgeFalmer.

Laurillard, D. (2001) *Rethinking University Teaching*, 2nd edition, London: RoutledgeFalmer.

Liber, O. and Olivier, B. (2003) 'Learning technology interoperability standards', in A. Littlejohn (ed.) *Reusing Online Resources: A Sustainable Approach to e-Learning*, London: Routledge.

Littlejohn, A. (ed.) (2003) *Reusing Online Resources: A Sustainable Approach to e-Learning*, London: Routledge.

Littlejohn, A. (2004) *The Effectiveness of Resources, Tools and Support Services Used by Practitioners in Designing and Delivering e-Learning Activities: Final Report*, JISC, www.elearning.ac.uk/resources/effectivefinal (retrieved 14 September 2006).

Littlejohn, A. H. (2005) 'Key issues in the design and delivery of learning and teaching', in P. Levy and S. Roberts (eds), *Developing the New Learning Environment: The Changing Role of the Academic Librarian*, London: Routledge.

Littlejohn, A. H. and Nicol, D. J. (2007) 'Supporting interdisciplinary studies using learning technologies', in B. Chandramohan and S. Fallows (eds) *Interdisciplinary Learning and Teaching: Theory and Practice in Contemporary Higher Education*, London: Routledge.

Littlejohn, A. H. and Peacock, S. (2003) 'From pioneers to partners: the changing voices of staff developers', in J. Seale (ed.) *Learning Technology in Transition: From Individual Enthusiasm to Institutional Implementation*, Lisse, the Netherlands: Swets & Zeitlinger.

Littlejohn, A. H., Campbell, L. M., Tizard, J. and Smith, A. (2003) 'From pilot project to strategic development: scaling up staff support in the use of ICT for teaching and learning', *Journal of Further and Higher Education* 27(1): 47–52.

Littlejohn, A., Falconer, I. and McGill, L. (2007) Characterising effective e-learning resources', *Computers and Education*, in press.

McAndrew, P. (2004) *Representing Practitioner Experiences through Learning Designs and Patterns*, report to the JISC e-learning programme, available online at www.jisc.ac.uk/uploaded_documents/practioner-patterns-v2.doc.

McAndrew, P., Goodyear, P. and Dalziel, J. (2005) 'Patterns, designs and activities: unifying descriptions of learning structures'. *Int. J.* (preprint), kn.open.ac.uk/public/getfile.cfm? documentfileid=6000 (retrieved 30 January 2007).

MacDonald, J. (2006) *Blended Learning and Online Tutoring: A Good Practice Guide*, Aldershot, UK: Gower.

McGill, L., Nicol, D. J, Littlejohn, A.H. and Greirson, H. (2005) 'Creating an information-rich learning environment to enhance design student learning: challenges and approaches', *British Journal of Educational Technology* 36(4): 629–642.

Margaryan, A. (2006) Report on personal resource management strategies survey. CD-LOR Deliverable 7. JISC, UK (retrieved 29 December 2006 from www.academy.gcal.ac.uk/cd-lor/CDLORdeliverable7_PRMSreport.doc).

Mason, R. (1994) *Using Communications Media in Open and Flexible Learning*, London: Kogan Page.

Mason, R. (2001) 'Time is the new distance?', Inaugural lecture, the Open University, Milton Keynes, 14 February.

Mayes, T. and de Freitas, S. (2004) 'Review of e-learning frameworks, models and theories: JISC e-learning models desk study', JISC, www.jisc.ac.uk/whatwedo/ programmes/elearning_pedagogy/elp_outcomes.aspx (retrieved 19 March 2007).

Meyer, K. A. (2003) 'Face-to-face versus threaded discussions: the role of time and higher order thinking'. *Journal of Asynchronous Learning Networks* 7(3): 55–65.

Murray, D. (2001) *e-Learning for the Workplace: Creating Canada's Lifelong Learners*, Ottawa: Department of Human Resources and Social Development, www. sdc.gc.ca/en/hip/lld/olt/Skills_Development/OLTResearch/learn_e.pdf (retrieved 30 January 2007).

Muter, P. and Maurutto, P. (1991) 'Reading and skimming from computer screens and books: the paperless office revisited?', *Behaviour and Information Technology* 10: 257–266.

Naeve, A. (1999) 'Conceptual Navigation and Multiple Scale Narration in a Knowledge Manifold', Royal Institute of Technology, Numerical Analysis and Computing Science, Kungl Tekniska Högskolan, Stockholm, www.cid.nada. kth.se/pdf/cid_52.pdf (retrieved 31 January 2007).

Nicol, D. and Littlejohn, A. (2005) 'Learning from digital natives: integrating formal and informal learning using technology', Paper presented at ALT-C 2005: Exploring the Frontiers of e-Learning: Borders, Outposts and Migration, 6–8 September, Manchester.

Nicol, D. J., Minty, I. and Sinclair, C. (2003) 'The social dimensions of online learning', *Innovations in Education and Teaching International* 40(3): 270–280.

Nicol, D. J., Littlejohn, A. H. and Grierson, H. (2005) 'The importance of structuring information and resources within shared workspaces during collaborative design learning', *Open Learning: The Journal of Open and Distance Learning* 20(1): 31–49.

Nipper, S. (1989) 'Third generation distance learning and computer conferencing', In R. Mason and A. Kaye (eds) *Mindweave: Communication, Computers and Distance Education*, Oxford: Pergamon.

Noble, D. (2003) *Digital Diploma Mills: The Automation of Education*, New York: New York University Press.

Norman, D. A. (1999) 'Affordances, conventions, and design', *Interactions* 6(3): 38–42.

Oblinger, D. (2004) 'The next generation of educational engagement', *Journal of Interactive Media in Education* 8 (Special Issue on the Educational Semantic Web).

OECD (2006) 'Education at a glance – 2006', Organisation for Economic Co-operation and Development, Annual Report, www.oecd.org/document/ 52/0,2340,en_2649_34515_37328564_1_1_1_1,00.html (retrieved 1 February 2007).

Oksman, V. (2006). 'Young People and Seniors in Finnish 'Mobile Information Society'. *Journal of Interactive Media in Education* 2006(02).www-jime.open. ac.uk/2006/02/oksman-2006-02.pdf (retrieved 19 March 2007).

Oliver, R. (2001) 'Exploring the development of critical thinking skills through a web-supported problem-based learning environment', in J. Stephenson (ed.) *Teaching and Learning Online*, London: Kogan Page.

Oliver, R., Harper, B., Hedberg, J., Wills, S. and Agostinho, S. (2002) 'Formalising the description of learning designs', *Proceedings of HERDSA Conference 2002*, www.ecu.edu.au/conferences/herdsa/main/papers/ref/pdf/Oliver. pdf (retrieved 31 January 2007).

Pegler, C. (2004) 'Learning objects in higher education: Changing perceptions of size and shape', in G. Richards (ed.) *Proceedings of World Conference on E-Learning in Corporate, Government, Healthcare, and Higher Education 2003*, Chesapeake, VA: AACE.

Pepicello, B. and Pepicello, S. (2003) 'Determining the significance of "no significant difference"', in G. Richards (ed.), *Proceedings of World Conference on E-Learning in Corporate, Government, Healthcare, and Higher Education 2003*, Chesapeake, VA: AACE.

Prensky, M. (2001a) 'Digital natives, digital immigrants', *On the Horizon* 9(5), October, www.marcprensky.com/writing/Prensky%20-%20Digital%20 Natives, %20Digital%20Immigrants%20-%20Part1.pdf.

Prensky, M. (2001b) *Digital Game-Based Learning*, New York: McGraw-Hill.

Rennie, F. and Mason, R. (2004) *The Connection: Learning from the Connected Generation*, Greenwich, CT: Information Age Publishing.

Reynolds, J., Caley, L. and Mason, R. (2002) *How Do People Learn?*, London: Chartered Institute of Personnel and Development.

Russell, T. L. (2004) *The No Significant Difference Phenomenon: A Comparative Research Annotated Bibliography on Technology for Distance Education*, Montgomery, AL: IDECC (The International Distance Education Certification Center).

Salmon, G. (2002) *E-tivities: The Key to Active Online Learning*, London: Kogan Page.

Schell, G. P. and Burns, M. (2002) 'Merlot: a repository of e-learning objects for higher education', *e-Service Journal* 1(2): 53–64, www.muse.jhu.edu/journals/ eservice_journal/v001/1.2schell.pdf.

Sener, J. (2002) 'Why are there so few fully online BA/BS programs in traditional "arts and sciences" disciplines?', *On the Horizon* 10(1): 23–28.

Seufert, S., Moisseeva, M. and Steinbeck, R. (2001) 'Virtuelle Communities gestalten' (Virtual communities outlined), in A. Hohenstein and K. Wilbers (eds) *Handbuch E-Learning* (Handbook of e-Learning), Cologne: Fachverlag Deutscher Wirtschaftsdienst.

Sharpe, R., Beetham, H. and Ravenscroft, A. (2004) 'Active artefacts: representing our knowledge of learning and teaching', *Educational Developments* 5(2): 16–21, and reprinted in *HERDSA News*, April 2005: 6–11.

Simpson, O. (2002) *Supporting Students in Online, Open and Distance Learning*, 2nd edition, London: RoutledgeFalmer.

Simpson, O. (2003) *Student Retention in Online Open and Distance Learning*, London: RoutledgeFalmer.

Skinner, B. and Austin, R. (1998). 'Computer conferencing: does it motivate EFL Students?', *English Language Teaching Journal* 53(4): 270–279.

Soon, L. and Sugden, D. (2003) '*Engaging Students through SMS Messaging*', in FERL Annual Conference 2003.

Syrian Virtual University (2003) University Prospectus 2003, www.svuonline.com/ sy/archive/Prospectus.pdf (retrieved 8 February 2007).

Thomas, C. (2005) 'Bodysnatching in cyberspace: dial 999 for co-constructed, patient centred, interdisciplinary learning', Paper presented at ALT-C 2005: 'Exploring the Frontiers of e-Learning: Borders, Outposts and Migration', 6–8 September, Manchester.

Thorpe, M. and Thorpe, K. (2005) 'CoUrse Versioning and REuse Project', retrieved on 6 June 2006 from www.kn.open.ac.uk/public/index.cfm?wpid= 5392.

Thorpe, M., Kubiak, C. and Thorpe, K. (2003) 'Designing for reuse and versioning', in A. Littlejohn (ed.) *Reusing Online Resources: A Sustainable Approach to e-Learning*, London: Routledge.

Twigg, C. (2003) 'Improving Learning and Reducing Costs: The Program in Course Redesign', in Seminar Proceedings *Balancing Quality, Access and Cost: Using ICT to Redesign Teaching and Learning*, Observatory on Borderless Higher Education and National Center for Academic Transformation, Westminster, May.

Universities UK (2006) *Universities UK's Position*, www.universitiesuk.ac.uk/ parliament/showBriefing.asp?id=37 (retrieved 8 February 2007).

Walker, D. F. and Schaffarzick, J. (1974) 'Comparing curricula', *Review of Educational Research* 44: 88–111.

Weinberger, D. (2002) *Small Pieces, Loosely Joined*, Cambridge, MA: Perseus Publishing.

Weller, M. (2003) *Learning on the Net: The Why, What and How of Online Education*, London: RoutledgeFalmer.

Weller, M.J. (2004) 'Models of large-scale e-learning', *Journal of Asynchronous Learning Networks* (JALN) 8(4), www.sloan-c.org/publications/jaln/v8n4/v8n4_weller. asp (retrieved 31 January 2007).

Weller, M., Pegler, C. A. and Mason, R. D. (2005) 'Students' experience of component versus integrated virtual learning environments', *Journal of Computer Assisted Learning* 21(4): 239–315.

Wenger, E. (1999) *Communities of Practice: Learning, Meaning, and Identity*, Cambridge: Cambridge University Press.

Wiley, D. (2004) 'Commentary on Downes', *Journal of Interactive Media in Education* 5, Special Issue on the Educational Semantic Web, 21 May, www-jime. open.ac.uk/2004/5/wiley-2004-5.pdf (retrieved 14 September 2006).

Wojtas, O. (2001) 'The e-learning revolution: myth or reality?', *The Times Higher Education Supplement*, September.

Zimmer, B. (1995) 'The empathy templates, a way to support collaborative learning', in F. Lockwood (ed.) *Open and Distance Learning Today*, London: Routledge.

Web sites

AUTC learning designs, www.learningdesigns.uow.edu.au

British and Irish Legal Information Institute, Law Reports online, www.bailii.org/

British Library 'Turning the pages' (incl. Leonardo da Vinci's diaries and Mozart's handwritten scores at the British Museum), www.bl.uk/onlinegallery/ttp/ttpbooks.html

Community Dimensions of Learning Object Repository (CD-LOR), www.academy.gcal.ac.uk/cd-lor/

Creative Commons, www.creativecommons.org

eLanguages at Southampton University, www.elanguages.ac.uk.

ePrints, www.eprints.org

Freedom Toaster, www.freedomtoaster.org/

Google, www.google.com

Horizon reports, www.nmc.org/horizon/

IMS Learning Design, www.imsproject.org/

IVIMEDS, www.ivimeds.org/

IVINURS, www.ivinurs.org/

Jorum repository, www.jorum.ac.uk

LAMS community, lamscommunity.org

Macquarie E-Learning Centre Of Excellence (MELCOE), www.melcoe.mq.edu.au

Massachusetts Institute of Technology open continent initiative, www.ocw.mit.edu

MERLOT (Multimedia Educational Resource for Learning and Online Teaching), www.merlot.org

MIT Open Courseware initiative, www.ocw.mit.edu/index.html

Mod4L, Models for Learning project, www.academy.goal.ac.uk/mod4l

Mudlarking at Deptford, www.futurelab.org.uk/showcase/mudlarking/

One laptop per child project,www.laptop.org/

Open University (UK), Open Content Initiative, www.open.ac.uk/openlearn

Open University, Study Strategies, www.open.ac.uk/skillsforstudy/

PROWE, Personal Repositories Online: Wiki Environments, www.prowe.ac.uk

Saltire Centre at Glasgow Caledonian University, www.gcal.ac.uk/thesaltire centre/

San Francisco Museum of Modern Art Podcasts www.sfmoma.org/education/edupodcasts.html

Syrian Virtual University, www.svuonline.org/

Teachandlearn.net, www.teachandlearn.net/

Virtual Frog dissection at the University of Virginia, www.frog.edschool.virginia.edu/

YouTube personal socialization software, www.youtube.com

Index